P9-AQL-630

WHAT IS HAPPINESS IN MARRIAGE FOR A WOMAN?

Is it to have a lovely home? Happy and healthy children? A successful husband? Time for talents? No money problems? Husband and wife having fun together? Is it the feeling of being a successful homemaker? Is it to be admired by her associates?

All of these things are important and some essential, but there is one need which is fundamental and it is *for her to be loved and cherished by her husband.*

Why is it that one woman may be happy, honored and loved, and another—no less attractive, no less essentially admirable and no less lovable—may be neglected, unhappy and disappointed? *Fascinating Womanhood* explains why and offers *every woman* an opportunity to learn the art of winning her man's complete love and adoration.

FASCINATING WOMANHOOD

A book of inspirational feminine secrets that can save your marriage and enrich your life . . .

WHAT IS A FASCINATING WOMAN?

Is she the coy coquette who flutters her eyelashes as she charms men with cute clichés? Is she the stunning sophisticate of the fashion magazines and charm schools? Does she selfishly manipulate the man in her life into satisfying her whims and fancies? Or, is she his slave, bent on catering to his every request? No, she is none of these superficial images.

She is a woman of strong and noble character, dedicated to high standards and values. Although she is submissive and giving, she does not allow herself to be trampled on or abused. She is the perfect wife, understanding her husband, his sensitive masculine pride, and his feelings of responsibility. She views her husband honestly and is aware of his faults, but concentrates on his virtues.

She is proud to be a woman, and does all she can to magnify her femininity, not by a mere outer showing of softness, but by a total personification of womanliness. This includes an outer femininity of appearance and manner and an inner femininity of attitudes and goals. She does not plan to be a man, to compete with him in his own field. She plans to be a feminine woman with a charm that knows no age.

Is she a free soul? Yes. She may devote most of her time to her family, but she does not regard herself as trapped in the household, a servant and a slave. She feels there is no greater work on earth than the work in the home, no greater goal than that of raising a successful family. Her career is a career in the home.

Her charms are not those of cleverness or sophistication but of freshness, wholesomeness and inner happiness. She is innocent and trustful with the playfulness of a child. She has a sort of bloom which comes from being loved, and adored by her husband. Only a woman so loved can be truly fascinating.

FASCINATING WOMANHOOD

Helen B. Andelin

BANTAM BOOKS
NEW YORK · TORONTO · LONDON · SYDNEY · AUCKLAND

*This edition contains the complete text
of the original hardcover edition.*
NOT ONE WORD HAS BEEN OMITTED.

FASCINATING WOMANHOOD
*A Bantam Book / published by arrangement with
the author*

PRINTING HISTORY
Pacific Press edition published March 1965
Bantam edition / March 1975
7 printings through November 1975
Revised Bantam edition . . . July 1980
2 printings through September 1981

A WORD OF EXPLANATION BY THE AUTHOR
*Many of the teachings of this book were inspired by a series of
booklets published in the 1920s, entitled* THE SECRETS OF FASCINATING
WOMANHOOD. *These booklets have long been out of print and the
authors unknown.*
Excerpts from the following books are reprinted by permission:

THE PRICELESS GIFT, *by Eleanor Wilson McAdoo. Copyright 1962
by Eleanor Wilson McAdoo. Reprinted by permission of McGraw-
Hill Book Co., New York, N.Y.*

THE EGO IN LOVE AND SEXUALITY, *by Dr. Edrita Fried. Copyright
1960. Reprinted by permission of Grune & Stratton, Inc., New
York, N.Y.*

THE POWER OF SEXUAL SURRENDER, *by Dr. Marie N. Robinson.
Copyright 1959 by Marie N. Robinson. Reprinted by permission
of Doubleday & Co., Inc., New York, N.Y.*

MARRIAGE FOR MODERNS, *by Henry A. Bowman. Copyright 1960.
Reprinted by permission of McGraw-Hill Book Co.*

WOMEN AND SOMETIMES MEN, *by Florida Scott-Maxwell. Copyright
1957 by Florida Scott Maxwell. Reprinted by permission of
Alfred A. Knopf, Inc., New York, N.Y.*

THREE WISE MEN OF THE EAST, *by Elizabeth Bisland. Reprinted by
permission of University of North Carolina Press.*

THE LAND OF POETRY, BOOK 2, *published 1930. Reprinted by
permission of James Nisbet & Co. Ltd., Welwyn, Herts., England.*

All rights reserved.
Copyright © 1963, 1974 by Helen B. Andelin.
Cover art copyright © 1980 by Bantam Books.
*No part of this book may be reproduced or transmitted
in any form or by any means, electronic or mechanical,
including photocopying, recording, or by any information
storage and retrieval system, without permission in writing from
the publisher.*
For information address: Bantam Books.

ISBN 0-553-27375-2

Published simultaneously in the United States and Canada

*Bantam Books are published by Bantam Books, a division of Bantam
Doubleday Dell Publishing Group, Inc. Its trademark, consisting of the
words "Bantam Books" and the portrayal of a rooster, is Registered in
U.S. Patent and Trademark Office and in other countries. Marca Regis-
trada. Bantam Books, 666 Fifth Avenue, New York, New York 10103.*

PRINTED IN THE UNITED STATES OF AMERICA

O   25   24   23   22   21   20   19   18

Contents

Acknowledgment

I would like to express a special acknowledgment to Verna Johnson who first opened the door of Fascinating Womanhood to me, helped me to see that any wife can be adored and cherished if she develops her feminine and fascinating nature.

Introduction

To be loved and cherished is a woman's heartfelt desire in marriage. This book is written to restore your hope in the fulfillment of this desire—and to suggest principles which you can apply in winning a man's genuine love.

The Sea of Darkness

Never before in history has there been a generation of women so disillusioned, disappointed, and unhappy in marriage as in our times. Many feel that married life does not offer what they had hoped and dreamed it would. Some feel neglected, unappreciated, and often unloved. When they search for the answers, they feel lost in a sea of darkness. Some are resigned to this condition, but others still hope and search for the answers.

There are, of course, many women who have achieved a high level of happiness, but in many cases it is not the happiness of which they once dreamed, and it falls short of their goals. They feel a need for a richer, fuller life. They, too, need light and understanding.

The Greater Darkness

In this vast sea of matrimonial darkness, there are other women who are in greater darkness, for they think they are happy when they are not. They live by the side of happiness, but are strangers to her beauty. They are satisfied to eat the crumbs which fall from the table, for they have never tasted the banquet; they think the weeds are pretty, for they have never seen beautiful flowers; and some are content with hell, for they have never known heaven.

A Woman's Heaven

What is happiness in marriage for a woman? Is it to have a nice home? Happy and healthy children? A successful husband? Time for talents? No money problem? Hus-

1

band and wife having fun together? Is it the feeling of being a successful homemaker? Is it to be admired by her associates?

All of these things are important and some essential, but there is one need which is fundamental, and it is *for her to be loved and cherished by her husband.* Without this one ingredient she will be unfulfilled. She may be a successful person in many ways and happy to a degree, but inside there will be something missing. She will not know heaven. She will enjoy weeds instead of flowers.

The Answer

Is there a light to bring her out of darkness and guide her to this earthly heaven? There *is* a light, and it is based upon fundamental law.

All life is governed by law. There is no such thing as chance. One woman succeeds in marriage because of obedience to law. Another fails because of disobedience to it. Neither may understand the law. Obedience is not always based upon understanding. But the result of obedience is invariably success, and disregard for it is always failure.

Through ignorance of the very simple operation of these plain laws, much unnecessary unhappiness exists. We find one woman happy, honored and loved; and another— no less attractive, no less essentially admirable and no less lovable—neglected, unhappy and disappointed. Why? This book tells why, for it explains the laws which she must obey if she is to be honored, loved and appreciated.

Fascinating Womanhood

Fascinating Womanhood is designed to teach women how to be happy in marriage. It will teach three essentials in creating the happy marriage:

1. *Love:* Since the cornerstone of a woman's happiness with her husband is to be loved, the essential aim of this book is to teach those principles which she must apply in arousing this love. Every woman can awaken her husband's feelings of love, no matter what her age and situation. Love is not reserved for the young, the single nor the beautiful. It is reserved for those who arouse it in a man. If a man does not love his wife with his heart and soul, it is the wife's fault. *A man ceases to adore and*

2

cherish a woman after marriage because she ceases to do the things which arouse these feelings. If she obeys the laws upon which love is based, she can kindle a deep and stirring feeling within his heart.

This book will teach *the art of winning a man's complete love and adoration.* It is not necessary for the man to know or do anything about the matter. This is not to say that men do not make mistakes or need to improve their behavior. But when women correct their own mistakes, they can bring about a wonderful loving response in a man. We should be thankful that we have this power to mend a relationship and cause it to blossom into love and tenderness, independent of any direct effort on the part of our husband.

The art of awakening a man's love is not a difficult accomplishment for women because it is based upon our natural instincts. However, in our complicated, highly civilized life of today many of our natural instincts may have become dulled or suppressed. We need but to acquire the traits which belong to us by nature.

2. *Human Dignity:* Also essential to her happiness in marriage is her human dignity. She cannot suffer hurt, humiliation, insults or unfair treatment by her mate without damage to her spirit. This book will teach her how to handle these difficult situations without pain, without friction. It will teach her how to react when treated unfairly, imposed on or ignored.

3. *Her Desires:* If a woman is to be truly happy in marriage she must also be able to have the things that are dear to her heart. She is a human being with human needs, longings and rights that need to be fulfilled. In Fascinating Womanhood she will learn how to obtain these things without causing a marital stir. She will learn how to cause a man to *want* to do things for her.

Within these pages I will point out those principles which she must obey if she is to be happy, loved and appreciated. My aim is to teach her how to become "The Ideal Woman," the kind she is designed to be, the kind a man wants. Remember, *a woman holds within her grasp the possibilities of a heavenly marriage. She can bring it about independent of any deliberate action on the part of her husband. So, a woman holds the keyes to her own happiness.*

In accomplishing this, she loses none of her dignity, influence or freedom, but gains them. And it is only then, that she can play her vital part in this world. The role of woman when played correctly is fulfilling, fascinating and full of intrigue. There never need be a dull moment. The practice of this art of womanhood is an enjoyable one and is filled with rich rewards, numerous surprises, and vast happiness.

What This Book Can Do For You

It will teach you:
1. The ideal woman, from a man's point of view.
2. What men find fascinating in women.
3. How to understand men, their needs, characteristics and pecularities.
4. How to treat a man when he is depressed, in order to build up his confidence and respect in himself.
5. How to arouse his deepest feelings of love and tenderness.
6. How to cause a man to protect you, and offer you his true devotion.
7. How to obtain those things in life which mean so much—things you are justified in having and for which you are dependent upon your husband, and how to add charm and love to your marriage by doing so.
8. How to bring out the best in your husband without push or persuasion.
9. How to understand the feminine role, and the happiness which comes with its fulfillment.
10. How to understand the masculine role, the respect due this divine calling, and the importance of such respect in the happiness of both husband and wife.
11. How to react when a man is thoughtless, unfair or negligent.
12. How to be attractive, even adorable, when you are angry.
13. How to keep the line of communication open in marriage so that a good feeling always exists.
14. How to gain true happiness in marriage, while placing your husband's happiness as a primary goal.

Please Note: Many success stories appear throughout this book. All of these are true and came to the author's attention either by direct conversation with the party involved or by unsolicited letter. Likewise, all of the illustrations and examples in the book are taken from true experiences.

5

1

Celestial Love

12.52

In the city of Agra in northern India stands the Taj Mahal. Although it was built in the seventeenth century, it is still one of the most beautiful buildings in the world and the most costly tomb in existence. It was built by the Indian ruler Shah Jahan in memory of his favorite wife, Mumtaz-i-Mahal, which means "Pride of the Palace." The Shah had other wives, but honored only Mumtaz with a Taj Mahal.

This is a chapter which deals with man's true love of woman, the kind of love that Shah Jahan had for Mumtaz. In trying to discover a single word to represent this kind of love, I discovered that such a word does not really exist. The word "love" itself has a broad meaning and "Christian love" is that charity of spirit which we owe to all mankind. The love between a man and a woman is not this broad type of love nor is it given out of obligation, but springs spontaneously from the depths of emotion.

I decided to call this type of love *Celestial Love*—a term to represent the highest kind of tender love a man can feel for a woman, and that a woman feels for a man. It lifts love out of the mediocre and places it in the heavens where love belongs. It is the flowers rather than weeds, the banquet rather than the crumbs.

Do you think that this type of love exists when a man tells his wife frequently that he loves her, remembers her birthday, takes her out to dinner often and is generous and kind? Not necessarily. These attentions are admirable, but they are not the attributes of real love. A dutiful husband may do or say these things without any actual feeling for his wife.

Celestial love is more intense, more spontaneous and dynamic than the passive actions just mentioned. When a man loves with his heart, he experiences a deep feeling within. It has been described as a feeling almost like pain. He may feel enchanted and fascinated. In addition, he feels a tender desire to protect and shelter the woman he

7

loves from all harm, danger and difficulty. Then there is the deeper, more spiritual feeling almost like worship. Even this, perhaps, cannot adquately describe the "many splendored thing" called love, but the following accounts are vivid examples of man's true love of woman:

John Alden and Priscilla

An illustration of Celestial Love is expressed in Longfellow's account of John Alden and Priscilla Mullens, in which John speaks tenderly of Priscilla: "There is no land so sacred, no air so pure and wholesome, as is the air she breathes and the soil that is pressed by her footsteps. Here for her sake will I stay and like an invisible presence, hover around her forever, protecting, supporting her weakness."

Victor Hugo's Love

An illustration of a tender, protective feeling of love is found in the words of Victor Hugo, written about the woman he loved in real life, Adele Foucher:

"Do I exist for my own personal happiness? No, my whole existence is devoted to her, even in spite of her. And by what right should I have dared to aspire to her love? What does it matter, so that it does not injure her happiness? My duty is to keep close to her steps, to surround her existence with mine, to serve her as a barrier against all dangers; to offer my head as a stepping stone, to place myself unceasingly between her and all sorrows, without claiming reward, without expecting recompense... Alas! If she only allow me to give my life to anticipating her every desire, all her caprices; if she but permit me to kiss with respect her adored footprints; if she but consent to lean upon me at times amidst the difficulties of life."

Woodrow Wilson

Probably one of the finest examples of true and enduring love is found in the love letters of President Woodrow Wilson, written to his wife Ellen. After being married for seventeen years, he writes, "All that I am, all that has come to me in life, I owe to you. . . . I could not be what I am, if I did not take such serene happiness from my union with you. You are the spring of content; and so

8

long as I have you, and you too are happy, nothing but good and power can come to me. Ah, my incomparable little wife, may God bless and keep you."

And after being married for twenty-eight years, he writes from the White House: "I adore you! No President but myself ever had exactly the right sort of wife! I am certainly the most fortunate man alive." And in another letter, "I can think of nothing while I write but only you. My days are not so full of anxiety and a sense of deep responsibility as they are of you, my absent darling, who yet plays the leading part in my life every minute of the day." These lines were taken from "The Priceless Gift," a collection of letters written by President Wilson to his wife Ellen. Each letter is a love letter, warm and intimate.

Some of you may believe your husbands are incapable of such feelings or at least incapable of expressing them. This is doubtful. The warm, tender letters of President Wilson were a surprise to many who knew his personality—that of an unemotional schoolmaster. Every man has the capability of being tender, romantic and adoring, if these passions are awakened by a woman.

Shah Jahan's Love for Mumtaz

I would like to now elaborate on the love Shah Jahan felt for Mumtaz, lady of the Taj Mahal. Theirs is a most serene and exquisite love tale, a *clean white flame*, and an excellent example of the Celestial love of which I speak. In describing their love I quote from the book Three Wise Men of the East, by Elizabeth Bisland:

"The young Indian ruler found in this Persian girl the realization of all his high dreams and imaginings. So closely were their lives interlaced, so supremely does she appear to have been his inspiration, that it is necessary to imagine one profile next to the other. And in a poet's words the Shah's feelings are expressed:

> He preferred in his heart
> The least ringlet that curled
> Down her exquisite neck
> To the throne of the world.

"In the culture of his day, practically no restraint existed either in law or public opinion to control the desires regarding women of a Mogul emperor . . . he was absolutely free to take women where he would and use them as he willed; yet never is there evidence that Shah Jahan gave his wife a rival. He had two other wives, but these were political marriages, not love matches."

During his lifetime Shah Jahan built for his wife a magnificent palace of white marble, probably the most perfect dwelling place that man had ever built at the time. It was exquisite, with light passing through delicate carvings of marble almost like lace and superb mosaics of birds and flowers in precious stones. Here, indeed, the emperor created a work of art in making a home for his beloved. And above the rich columns holding up the ceiling in beautiful Persian script in pure gold is the famous inscription, "If there is heaven on earth, it is this, it is this, it is this."

Mumtaz died at the birth of their fourteenth child. From an old Persian manuscript is the following account: "When the emperor learned that she was to die, he wept bitterly because of the great love he bore her, and one would have said that the stars fell in heaven and the rain upon the earth. Such lamentation arose in the palace that one would have said the Day of Judgment had arrived. The emperor, weeping and striking his breast, repeated the words of the poet Saadi, 'God will not rest in the hands of a prodigal nor patience in the heart of a lover more than water in a sieve.' But grief stirred his genius to its supreme accomplishment. He resolved that upon the grave of his beloved should be laid love's perfect crown."

"The great buildings of the world have been monuments of the pomp and pride of kings, or temples to gods, or records of rich and haughty cities. But he, in the beauty of white marble, for the first time gave utterance to man's love of woman. Not physical desire, but the mating of spirit with spirit. No pains were spared to bring to perfection the last dwelling place of his beloved Queen. Twenty thousand laborers toiled upon it for seventeen years." And take note of this thought: Mumtaz was of a culture where women were subservient, dependent, and kept their place in the feminine world. It was not a culture where women dominated and demanded and tried to be equal with men. And yet her husband gave to her the greatest token of love that man has ever given to a woman, in the Taj Mahal. And we may well ask ourselves. "Are we worthy of a Taj

Mahal? Have we earned such love and devotion from our husband?"

Is It Selfish?

Do not think it selfish to want to be loved with great tenderness. A man's feeling of tender love for his wife is a source of great joy to him and he is more of a man because of it. It provides him with greater incentive to succeed in life, giving him something to work for, to live for and if necessary to die for. The woman who awakens her husband's love helps him find greater happiness and fulfillment. The woman who does not, robs him of one of his finer joys.

Benefits come to the woman, also. Her husband's love is the center of her happiness in marriage. A marriage without this love is an empty shell, as every woman who has suffered such a lack will readily admit. When she is loved and happy she can more adequately devote herself to her responsibilities of family life.

Love in marriage is the most important element in its success, and a happy marriage the foundation of a successful home. There is simply no way a man and woman can create a truly successful home without creating a happy marriage based upon a true and abiding love for each other. Love, then, becomes not only the fulfillment of a desire, but a responsibility. When the marriage is happy we have happy children who can develop normally and be prepared for the life ahead. The happy home becomes a worthy contribution to the well being of society, bringing peace to the world rather than the discord that arises from lack of love.

For a true state of Celestial Love to exist, both the man and the woman should love each other dearly. Since we study only those principles which awaken the husband's love for his wife, how then is her love for him to deepen? The common answer is that *he* must do something about it by being a better man. Although it is undeniably true that a man's initiative to improve himself would increase his wife's love for him, the miracle of Fascinating Womanhood is this: 1) When the wife applies these teachings, she gains a greater understanding and appreciation for him, learns to see his finer side and therefore learns to love him more fully. 2) By living the principles of Fascinating

11

Womanhood, she becomes a better woman and brings new life and romance into their relationship. This gives the man more incentive to strive, to make something more worthwhile of his life. Thus, he becomes a better man, one she can love more completely.

Celestial love is what every woman has longed for since the world began. Even in childhood, little girls have tender dreams of romance in which they are the beautiful princess who is sought after by the handsome prince. Snow White and Cinderella are favorites of little girls. All during youth, uppermost in a young girl's mind is finding a man who will love and cherish her. This tender love has long been the theme of great operas, novels and songs. Romantic love, one of the most moving forces in life, rightfully deserves our study and consideration.

As we conclude this chapter, you may ask, "What can I do to inspire Celestial Love in my husband's heart?" To know we must learn the principles which awaken a man's love. We must study "The Kind of Woman a Man Wants," the kind which awakens his emotions of worship, adoration and love.

2

"The Ideal Woman" from a Man's Point of View

To understand the masculine viewpoint, we must learn to view the ideal woman through a man's eyes and realize that his ideas of feminine perfection are *different from our own*. The things we women admire in each other are rarely attractive to men. On the other hand, the characteristics which the average woman ignores or condemns in another woman are sometimes just the characteristics which make her fascinating to men. Women are blind to their own charms which is the reason it is often difficult for them to realize what a man wants.

Haven't you been puzzled at times to know what a certain man sees in a particular woman? To you she doesn't hold any appeal, yet the man may be completely enamored. The fascination men feel for certain women seems to be an eternal riddle to the rest of her sex. Even when asked "why," . . . the man finds himself at a loss to explain the spell cast upon him. And haven't you also known women who appear to have all of the qualities which ought to please a man, yet they are unappreciated, neglected and often unloved? So in our study of the ideal woman, remember that *a man judges with a different set of values*.

Women are inclined to appreciate poise, talent, intellectual gifts and cleverness of personality, whereas men admire girlishness, tenderness, sweetness of character, vivacity, and the woman's ability to understand men. A marked difference is in regards to appearance. Women are inclined to be attracted to artistic beauty such as the shape of the face, the nose, and artistic clothes. Men, however, have a different interpretation of "what makes a woman beautiful." They place more stress on the sparkle in the eyes, smiles, freshness, radiance, and the feminine manner.

The ideal woman from a man's point of view is divided into two parts. The one part is her spiritual qualifications. We will call this side of her the Angelic. The other part relates to her human characteristics. We will call this side of her the Human.

The Angelic side of a woman has to do with her basic good character, her ability to understand men, their feelings, needs, and sensitive nature. It also includes her domestic skills and the ability to succeed in her feminine role in the home. It includes a quality of inner happiness or tranquility of spirit which is a part of womanly beauty.

The Human side refers to a woman's appearance,

Angelic   Human

manner, and actions and includes the charms of femininity, radiance, and a quality of dependency upon men for their care, protection, and guidance. It also includes good health and a feminine dignity of spirit or spunk. The Angelic and the Human combine to make the perfect woman from the man's point of view. They are both essential in winning his genuine love.

These two distinct qualities in women awaken different feelings in a man. The Angelic awakens a feeling almost like worship and brings him a feeling of peace and happiness. The Human side fascinates and enchants him and awakens a tender feeling, a desire to protect and shelter her from harm and danger. When a woman has both the Angelic and the Human qualities, she becomes a man's ideal woman, one he can *cherish*.

For illustrations of the Angelic and the Human in women, I would like to refer to examples from classic literature. Although these women were from fiction, we must realize that skilled authors always draw their characters from living examples, from people they knew or observed in real life. So these women I will refer to were actually living examples in the author's lifetime.

Also, I am referring to literature of over 100 years ago. The reason I have done this is because they are such excellent examples of what I teach. But just because they were figures from the past does not mean they do not apply fully to present times. Human nature does not change, nor do the needs of human beings. The human family has always been pretty much the same, especially in their relationships, which is why characters from the Bible have such eternal application. Let us now turn to these examples of the past for a view of the Angelic and the Human in women.

David Copperfield

A perfect illustration of the Angelic and the Human in woman is in the story of David Copperfield, by Charles Dickens. Our ideal, however, is not represented by one woman, but by two, Agnes and Dora.

Agnes

Agnes represents the Angelic side of our ideal, the side which inspires worship. David Copperfield knew Agnes from childhood and worshipped her from the time he first beheld her. The following is a description of their first meeting:

"Mr. Wickfield (Agnes' father) tapped at a door in a corner of the paneled wall and a girl of about my age came quickly out and kissed him. On her face I saw immediately the placid and sweet expression of the lady whose picture had looked at me downstairs (her mother). It seemed to my imagination as if the portrait had grown womanly and the original remained a child. Although her face was quite bright and happy, there was a tranquility about it, and about her—a quiet good calm spirit—that I never have forgotten; that I never shall forget. 'This was his little housekeeper, his daughter, Agnes,' Mr. Wickfield said. When I heard how he said it, and saw how he held her hand, I guessed what the one motive of his life was. She had a little basket trifle, hanging at her side with keys in it, and she looked as staid and as discreet a housekeeper as the old house could have. She listened to her father as he told her about me, with a pleasant face; and when he had concluded, proposed to my aunt that we should go upstairs and see my room. We all went up together, she before us. A glorious old room it was with more oak beams and diamond panes; and the broad balustrade going all the way up.

"I cannot call to mind where or when, in my childhood, I had seen a stained-glass window in a church. Nor do I recall its subject. But I know that when I saw her turn around in the grave light of the old staircase and wait for me above, I thought of that window; and I associated something of its tranquil brightness with Agnes Wickfield ever afterwards."

David and Agnes became the closest of friends. She gave him comfort, understanding, true sympathy and comradeship. "As if," he writes, "in love, joy, sorrow, hope, or disappointment, in all emotions, my heart turned naturally there and found its refuge and best friend."

Agnes always had a sacred and peaceful influence on David. At one time, while under great stress and tension, he said, "Somehow as I wrote to Agnes on a fine evening by my open window, and the remembrance of her clear calm eyes and gentle face came stealing over me, it shed such a peaceful influence upon the hurry and agitation in which I had been living lately . . . that it soothed me into tears." But, although he had known Agnes since childhood, although he had worshipped her from the time he first beheld her, and although he senses all along that she alone is equipped to give him true sympathy and comradeship, he becomes madly infatuated, not with Agnes, but with Dora.

Dora

—Dora represents the Human side of our ideal, the side that fascinates, captivates and inspires an overwhelming tenderness in a man's heart and a desire to protect and shelter. David describes her in the following words:

"She was a fairy and a sylph. She was more than human to me. I don't know what she was—anything that no one ever saw and everything that everybody ever wanted. She had the most delightful little voice, the gayest little laugh, the pleasantest and most fascinating little ways that ever led a lost youth into hopeless slavery. She was rather diminutive altogether . . . she was too bewildering. To see her lay the flowers against her dimpled chin was to lose all presence of mind and power of language in feeble ecstacy."

Her childlike ways, her dear little whims and caprices, her girlish trust in him, her absolute dependency upon others to provide for her, made an irresistible appeal to David's gentlemanly and chivalrous heart. She fascinated him, for he writes: "I could only sit down before the fire, biting the key of my carpet bag, and think of the captivating, girlish, bright eyed, lovely Dora. What a form she had, what a face she had, what a graceful, variable, enchanting manner."

Married To Dora, David Turns to Agnes

Yet even while such feelings toward Dora are at their highest, he misses the comfort, the understanding, the appreciation and the sacred influences of Agnes. "Dora," he tells Agnes, "is rather difficult to—I would not for the world say, to rely upon, because she is the soul of purity and truth—but rather difficult to—I hardly know how to express it. Whenever I have not had you, Agnes, to advise and approve in the beginning, I have seemed to go wild and to get into all sorts of difficulty. When I have come to you, at last, as I have always done, I have come to peace and happiness."

Dora's Homemaking

In marriage, Dora also failed as a homemaker. Their home was in constant clutter: "I could not have wished for a prettier little wife at the opposite end of the table, but I certainly could have wished when we sat down for a little more room. I did not know how it was, but although there were only two of us, we were at once always cramped for room, and yet had always enough to lose everything in. I suspect it could have been because nothing had a place of its own." Dora could not manage the household finances, nor the household help, although she tried. Nor could she cook, although David bought her an expensive cookbook. But she used the book to let her little dog stand on.

The Void in His Life

While married to Dora he continued to love her. She fascinated and amused him, and he felt tenderly towards her. But it was not a complete love, nor did it bring him genuine happiness, for he said: "I loved my wife dearly, and I was happy; but the happiness I had vaguely anticipated once was not the happiness I enjoyed, and there was something wanting. An unhappy feeling pervaded my life, as a strain of sorrowful music, faintly heard in the night." And he said, "I did feel sometimes, for a little while, that I could have wished my wife had been my counsellor; had had more character and purpose to sustain me, and improve me by; had been endowed with a power to fill up the void which somewhere seemed to be about me."

Later on in the story Dora died and David turned to Agnes. When married to Agnes, David enjoyed real peace and happiness, for she filled up the void in his life. She was a wonderful homemaker and gave him true understanding. They had children and a wonderful home life. His love for Agnes was holy, but—it was not complete. During his marriage to Agnes he still had tender recollections of Dora that played upon his emotions. In thinking of her he writes: "This appeal of Dora's made such a strong impression on me. . . . I look back on the time I write of; I invoke the innocent figure that I dearly loved to come out of the mists and shadows of the past and turn its gentle head toward me once again."

On one occasion his little girl came running in to her father with a ring on her finger very much like the engagement ring he had given to Dora. The little ring—a band of forget-me-nots, with blue stones, so reminded him of Dora, that he said, "There was a momentary stirring in my heart, like pain!"

The feeling David had for Agnes was one near worship. She had a sacred influence on him. She brought him peace and happiness, and without her he seemed to "go wild and get into difficulty." Thinking about her "soothed him into tears." He felt as though she were a part of him, "as one of the elements of my natural home."

The feeling he had for Dora was different. She fascinated and amused him; "she was more than human to me"; "she was a fairy and a sylph"; "I don't know what she was—anything that no one ever saw and everything that everybody ever wanted." All of her delicate and bright mannerisms aroused his irresistible longing to shelter and protect her.

I would like to stress that David Copperfield felt two distinctly different types of love for these two girls. David experienced a type of love for Agnes all along, but it was not strong enough to bring him to marriage. And even though this type of love brings men the greatest peace and the truest and most abiding happiness—it is not the most driving.

The kind of love David felt for Dora was forceful, consuming and intense. He felt like "biting the key of his carpet bag" when he thought of her; he was "in fairyland." He was "a captive and a slave." This type of love, however, was not complete, nor did it bring him real happiness, for he said, "I loved my wife dearly and I was happy; but the happiness I vaguely anticipated once was not the happiness I enjoyed and there was something wanting. An unhappy feeling pervaded my life, as a strain of sorrowful music, faintly heard in the night."

While married to Agnes, he experienced peace and happiness and he loved her dearly, but he still had tender recollections of Dora which sent stirring feelings through his heart. David Copperfield never had the satisfaction of loving completely, for his feelings were inspired by two different women. Neither was the whole of our ideal, so neither could arouse his love in a complete sense.

There are many women such as Agnes, in this life— women with inspiring characters. They make wonderful mothers and homemakers and are good citizens. They are greatly appreciated, but if they lack the adorably human qualities that so fascinate men, they will undoubtedly fail to win the true love of their husband. A man wants more than an angel. On the other hand, there are some women such as Dora, who are tender, childlike and gay little creatures, but if they have not the depth of character and purpose, if they are too self-centered to be good homemakers and mothers, and if they lack the ability to understand men, they will only win a part of their husband's love.

There is no reason why a woman cannot be both an Agnes and a Dora, for the Angelic and the Human qualities do not conflict. Both are a natural part of femininity and are essential to real feminine charm. Both the Angelic and the Human qualities are essential in winning men and in keeping them happy after marriage— thereby sustaining their love and devotion. Your complete happiness in marriage depends upon your development of both sides of our ideal.

Comparing the Two

If Agnes had had the girlishness, the adorable human and childlike manner of Dora, and her complete dependency upon man for protection and guidance, David would never have made the mistake of marrying another. His worship for Agnes would have turned into genuine love, into the desire to protect and shelter. On the other hand, if Dora had had the sympathetic understanding, the appreciation of his highest ideals and the depth of character that Agnes had, and had given his home order and peace, David's mad infatuation for her would have developed into everlasting adoration and love. Neither of the two, unfortunately for them, represents the whole of the Angelic and the Human. Each of them made mistakes, each of them won and lost David, but each of them is well worth emulating in some respects.

Analyzing Agnes

What She Had:

Agnes had four outstanding qualities that appeal to men, and they were all on the Angelic side of our ideal.

1. *She had a pure and lovely character,* for David always associated her with a "stained-glass window of a church," and said she had a sacred influence on him.

Perhaps the greatest test of her character came when David married Dora. Even though Agnes herself loved David, she did not become bitter or resentful toward either of them, but continued her unselfish friendship to David, and became a friend to Dora as well. She had the courage to keep her love a secret and to live a useful life in spite of her own disappointment. Further evidence of her character is shown in her devotion to her father and the sacrifice of many of her own pleasures for his sake.

2. *Agnes understood men.* She gave David true understanding. She knew how to rejoice with him in his triumphs and sympathize with him in his difficulties. She brought him comfort, peace and comradeship.

3. *She was a capable housekeeper.* From the time she was a child, Agnes was a "discreet little housekeeper." She took care of the meals, the house and her father, with womanly efficiency.

4. *Inner happiness.* As a result of her pure character, Agnes had a "tranquility about her, and a good calm spirit," which indicates peace, or happiness within.

What Agnes Lacked:

1. *She was too independent.* She was too hesitant to lean on David or to need him. She was too unselfish, for David said, "Agnes, ever my guide and best support—if you had been more mindful of yourself, and less of me, when we grew up together, I think my heedless fancy never would have wandered from you." Because she hesitated to lean on him for anything, this made her appear to be too independent. She did not appear to need his manly care and protection.

2. *She lacked the girlish, childlike, trusting qualities.*

3. *She lacked the gentle, tender, fascinating little ways that stir a man's heart.*

Analyzing Dora

What She Had:

1. *She had an enchanting manner.*

2. *She was childlike, girlish.* At times he would refer to her as his "child-bride." At times she would shake her curls as little girls do. Her attitude was childlike, trusting.

3. *She had tender little ways.* The way she laid the flowers against her dimpled chin, or the way she patted the horses or spanked her little dog, fascinated David.

4. *She was gay.* She had a gay little laugh, a delightful little voice, and the pleasantest little ways.

5. *She was bright-eyed.*

6. *She was dependent.* She was helplessly in need of masculine protection and guidance. She had a girlish trust in David.

What Dora Lacked:

1. *She was a poor homemaker.* She could neither keep house, nor cook, nor manage household expenses.

2. *She lacked character.* Dora was good, pure and kind, but she was very self-centered. David said, "I wished my wife had had more character and purpose to sustain me." She was too absorbed in her own little problems, cares, and whims to make a good wife.

3. *She did not understand men.* This was her greatest lack. She did not know how to offer sympathy, understanding, appreciation or intellectual comradeship, for he writes, "It would have been better if my wife could have helped me more, and shared my many thoughts in which I had no partner."

Deruchette

An example of a girl who had both the Angelic and the Human qualities is Deruchette, heroine of the novel *Toilers of the Sea,* by Victor Hugo:

"Her presence lights the home; her approach is like a cheerful warmth; she passes by, and we are content; she stays awhile and we are happy. Is it not a thing of divine, to have a smile which, none know how, has the power to lighten the weight of that enormous chain that all the living in common drag behind them? Deruchette possessed this smile; we may say that this smile was Deruchette herself.

"Deruchette had at times an air of bewitching languor; and certain mischief in the eye, which were altogether involuntary. Sweetness and goodness reigned throughout her person; her occupation was only to live her daily life; her accomplishments were the knowledge of a few songs; her intellectual gifts were summed up in simple innocence; she had the graceful repose of the West Indian woman, mingled at times with giddiness and vivacity, with the teasing playfulness of a child, yet with a dash of melancholy. Add to all this an open brow, a neck supple and graceful, chestnut hair, a fair skin, slightly freckled with exposure to the sun, a mouth somewhat large, but well defined, and visited from time to time with a dangerous smile. This was Deruchette."

"There is in this world no function more important than that of being charming—to shed joy around, to cast light upon dark days, to be the golden thread of our destiny and the very spirit of grace and harmony. Is not this to render a service?"

In another place Hugo compares Deruchette to a little bird that flits from branch to branch as she moves about the house from room to room, coming and going, stopping to comb her hair as a bird plumes its wings, and "making all kinds of gentle noises, murmurings of unspeakable delight. She is, as it were, a thread of gold interwoven in your somber thoughts. She is fresh and joyous as the lark," and "She who is one day to become a mother is for a long while a child."

You may think at this point that Deruchette is a bit insipid. Remember, however, that Victor Hugo was a man, a rugged man who wrote challenging sea stories, speaking more the language of men than women. But here is a peek into his masculine viewpoint of true femininity.

When the young clergyman in the story proposed to Deruchette, he gave indication of her angelic qualities when he said, "There is for me but one woman on earth. It is you. I think of you as a prayer—you are a glory in my eyes. To me you are holy innocence. You alone are supreme. You are the living form of a benediction."

Analyzing Deruchette

Her Angelic Qualities:

1. *Her Character:* "Sweetness and goodness reigned throughout her person." She had a character which was mindful of the needs of others, for she "cast light upon dark days," and had a "smile which had the power to lighten the enormous chain." Further evidence of her character is in her lover's statement that she is "holy innocence," "is like a prayer" and the "living form of a benediction."

23

2. *Domestic:* She was capable in her domestic duties, for "her occupation is only to live her daily life," and "her presence lights the home."

3. *Inner happiness:* Similar to Agnes, Deruchette possessed inner happiness, or she could not possibly have had such ability to radiate it to others.

Her Human Qualities:

1. *Childlikeness:* Like Dora, Deruchette had childlike ways. "She who is one day to be a mother, remains for a long while a child." She had "certain mischief in the eye," and at times "the giddiness and vivacity, and the teasing playfulness of a child."

2. *Changefulness:* Deruchette was not at all times the same. Sometimes she was radiantly happy and full of giddiness and vivacity; at other times she had an air of "bewitching languor." Although she was sweet and good, at times she had "a certain mischief in the eye." Sometimes she was full of teasing-playfulness, and at other times, "a dash of melancholy." Changefulness is also a childlike quality.

3. *Fresh appearance:* "She is *fresh* and joyous as the lark."

4. *Gentle:* Her gentle qualities are described in her voice; "She makes all kinds of gentle noises, murmurings of unspeakable delight."

5. *Radiates happiness:* The most notable quality she had was her ability to radiate happiness. This was a part of her character, manner and actions.

    a. She was fresh and joyous as the lark.
    b. She shed joy around.
    c. She cast light upon dark days.
    d. Her presence lights the home.
    e. Her approach is like a cheerful warmth.
    f. She passes by and we are content.
    g. She stays awhile and we are happy.
    h. She has a smile which had the power to lighten the weight of that enormous chain which all the living in common drag behind them—a dangerous smile which was Deruchette herself.
    i. At times she had giddiness and vivacity.

6. *Grace:* Not mentioned before, but similar to gentleness and tenderness is that of grace. Deruchette was the

very spirit of grace and harmony and had the "graceful repose of the West Indian woman." Her neck was supple and graceful.

Amelia

Another example in literature of a girl who was both Angelic and Human is Amelia, from the novel *Vanity Fair*, by Thackeray. Thackeray says that Amelia is a "kind, fresh, smiling, artless, tender little domestic goddess, whom men are inclined to worship." A few pages further he calls her "poor little tender heart." In another place he attributes to her "such a kindly, smiling, tender, generous heart of her own." He admits that others might not consider her beautiful:

"Indeed, I am afraid that her nose was rather short, than otherwise, and her cheeks a good deal too round for a heroine; but her face blushed with rosy health and her lips with the freshest of smiles, and she had a pair of eyes which sparkled with the brightest and honestest of good humor, except indeed when they filled with tears, and that was a great deal too often; for the silly thing would cry over a dead canary, or over a mouse that the cat haply had seized upon; or over the end of a novel, were it ever so stupid."

Amelia had a "sweet, fresh little voice." She was subject to "little cares, fears, tears, timid misgivings." She trembled when anyone was harsh. Altogether, she was "too modest, too tender, too trustful, too weak, too much woman," for any man to know without feeling called upon to protect and cherish.

Analyzing Amelia

Amelia had several qualities worthy of our attention.

Her Angelic Qualities:

1. *Her character:* She had a generous heart and was kindly, and since "men are inclined to worship her," she evidently had a worthy character.
2. *Her domestic qualities:* Thackeray calls her "a little domestic goddess."

1. *Her freshness:* She had the freshest of smiles, and her face blushed with rosy health. She had a pair of eyes that sparkled. She had a sweet, fresh little voice.

2. *She had childlike emotions:* Her eyes would often fill with tears. She would cry over a dead canary, or a mouse or a novel. She is subject to little cares, tears, fears, timid misgivings. She trembles when anyone is harsh.

3. *Tenderness:* She was a "tender little domestic goddess." She was "too tender, too weak, too much woman."

4. *Trustfulness:* "She was too trustful."

Is Beauty Necessary?

As we come to the end of our study of these four women, we can see that they had many qualities which men admire in women. But it is interesting to note that none of these authors placed importance upon natural beauty. Amelia, for example, was chubby and stout with a very imperfect nose—"her nose was rather short than otherwise—and her cheeks a great deal too round for a heroine." Deruchette's complexion was marred by freckles, and her mouth was too large for perfection. So far are the authors from claiming beauty for these young charmers that aside from pointing out the defects mentioned, they make no attempt to describe outward appearance. Agnes and Dora were both beautiful girls, so David's choice was based upon other qualities. Realizing how men regard beauty, we can see that we will have to rely upon men's opinions in guiding us to what they admire in women. The four women we have studied thus far have been classic examples from literature. There are, of course, and always have been living examples from history. One worthy of our review is that of Mumtaz, the lady of the Taj Mahal. Again I quote from *Three Wise Men of the East,* by Elizabeth Bisland.

Mumtaz

Mumtaz was described as "exquisitely lovely." "Her glassy black hair hung in two plaits over her shoulders. Her large eyes were perfect in shape and of soft deep black; the delicately arched eyebrows were like a swallow's wing, and long silky lashes added to their beauty. Her velvety skin was fair as a lily." But, although she had uncommon external beauty, if Shah Jahan was as other men, it was her qualities within that made her superior to other women.

"She had a pure, simple and generous mind. She was amiable in nature (sweet in temper, kindhearted, etc). She was affable (easy to speak to, courteous). She had indomitable patience which would not give way even under the most trying circumstances. For example, during one period of their lives before her husband ascended to the throne, there was an attempt made to oust him from his position. Chased by the Imperial Army, he had to move from place to place for shelter. Mumtaz accompanied her husband everywhere, from the forests of Telingana to the plains of Bengal, suffering with a patient, cheerful resignation all of the miseries and hardships of a fugitive's camp life. Many of the prince's friends and advisers deserted him in the course of these events, but she clung to him with a most sincere devotion."

"Mumtaz was a wise, prudent and sagacious lady, and the Emperor had implicit confidence in her in private as well as State affairs. He used to consult her on many important affairs of the Empire, and she discharged this function of adviser admirably well." She was charitable and kind. "Many suppliants used to come to her and she never turned a deaf ear to any suitor worthy of attention. Her intercession saved many a vicitm from the scaffold and reinstated many who had incurred royal displeasure. Orphans, widows and other indigent persons won her assistance."

"Mumtaz also had a lofty sense of conjugal duty and proved to be an ideal wife. She fascinated the mind of her husband. With all of her beauty, wisdom and grace, she was the consummate flower of her gifted family. If she used all of these potent charms to bend her husband to her will, it was done with such entire art that the world had no vision of the process. From the story of their lives, however, it is evident that this woman was a strong factor in the life of this man." Perhaps her feminine influence was the reason for the extended period of peace during the reign of Shah Jahan. In his long reign of forty years, but three wars took place and these were to suppress attacks or revolts. Public affairs flowed so smoothly that chroniclers find no episodes of blood or violence to record. His

27

extremely successful foreign policy, too, was a measure of the success of his reign as was his domestic jurisdiction.

"In historical records, only by inference do we have the suggestion that Mumtaz helped to shape the life of Shah Jahan, but it must be supposed that she affected his life profoundly. Not that we have any record of his words. One hears nothing of any public action of hers. We get only a most fleeting glimpse of a lovely figure, enshrined like a jewel in a marvelous setting of splendor."

Analyzing Mumtaz

Her Angelic Qualities:

1. *Her character:* She was pure, simple and generous. She was sweet tempered and kindhearted, affable and courteous. She had indomitable patience, in the most trying circumstances. She was compassionate to the needy, assisting them in their desperate circumstances. She was intelligent and had great wisdom and prudence.

2. *Her domestic qualities:* She had a lofty sense of duty to her husband and proved to be an ideal wife. She bore him fourteen children. (Only eight lived, however, four sons and four daughters.)

Her Human Qualities:

1. *She was feminine:* She had a profound influence on her husband's life, but it was done with a subtle feminine art. She played her submissive role admirably.

2. *Radiance:* There was a cheerfulness about her in spite of trying circumstances.

3. *Fascinating:* She fascinated the mind of her husband.

We can find other examples from history of women who had Angelic and Human qualities. Cleopatra's charm changed the course of history. Helen of Troy was so treasured as to have caused a major war. Ellen Wilson, wife of the President, would be worthy of intensive study. As for modern examples, there are undoubtedly many. However, intimate descriptions of their charms are scarce. Tradition seems to be that one must die before virtues are revealed. Only recently have the love letters of Woodrow Wilson been made public. But we do know that there are many lovely women in our world, fascinating women such as Princess Grace of Monaco, the Queen of Thailand, actresses Helen Hayes and Ann Blyth, Maria Von Trapp, Lady Bird Johnson, and many others, women who have goodness of character, domestic virtues, and fascinating charm. A study of their lives would reveal angelic and human qualities, as in the examples of this chapter. There are, of course, many fascinating women unknown to the public, but just as worthy of admiration.

As we come to the end of our study of the Angelic and the Human, I will blend these appealing qualities into one whole, the total woman. On the following page is a diagram of the ideal woman, with the essential qualities which men find appealing. Although she is divided, we should always think of her as one, the Angelic and the Human combined. Together they form the ultimate in feminine charm.

You may wonder how you can come to know if these teachings are true, if these are indeed the qualities that man find fascinating, and if they will for certain awaken his tender feelings of genuine love. Experience with thousands of women has proven without question that these teachings bring the results claimed. Many thousands of women have both read the book and taken classes on the subject. Results have been unbelievable. Women who have thought they were happy before have found a new kind of romantic love come to their marriages. Women who have felt neglected and unloved have seen their marriages blossom into love and tenderness, and women who have all but despaired over their situations have found the same happy results. Time and experience have proved these teachings to be true, that whenever these principles are applied, women can be loved, honored and adored, marriages flourish, and homes are made happier.

However, an even more convincing way to truth is to apply these teachings in your own life. Acquire some of the qualities given in this chapter and see for yourself the loving response in your husband. Study the forthcoming chapters, applying the assignments at the end of the lessons and observe the convincing evidence. During this time it is best if you do not inform your husband on the subject. If you apply these principles without his awareness, you will be able to see more clearly his automatic response to Fascinating Womanhood. This will be further proof of its truth.

Angela Human

The Ideal Woman from a Man's Point of View

Angelic Qualities	Human Qualities
1. Understands Men	1. Femininity
2. Has Deep Inner Happiness	2. Radiates Happiness
3. Has A Worthy Character	3. Fresh, Radiant Health
4. Is A Domestic Goddess	4. Childlikeness

The angelic side of woman arouses in man a feeling approaching worship. These qualities bring peace and happiness to man.

The Human side of woman fascinates, amuses, captivates and enchants man. It arouses a desire to protect and shelter.

Together He Cherishes
Both are Essential to His Celestial Love

Assignment

1. Write down the following:
   A. The Angelic qualities you have.
   B. The Angelic qualities you lack.
   C. The Human qualities you have.
   D. The Human qualities you lack.

2. Make a chart of Angela Human. List the eight main qualities, leaving considerable space in between. Fill in specific qualities *you have*, referring to the list you have made. After you finish reading this book, you will probably be able to list more qualities, and after you have lived these teachings for a year, you will, no doubt, be able to list many more.

Happy with the
Simpler things
in life.

Always happy
go lucky

Keep our home
neat clean
could be more
orderly

Part I

The Angelic Qualities

1. *Understands Men*

2. *Has Deep Inner Happiness*

3. *Has A Worthy Character*

4. *Is A Domestic Goddess*

The Angelic arouses in man a feeling near worship, and brings him peace and happiness.

To become "The Ideal Woman" from a man's point of view, a woman must have Angelic qualities, or qualities of character. No man completely loves a woman who is not somewhat of an angel. A woman less angelic might fascinate him, but he will not feel for her love in all its fullness. These four qualities are separate, and yet they are one, for they are all spiritual. The following chapters in Part I are devoted to a study of these Angelic qualities and how to acquire them.

We begin our study of the Angelic side by learning to understand men. The first thing to learn is that *men are different from women,* so different in nature and temperament that it is almost as though they came from another planet. Men do not think like women do, approach a problem in the same light, nor do they have the same needs or the same sense of values as we do. Even those needs which may be similar in a man and a woman, differ widely in essential value. For example, love is essential to both. To be admired is essential to both. But, *to be loved is more important to a woman* and *to be admired is more important to a man.* Because we fail to understand these differences, we often supply men with the things *we* need, rather than the things *they* need and are baffled when they fail to respond as we anticipated.

In the following chapters we will study the masculine needs, characteristics and peculiarities. This knowledge should be a basic part of every woman's education. Without a thorough understanding of the masculine nature, how can we hope to build a good relationship with our husband and sons? The following are the six characteristics of men we will study in learning to understand men:

Six Characteristics of Men

1. His need to be accepted at face value.
2. His need to be admired.
3. His sensitive pride.
4. His need for sympathetic understanding.
5. His need to be number one in importance to his wife.
6. His need to be the guide, protector and provider for his wife and children.

3

Accept a Man
at Face Value

Characteristic No. 1

Several years ago Dr. Norman Vincent Peale, author of *The Power of Positive Thinking*, delivered a lecture in our community. After the lecture, as was customary with Dr. Peale, he allowed time for questions. One of the questions went something like this: "I have tried to make a good home, be a good mother and devoted wife, but things have not worked out very well. The trouble is that my husband has not put forth equal effort to make our marriage successful." She then listed his faults, some of which were, "He neglects the children, spends money foolishly, drinks, is cross and difficult to live with." Her question to Dr. Peale was, "After twenty-five years of marriage, is there any hope that he will change?"

Dr. Peale looked at the audience and said with a firm conviction, "Don't you know that you must always be willing to accept a man at face value and never try to change him!" Dr. Peale's marvelous advice is one of the secrets of a happy marriage and the foundation of Fascinating Womanhood. A man's most fundamental need in marriage is for his wife to accept him at face value and not try to change him.

What Does Acceptance Mean?

Acceptance means that we accept him for the man he is. We accept his ways, his hopes and dreams or his lack of dreams. We accept his ideas, his interests and his weaknesses. We accept the little quirks in his personality, his religious views and his political views and any traits he may have, for better or for worse. We are doing more than accepting him—we are accepting *his right to be himself*. We may not agree with his ideas, but we respect his right to his own viewpoint. We may notice his weaknesses, but we accept this as normal in a human being. We accept him as he is and look to his better side.

Acceptance means that we recognize him as a human being who, like ourselves, is part virtue and part fault. With this honest viewpoint we realize that his faults exist, but we also see his virtues. We accept the total man with all of his potential goodness and all of his human frailties. This is not to say that the man should not take his own faults seriously and try with all diligence to overcome them. But this is his responsibility.

Acceptance does not mean tolerance, or "putting up with him"; nor does it mean dishonesty—that we must convince ourselves he is perfect when he is not. Nor does it mean resignation. Acceptance is a happy state of mind when we realize that our responsibility is not in making him over, but in appreciating him for what he is.

Acceptance will be easier to understand if you will form a mental picture of a man painted in two colors, one bright and the other dull. Paint one side of him in the bright color to represent his virtues. Paint the other side in a dull color to represent his faults. Then turn the dull side out of view so you see only his virtues. You know the dull side is there, but you are not looking at it. You see only the bright side. Acceptance means, then, *to accept the man as a human being, part virtue and part fault, to stop worrying about his faults and look to his better side.*

What Faults do Men Have, That Women Try to Change?

The common masculine faults fall into the following categories:

1. *Personal Habits:* These include poor eating habits, poor table manners, neglect of appearance, poor spelling and grammar, bad temper, depressed moods, careless driving, untidy habits, especially in leaving things around the house and failure to hang up things or put things away in the proper place, lack of courtesy, swearing, smoking, drinking, and many others.

2. *How They Spend Their Time:* Spend too much time watching television, in the bathroom, or napping on the sofa. Spend too much time away from home with the boys in sporting events, church responsibility or other outside activity. Are too involved in too many things,

always in a hurry. Fail to come home on time or to call if they are going to be late.

3. *Duties:* Neglect home duties such as home repairs, yard work, painting, fixing. Fail to pay bills, neglect church responsibility, fail to follow through in responsibility. Undependable in their jobs and therefore are unsuccessful. Lazy, shiftless and irresponsible about their duties.

4. *Social Behavior:* Brag too much in public, talk too much, talk too little, careless in conversation, crude or loud in conversation. Lack courtesy and social graces. Do not choose friends that the wife can accept. Fail to accept wife's friends.

5. *Desires and Dreams:* Have no ambition or zest for living, do not have a desire to better themselves, underestimate themselves, lack confidence, cannot make up their minds what they want out of life, move from one dream to another. Let good opportunities go by, have no imagination about getting ahead. Some men have dreams that are too impossible to fulfill or take too much risk.

6. *Manly Qualities:* Are not masculine enough, are indecisive, vacillating, fail to lead the family firmly, too soft on the children, worry too much about past mistakes, too fearful of launching out on something new, do not have good ideas.

7. *Money:* Do not manage money well, spend money foolishly, are stingy with money, spend large amounts without consulting wife.

8. *Neglect of Children:* Ignore children when they come home, do not play with the children or take them any place, do not help children with their homework or take part in care and training of children. Complain about normal noise and contention of little children.

9. *Religion:* Will not attend church, will not listen to religious ideas, are not interested in religion. Take children on fishing trips or to amusement parks instead of to church.

Why do Women Try to Change Men?

1. *For Her Own Good:* In most cases a woman will try to change a man because his faults bring problems and deprivation into her life, robbing her of some of the things she really wants. She may feel that if the man would change, her life would be better and happier. If you will

review the list of men's faults just covered, you will see how this can be true, how her desire for comforts, money, material goods, prestige, pleasure and other benefits to herself can make her anxious to change her husband.

2. *For His Own Good:* Another reason for trying to change a man is *for his own good.* Many well meaning women will say, "If you really love and care about someone, it is important to see that they get the best out of life. Therefore, I must change my husband for his own good." Women such as this feel it is their *responsibility* to change their husband. A woman of my acquaintance began marriage by making a long list of her husband's faults which she tried to change. She thought it was her duty to improve him.

Is it our duty? Are we responsible for making our husband into the man he ought to be? In answer, if a man is blind to his own faults and this blindness causes him to get into difficulty or to fail to reach success, it is important for his wife to *wake him up,* as I will explain later in this chapter; but once he realizes his mistakes or faults, if he chooses to continue, she should not persist in the matter, but should accept him as he is. It is not her duty to push him to success. "But," his wife may say, "my husband's faults are robbing him of basic happiness; therefore I must change him so that he can be happy." This seems like a worthy aim. What possible reason could one have against it? There are four reasons why women should not try to change men and they are the following:

1. It creates marriage problems.
2. It can destroy love.
3. It can cause a man to rebel.
4. It doesn't work.

1. It Creates Marriage Problems:

Even though a wife may set out to remake her husband with the best of intentions, it can bring marriage problems with serious consequences. In the first place, it can create a terrible tension in the household. The wife may suffer tension because of her concern for her husband's faults. She may worry about the consequences of his behavior. Then, when she sets out to change him she creates additional tension in that he resists the change. Children, too, suffer when they become aware of the tension existing between the parents.

When a woman tries to change a man she is, in effect, indicating that she is not satisfied with him as he is. When a man feels his wife's lack of approval, he is apt to form resentments toward her, affecting his feelings for her and bringing discord into their relationship. His resentful attitude can cause him to become withdrawn and cool towards his wife and may be the beginning of a break in their communications. He may avoid the situation by spending a great amount of time away from home, with his friends or in other interests or pursuits.

Another problem is in regards to his ego. His realization that his wife is not satisfied with him is deflating to his ego. *A man is proud in spirit* and adversely affected when his spirit is wounded. He knows his weaknesses, but would like his wife to evaluate him from his better side. Her inference that he is not fully acceptable threatens his security, just as the wife would feel insecure if she felt unloved.

The tension, resentments, lack of communication and cooled attitude should cause the wife to question *if her objectives are worth it.* Does what she hope to accomplish in improving her husband compensate for the discord in her home and the damage to her marriage relationship? Which is more important to her children, to herself and her husband? Isn't love and harmony in marriage of greater value?

2. It Can Destroy Love:

Not only can love be cooled, in some cases it can be *destroyed.* When a wife constantly pushes and nettles her husband, it can cause the destruction of a happy marriage. One of the most tragic cases in history is that of the Russian novelist, Count Leo Tolstoi and his wife.

In the beginning of their marriage, Tolstoi and his wife were so blissfully happy that, kneeling together, they prayed to God to continue the ecstasy that was theirs. Tolstoi is one of the most famous novelists of history. Two of his masterpieces, *War and Peace* and *Anna Karenina,* are considered literary treasures. He was so admired by his people that they followed him around day and night and wrote down in shorthand every word he uttered.

Although he was a man of wealth and fame, after studying the teachings of Jesus and other moralists, he gave away his property, worked in the fields chopping wood and pitching hay, made his own shoes, ate out of a wooden bowl, and tried to love his enemies. He gave away the publishing rights to his books and had the courage of his convictions to live a life he believed in.

But his wife never accepted his simple philosophy of life. She loved luxury and he despised it. She craved fame and the esteem of society, but these things meant nothing to him. She longed for money and riches, but he thought these things a sin. For years she made every effort to change him and his views. When he resisted her and went his own way, she screamed at him and threw herself into fits of hysteria or threatened to kill herself or jump down the well.

After forty-eight years this man who had adored his wife when he married her could hardly bear the sight of her. And one of the most tragic scenes was when Countess Tolstoi, heartbroken and old and starving for affection, would kneel at her husband's feet and beg him to read aloud the exquisite love passages that he had written about her in his diary fifty years previously. And as he read of those beautiful happy days that were now gone forever, both of them wept. His dying request was that she should not be permitted to come into his presence. There have been, of course, many marriages that began by being romantic and tender, but were destroyed because of the wife's inability to accept her husband or allow him to be himself. Such are the real tragedies of history.

3. It Can Cause Rebellion:

Pressing a man to change can bring out a streak of rebellion in him. This is caused by his struggle to preserve his freedom to be himself. For example, I have a young son who sometimes says, "Mother, don't tell me to do it or I won't want to." This indicates how men feel about their precious freedom and how they will sometimes turn against the very things they want because of it. An illustration of this is in the following true experience:

Escape Out the Bathroom Window

A woman became converted to a particular religion which she was very devoted to. She, therefore, tried to interest her husband, but he did not respond. She kept after him night and day, but each effort failed. One evening she arranged secretly for the missionaries of her church to drop by at dinnertime, thinking that her husband would feel obligated to invite them in and be friendly. She also arranged for them to bring books, tapes, a film and other materials from which they could preach to him after the meal.

Everything went exactly as planned. Just as the family was sitting down to the table, the missionaries rang the doorbell. After an enjoyable meal, the wife said, "Wouldn't it be nice if these two gentlemen explained a little about the church." Due to moral pressure and courtesy, the man agreed. As the missionaries were assembling their materials, flannel board, books and pictures, the poor husband felt trapped. He excused himself to go to the bathroom, climbed out of the bathroom window and disappeared. He was gone for three days.

After three days of searching, the desperate wife turned to her church for help. Several of the leaders came to her rescue and began looking for the husband. After an extensive search, he was found. In questioning him, it was discovered that he had no intention of returning home at all. However, due to the kindly persuasion of the gentleman who found him and his wife's promise that she would never mention religion again, he returned home. The wife kept her promise, and the man began to relax in peace.

The impressive part of this story is the following experience. The gentleman who found the husband became quite well acquainted with him. In their conversation the husband confessed, "I have wanted to know more about it, but *not from my wife*." Secretly he learned more about his wife's religion, became converted to it and secretly became a member of it. Then one morning in church the minister arose and announced that there was a new member of his congregation, gave his name and asked him to come to the rostrum. When her husband arose, the wife was so overjoyed that she burst into tears.

Another woman caused a rebellious streak to appear in her husband by doing the following: When she first married him, she made many suggestions about trival matters. She tried to reform his eating habits, encouraged him to take more baths and to take better care of his appearance. She cooked many health foods. Her husband came from a family that thought nutrition unimportant, so it was especially irritating to him to be deprived of the foods he was used to. This infringement upon his freedom caused him to eat especially unwholesome foods while he was away from home. He also began drinking. Her suggestions were towards health, so his rebellion was against health, and he has almost ruined his once strong body by his unwholesome eating habits. In a sense his attitude has been *give me liberty or give me death*.

4. It Doesn't Work:

The final reason women should never try to change men is that *it doesn't work*. Women's suggestions and pressures do not change men. Did Countess Tolstoi succeed in changing her husband? Did the wife who was anxious about her religion succeed in having the missionaries preach to her husband? Did the wife who cooked health foods succeed in reforming her husband's eating habits? No, men do not change in this way.

Now in some instances a woman claims credit for her husband's improvement, saying his change was a result of her own efforts. Do not let this mislead you. If you could possibly know the details, you would find that the man changed, not due to his wife's persuasion, but because he found another incentive for changing, a reason that she does not realize. Or he was intelligent and wise enough to see the folly of his ways without her help. The man would undoubtedly have changed sooner without her push.

As you can see from the four problems just illustrated, women's efforts to change men are unsuccessful in that they lead to marriage problems, tend to destroy love, bring out a rebellious streak, and do not bring any change in the man.

How You Can Help a Man to Change, or Improve Himself

If you accept a man at face value, is there any hope that he will change? Who is to say? You must accept the fact that he may not. But in a miraculous way men are apt to improve when they are fully accepted. *The only hope that a man will change is for you not to try to change him.* Others may try to change him, teach him, and offer suggestions, but the woman he loves must accept him for the man he is. However, there are three things a woman can do which will encourage his growth to his better self:

42

1. *Give Him His Freedom:* You can help a man to improve himself by giving him his freedom to be himself, to worship God according to the dictates of his own conscience, to follow his own interests and objectives, to do the things he wants to do, to dress as he wishes and eat what he wants. When given this personal freedom, his mind can function without obstacles and his spirit will be released. His mind will be receptive to ideas, even your own. He will be encouraged to be his better self.

2. *Look To His Better Side:* You can further encourage his growth and improvement by looking to his better side. Express appreciation for this better side and he will be encouraged to grow to be a better man and strive more diligently to overcome his weaknesses. Only by looking to a person's better side can we help a child, a man or any individual to grow to a higher potential.

3. *Live All of Fascinating Womanhood:* One of the miracles of Fascinating Womanhood is that when you live all of these principles, the man's faults tend to disappear and he becomes a finer, better person. I have seen this happen again and again. Women have told me that their husbands have been so obnoxious that they, or anyone else, have not been able to stand them; but when the wife lived Fascinating Womanhood, in an almost magical way the man dropped his obnoxious traits and became quite a man. Of course, there is no guarantee, but a wholehearted effort to live Fascinating Womanhood *can* cause a man to change for the better. So, remember that there are three means of encouraging a man's improvement. I would like, now, to elaborate on the first by explaining the man's great need for freedom:

The Man's Great Need for Personal Freedom

Free agency is one of the most fundamental laws of life. Mankind does not develop nor experience happiness without it. God was fully aware of this eternal principle when he created man and placed him on the earth. He allowed the forces of evil to be present, although he knew from the beginning that many of the precious souls of men would fall into sin and reap the bitterness which comes from disobedience. But he also knew that without freedom, mankind could not develop. Man has to be given a choice and has to make that choice himself. If God could risk man's future happiness and well being in order to

43

extend to him his precious freedom, *why then cannot women allow men this same privilege? Why not let a man do the things he wants to do and be the kind of a man he wants to be without interference?*

A man is particularly in need of *religious* freedom, as all men everywhere have always been. Our nation was founded upon this principle; the pilgrims left Europe because of it, and it is still just as important to each one of us today. Each individual has a right to his own religious views; it is his God-given right. And a man certainly has a right to his personal feelings about religion. When a wife preserves his religious freedom, rewards follow. His mind will function without barriers, and he is more apt to consider another viewpoint. Let me illustrate by the following experience:

A girl was engaged to marry a man of a different religion from her own. Her religion was very important to her, and she hoped that if she married him he would eventually join her church. She sought counsel from a wise man who told her, "If you marry this man, make nothing of his religious differences to him openly. Do not attempt to change his views, but rather recognize his religious freedom. If he wants to go to his church, go with him. Give him complete freedom, but hold to your own ideals and be the living example of what your religion teaches."

She did marry the man, and she followed the wise man's counsel. He did ask her to attend his church with him, which she did willingly. In return, he was willing to attend hers. By comparing the two, he soon became convinced that his wife's church was superior to his own and he became a member of it.

Men are so touchy about religious freedom that they resist even a gentle hint. For example, a young wife told me that each Sunday morning she merely asked her husband, "Are you planning to attend church this morning?" This gentle hint so irritated him that he stayed home just to hold to his freedom. He had nothing against the church, but if he attended, he wanted it to be his idea. As soon as she stopped hinting, he began to attend more regularly. When we attempt to drive men to church, we more often drive them away. The few women who have supposedly pushed their husbands to church have taken credit for it under a false illusion. Their men have found some other reason for attending church than the woman supposes, and

44

they would have come into activity sooner with freedom and a shining example.

In addition to religion, a man needs other freedoms— the freedom to follow his own interests, to spend his time, money and energy as he sees fit, and in general be the kind of man he wants to be. He is quite sensitive about freedom of dress, how he wears his hair and other things about his appearance. He guards his right to eat as he chooses. When this right is infringed on, he can be rebellious as I pointed out in a previous example; but when freedom is extended, the man sometimes changes for the better, as in the following example:

A girl of my acquaintance was devout in eating *health foods*. But she married a man who was not interested in nutrition and has been used to eating pies, cakes, jams, candy and white bread. Soon after they were married, she said sweetly to him, "Honey, I know that you have been trained to eat a different way than I, but do you mind if I prepare for myself the foods I want and I will do the same for you?" He agreed, and she did this for many months. But after awhile he adopted her good eating habits and was preaching their value to his own family. Men are usually wise enough to want what is right and best for themselves, but more than anything, they want their precious freedom.

Although a man loves the freedom to be himself and do the things he wants to do, he will sometimes sacrifice this freedom for one thing: peace in the household. For example, a young couple who were guests in my household planned a day at the beach. As they were leaving, the girl asked her husband if he was going to wear his dark glasses. He told her that he deliberately left them for he did not want to be bothered. She tried to insist, but he held his ground. After they were in the car I heard a car door open, and the man came back for his glasses. All he said was, "Anything to keep peace." She, of course, wanted him to wear his glasses "for his own good." In our efforts to pamper and serve our men, we often infringe on the very thing which is most important, their freedom.

There are other situations when a man sacrifices his freedom for peace. He may go places he does not want to go, give up interests, spend money against his better judgment, yield to the children, and numerous other things he does not believe in or want to do, just to keep peace in the household. But the wife pays a dear price for having things her way—*loss of love and tenderness.*

How Women Try to Change Men

Sometimes women try to change men by an element of force in the form of demands, ultimatums or threats, but more frequently by criticism, nagging or pushing. Even more frequently women use the more subtle methods such as moral pressure, disapproval, a carefully worded suggestion or a gentle hint. Another subtle way is by using other men as shining examples. She may express admiration for her father, brother, another man in the community or even a famous man from history. If she does so with the intent of impressing on her husband's mind the other man's superior virtues, hoping he will try to be more like the other man, she can cause her husband to feel she is dissatisfied with him as he is. So it is in the following ways that women try to change men:

1. By demands
2. By ultimatums or threats
3. Criticism
4. Nagging
5. Pushing
6. By moral pressure
7. Disapproval
8. Suggestions
9. Hints
10. Using other men as shining examples

Provoking a Man to Righteousness

Some Christian women have been taught that if necessary, they should "provoke their husbands to righteousness" and have interpreted this to mean to "nettle or to push" the man to a more righteous form of living. Their mistake lies in an incorrect definition of the word "provoke." At the time this religious instruction was given, the dictionary meaning of the word "provoke" was different than today and meant to "inspire or incite," whereas the word today means "to nettle or to push." The correct way, therefore, to interpret the word "provoke" in this religious instruction is "to inspire or to incite a man to righteousness," and this apparently would be by her example.

46

When women try to change men, it indicates a serious fault within themselves, the fault of self-righteousness. A self-righteous woman will feel that she is better than her husband. She may love and respect him, but in the overall, considers herself a little finer, smarter, more alert, more diligent and more careful than he. She may feel that she is more devoted to the church, more faithful in living her religion and doing what is right and therefore a more righteous person than he. This same attitude of self-righteousness was observed among the Sadducees and the Pharisees in Biblical times. They were proud of their faithfulness to attend church, pay tithes, pray, read the Scriptures, fast, observe the Sabbath and attend to any number of rituals—but the Savior condemned them, not for their faithfulness, but because of their self-righteous attitude about their faithfulness.

The woman who condemns a man for his faults is puting herself in the position of being a judge. She should ask herself if she is qualified to judge a man's worth, *or* her own. Is she really a better person than he is? One day a woman complained to me of many of her husband's faults, some serious. Then I said to her, "Do you really think you are a better person than he is?" She looked at me with indignation, then, after quiet meditation she lowered her head and said humbly, "No, I don't think I am a better person than my husband. I know he is a fine man at heart."

One thing that makes it difficult to overlook a fault in a man is that you may not have his particular fault—your faults are likely *different from his*. For example, he may be disorganized and messy, whereas you may be neat and orderly. He may be forgetful and you may be alert. On the other hand, you may be critical whereas he is inclined to be forgiving. He may be prompt and you may be late. Because your faults are different, you may focus on his and overlook your own, creating an attitude of self-righteousness. The next time you are troubled by a fault in your husband, say to yourself, "He has this fault, but he is better than I am in other ways."

If we have any duty to God it is not to improve our husbands but to look to ourselves for failings. The heart of Christian doctrine and other sound religions and philosophies is *"It is ourselves we must change,"* or "cast out the

47

beam from our own eye first that we may more clearly see the mote in our brother's." Only through this humility of spirit can we build a successful relationship with another person. Remember the Bible account of the man who lifted up his head in pride saying that he was glad he was not sinful as other men, but Jesus approved the humble man who smote his chest saying, "Oh, God, be merciful to me, a sinner."

The Virtue Behind His Faults

2.02

In discovering a man's better side, understand that there are virtues behind many of men's faults. For example, an obnoxious man is often a sign of a high caliber man who is not appreciated, not accepted, not given his freedom or in some way mistreated by his wife. A man who is moody and discouraged is often a man with extremely high aspirations that are not being met. A man who is forgetful, negligent, thoughtless, is often a man who has great mental capacity and is using his mind for greater things than what appear to be important details to you. A man who appears lazy and negligent at home may be a man who is putting all of his energies away from home towards being successful and a good provider. Look beyond these faults and you will find the better, finer man.

Is There Ever a Time When I Should Try to Change Him?

In answer, "No," there is never a time when you should try to change the man you love, but there are times when you should respond to his faults, or deal with them in a certain way, as in the following situations:

1. *When A Man Is Blind To His Own Mistakes:* Sometimes a man is blind to his own mistakes, and such blindness causes him to get into difficulty and even fail to reach success. Take for example the salesman who uses a poor approach, the department supervisor who is too dictatorial, or the doctor who is losing his patients because he appears unfriendly. On these occasions his wife should wake him up. She may be the only one who cares enough to help. Often others who observe his mistakes are not interested enough to help or may not feel it their business to do so.

In waking up the man who is blind, keep in mind that

you do accept him. It is the world that does not. Others are offended, not you. Tell him that you have a few ideas that might prove helpful. Let him know that you are not close to the situation as he is and that you could be wrong, but "could this be the cause of your trouble?" Assure him that you admire him and isn't it regrettable that others do not esteem him for his true worth. Once you have opened his eyes, do not persist in the matter. Drop it completely. If he continues to make the same mistakes, fully aware of them, you will have to allow him this freedom.

Be certain that he is actually unaware of his mistakes and also be certain that it is causing him difficulty. A woman asked me if she should correct her husband's grammar, which was obviously poor. In inquiring about him, I found that he was extremely successful and had approval of many friends. I told her that I felt it unnecessary to say anything about it. When you give your opinions or corrections to your husband, be feminine. Don't appear to know more about his business than he does; don't be motherly, and don't talk man to man. (Refer to Chapter 8—How To Give Feminine Advice.)

2. *When He Mistreats You:* Should you try to change a man's behavior when he mistreats you? I am referring to times when he may be thoughtless, unfair, insulting or even harsh or critical. In answer, let me say this: A man is entitled to many freedoms, but he does not have the right to mistreat you. You are not a doormat. You are a human being worthy of the highest respect and consideration, and it is important to both of you and to your relationship for you to maintain your self-dignity. It is, in fact, difficult for a man to feel kindly towards a woman he can mistreat. The method of handling these difficult situations is not one of remaking the man, but of preserving dignity and easing tension. It is one of the charming arts of Fascinating Womanhood and will be taught in Chapter 20.

3. *When A Man Does Something Wrong:* Another time to respond to a man's faults is when he is dishonest, unkind, weak, sinful, or in any way shows a lack of character. If you overlook his weakness, you display a lack of character yourself. The way to respond to his improper conduct is this: At first show reluctance to believe it. Say that you thought it was impossible for a man such as he to do such a thing. If you are compelled to believe it, indicate that you know it is contrary to his true nature and was only the result of carelessness or thoughtlessness. *You*

must be immensely disappointed at his temporary lapse, but your faith in his better side must be unshaken.

And do not make the mistake of lowering your standards to his. When a man errs, the woman may be tempted to fall to his level so that he will feel more accepted. This is a serious mistake. A man always considers a woman to be better than he and would be disappointed to see her fall from her level to his. He expects her to hold to her ideals and standards, even under trying circumstances.

Some Special Problems

1. *The Alcoholic Husband:* Many women ask, must I accept alcoholism in my husband? Alcoholism is one of the most difficult of faults for a woman to accept in a man, due to related problems of squandering money, ugliness of disposition, dishonesty, unreliableness, other women, and the deterioration of the home. Women almost despair over this problem. Many have asked me, "How can I accept what he has done to our life?" In answer, "you must accept this," but let me stress some points which will make this acceptance possible.

First, realize that alcoholism is one of the most difficult of all weaknesses to overcome. You will have to gain an understanding of the depth of the problem and a sympathy for what the man faces. I know you have been told this before, but here is what you can do to make sympathy real. Once a month fast for three days—going without all food or beverage—nothing but water, or give up smoking, coffee, sweets or other binding habits. You will soon get the picture of what you are expecting of a man when you ask him to give up his enslaving habit.

Next, try to gain a humility of spirit in the following way: Take a look at *your reaction to his problem.* Even though you have known better, you have probably yelled, nagged, insulted and abused him for the mess he has made of your lives. When he acts like he does, you have had a bad attitude, lost patience and exploded. You may have tried to live the principles of Fascinating Womanhood, but time and time again you have failed to apply them.

If you can admit such weakness in yourself, the inability to control yourself and a failure to do what you know you should do, then can you condemn your husband for his weakness, a most difficult human weakness to overcome? Your weaknesses are relatively easy to overcome. His are almost impossible. If you will "cast out the beam from your own eye first," then you will be able to see the terrible enslaving bond of alchoholism that your husband is under.

2. *Cruelty To Children:* If a man is dangerously cruel with his children in that he would harm either body or spirit, the wife has a moral and sacred obligation to protect her children by taking them out of his presence or even out of the household and remaining away until all danger is past. This step can be taken kindly but firmly, not condemning the man, but protecting the children. You will have to accept even cruelty as a human weakness and not judge the man, but try to understand the causes of his cruelty. Your own kind but firm spirit may be the means of bringing him to reality.

3. *Other Women:* There are two things a woman can rightfully expect in marriage, and they are *fidelity* and *financial support*. If the husband is involved with another woman, I suggest that the wife deal with the problem in the following way:

First, face your part in the problem by asking yourself what you did to drive him away. After a study of Fascinating Womanhood, you will see many of these mistakes. Correcting these errors can be the means of winning him back, and in many cases this has been done quickly and under difficult circumstances.

After you have eliminated your mistakes and become a wonderful wife, if he continues immoral practices, it will be time to bring him to a showdown, stating clearly but firmly that he will have to make a choice and that if he does not give her up you will have to leave him. And be prepared to keep your word.

It is morally wrong for a woman to continue to live with a man who is immoral. It can actually prevent his repentance, for if he has both of you, he does not have the incentive he needs to give her up. This step can be taken with understanding and humility, accepting the sin as a great human weakness, extremely difficult to overcome. This can be done without condemning or judging him. A woman cannot turn her back on her husband's infidelity with a clear conscience. She has a moral obligation to make an effort to win him back, for as long as he lives in sin he is on the way to destruction. By winning him back, you not only save a marriage, but a soul!

4. *Nonsupport:* The second thing a woman can expect in marriage is financial support. This means an income to cover necessities and a home of her own—a house, apartment or respectable dwelling place away from any other family. If the man does not provide these things, there is justification for action.

Since women are not inclined to let the children suffer hunger or want, many solve this problem by going to work. This step, however, will weaken the man's incentive and increase the problem. If she provides the income, he is removed from the weight of his responsibility. If the wife refuses to work, an indolent man may walk out on his responsibility and leave the wife to face her problems alone. In this case, the wife has no choice but to support the family but should refuse to have the man return until he arranges for their support. I am not implying that there are not certain circumstances and emergencies when the wife should work, but the responsibility is the man's as we will learn in a later chapter.

Acceptance Is Not Easy

I realize that when I teach women to accept their husbands at face value, I am not asking them to do something easy. Some women have found it so difficult that they have stopped trying. I learned that two women talked over their back fence about this one day. They agreed that accepting their husbands' faults was so difficult that it was too much to ask of themselves, and they decided to disregard this principle.

Try to realize that any advancement to a better, happier life is difficult. For example, living the Christian religion is not easy—loving your enemies, doing good to those that hate you and trying to become "perfect." But, a devout Christian does not set aside these goals, just because they are difficult. The ladies talking over the back fence might as well have decided to give up being a Christian because it is difficult, as to give up accepting a man at face value for this reason. Acceptance is the most fundamental principle taught in Fascinating Womanhood; therefore, your success will be dependent upon your living this part of the subject.

I can promise you tremendous rewards if you will accept your husband at face value. The response in your husband will likely be moving. For years he may have suffered the plaguing thought that you are dissatisfied with him as he is. Your assurance that you accept him as he is will remove a terrible doubt from his mind and come as a relief. His appreciation for you and his tender response can be almost earth shaking, as in some of the following true experiences:

The Years That the Locust Had Eaten

"Marriage, for me, at age twenty was an arrangement in which I could begin to change my new husband into the man I wanted him to be and get out of it all that I possibly could. I had been taught that marriage is a fifty-fifty proposition and that I was to do all that I could to be sure that my part of the proposition was secured.

"Seven stormy years later I began to view the shambles I had created—a very unhappy belligerent husband who had retreated into himself and children that also reflected the home situation. I began to ask the Lord what was wrong, and slowly but clearly as I searched the Scriptures I began to see the wonderful role that God had created for the woman in being a "help-meet" for her husband and of his place of leadership in the home. Mental assent was given to these truths; yet as to how to put them to practice eluded me. Some improvement was made in our home situation, but my husband remained behind his wall and after a long period of time, I became very discouraged and began to doubt the truths I had previously learned.

"At this point I heard of the Fascinating Womanhood course, feeling that this would perhaps give some of the answers I longed and prayed to know. Within six weeks of the course, I sought to put into practice what was being taught and saw my husband really begin to shower attentions upon me, so by the end of six weeks our life together was sweeter and richer than it was on our honeymoon. Whereas before I was occupied with his faults, now these same faults somehow were the points I could actually admire, finding myself in the freshness of a new love for him. He began to tell me that he loved me for the first time in years. Since then our life together is continuing to improve and grow in love and fellowship. For the first time I feel satisfied and fulfilled as a woman with much thanksgiving for the wonderful gift of womanhood God has given to me and to all women.

"It is written in the book of Joel ' ... I will restore to you the years that the locust has eaten ... and you shall eat in plenty and be satisfied and praise the name of the Lord your God that has dealt wondrously with you ...' (Joel 2:25, 26) I can say with all confidence that this promise is being fulfilled in my life as by the strength of Christ I continue to put into practice the principles in both the Scriptures and amplified in Fascinating Womanhood."

His Little Angel

"My husband and I have been married 21 years. I had always thought we had a wonderful marriage, that is, for the first half of it. Then things began to happen. We have seven children whom we love very much, but this was not enough to hold our marriage together. A friend and sister had been trying to get me interested in Fascinating Womanhood, so in desperation I thought I would try, so I borrowed a book and began to read. To me it was revelation upon revelation.

"My husband at the time was planning to leave me. I told him I thought he should as we had nothing in common anymore. He was 200 miles away looking for work which would take him further away, so I had to work fast. The night he came home I applied the first assignment, to accept him and tell him so and told him I would like very much a chance to prove to him that I would improve. He said nothing. The next night I asked him if he had thought about it and he said 'yes,' but he was convinced it wouldn't work. He was so discouraged, disillusioned and unhappy that he thought the only thing to do was to go away by himself. I tried to convince him otherwise but nothing would change his mind. Well, with my life at an end, so I thought, I cried the whole night.

"The next morning he asked me if I really meant what I said and I said 'Yes.' He told me that he had always loved me, that he really didn't want to leave and that his boss had offered him a raise if he would stay. He held me in his arms as if he would never let go. I am remembering our first year of marriage when he kissed my feet and called me 'his little angel,' and I am wondering how I could have been such a fool as to let him down as I have. But I feel very blessed to be given another chance, and by applying Fascinating Womanhood, I am praying that I will be able to arouse these feelings again in him."

A Blow to Self-Sacrificing Me

"Before taking Fascinating Womanhood I had practically given up on my marriage. In fact, two days before my first class I had consulted a lawyer about getting a divorce from my unbearable husband. He drank too much, had no interest in us and each weekend would take off to some extravagant city and spend his entire paycheck. When he learned I had seen an attorney, he begged me with tears in his eyes not to leave him. 'I'll change, I'll do anything,' he pleaded. Finally I was satisfied for he had promised to change.

"Then I had my first Fascinating Womanhood lesson on acceptance. It was a blow to self-sacrificing me. I had to admit I made mistakes too. Could it have been my fault all along for not accepting him? I went home and told him I accepted him the way he was. I said I had made a lot of mistakes in our marriage and would sincerely try to do better. A wonderful shocked expression appeared on his face and he said, 'You mean I can go out and spend all the money and you won't care?' I said with a smile, 'If you still want to after I am fascinating, go ahead.' He hasn't gone out one time since I have been practicing this philosophy. I still have a lot of work to do, but our marriage has become better each week."

Out of the Cellar

"I have a wonderful husband but he has some habits I disapproved of, especially his use of tobacco. I always insisted he go into the cellar to smoke even though I accepted this habit in him when we were married. After learning the principle of acceptance, I realized how awful I had been. When he came home that night I confessed my feelings, asking forgiveness for the terrible way I had treated him and told him that I accepted him as he is. My husband was so tenderly touched that he cried. Later that evening he told me that he loved me for the first time in two years and he slept with his arm around me all night."

How to Bring a Man Home

"My husband has been quite a fellow to go out with the boys, almost every night until dawn. Each time I have been extremely aggravated with him. After understanding the principle of acceptance, however, I tried a different approach. One night I had dinner on the table and had called him to eat when one of his buddies came to the door, wanting him to go out for awhile. He got his coat on and told me where he was going and not to wait up for him. Although my first impulse was to hit the ceiling, I caught myself and said instead, 'Oh, I think that is a good idea. You really need to get away for awhile. Have a good time and I'll have something for you to eat when you come home.' His reaction was one of great surprise. He did go, but in about 45 minutes was back home in very happy spirits and with a box of candy for me. He spent the rest of the evening just talking with me and helping me."

Rules for Acceptance

1. Get rid of self-righteous attitude.
2. Accept him as part virtue, part fault.
3. Give him his freedom to be himself.
4. Don't try to change him.
5. Don't use other men as shining examples.
6. Look to his better side.
7. Express your acceptance in words.

Assignments

1. Tell him something like the following: (An Ice Breaker) "I am glad you are the kind of man you are. I can see that I have not understood you in the past and that I have made many mistakes. But I am glad that you have not allowed me to push you around. You have not been like putty in my hands, but have had the courage of your convictions. Will you forgive me for not understanding you and let me prove to you that I am happy you are the kind of man you are?" At first you may feel insincere by telling him these things for all of your critical attitudes may not have disappeared. But do tell him and look to his better side and your acceptance will continue to grow.

2. **Look to his better side:** Spend some time thinking of his better side, listing all of his virtues you can think of. Express sincere appreciation to him for these virtues.
3. Make or buy a little "Love Booklet" to write down the loving things your husband says or does as you begin to apply the principles of Fascinating Womanhood. Write down any favorite reaction to the above assignments.

4

Admiration

The center of a woman's happiness in marriage is to be loved—but the center of a man's is to be admired.

Characteristic No. 2

Deep in his heart every man longs for admiration—of his abilities, his ideas and his dreams. This admiration is a source of great happiness, and the lack of it one of his most distressing miseries. Although it is all important to him, it isn't something he can get for himself. It must be given him by those who respect and love him. He likes receiving it from any and every source, but it is most essential from the woman he loves.

A man will often do and say things deliberately in the presence of a woman, hoping to receive admiration. But these things often go unnoticed. Usually a woman is too busy or too mentally occupied with her own world and problems to notice anything to admire. We don't often notice or bother to find out what is in a man's heart, what he thinks and dreams about. The woman who offers the perfect admiration is the woman who wins his deepest affection.

The Young Boy

This need is manifest in the young boy and is essential to his confidence and growth into manhood. It helps him to experience love for his parents. Unfortunately there are many young boys whose parents fail to admire them. A life of correction without praise some young men endure, but the longing is always there. When such a boy matures, he needs admiration more than ever, for doing without it in his youth has caused a lack of confidence. If the woman he marries can offer the needed admiration, his troubles are over. If not, he often becomes a lonely creature.

The Young Man

Especially is the need for admiration apparent in the young man just beginning his career. He expects to be an all-conquering success; no project is too wild, no dream too fantastic. He is full of plans and proposals, assurance and enthusiasm. What he doesn't expect to do, after a little preliminary preparation, of course, simply isn't worth doing. He can find a hundred flaws in the way older heads are managing things now—but wait until he gets his chance and revolutionizes matters. Meantime, life isn't worth living if he can't find someone to whom he can tell all of this, how things ought to be, how they will be when he gets his chance. Most of his youthful associates are too much occupied with their own aspirations to listen to his. Older people will only laugh at him. Where can he find an uncritical listener and confidante? *The cry of his soul is for admiration.* The woman who gives it to him is no less than an angel.

The Older Man

As a man grows older, if he has not been admired, he often learns to do without it. He becomes, it would seem, hardened, incredulous and less sensitive to the lack of admiration. The older a man becomes, however, the more bitterly he resents this apparent indifference to the bigger and nobler elements of his character. He represses his craving for admiration because he does not believe it is to be had, but the craving for it is just as strong and persistent as it is in the younger man.

What He Wants You to Admire

What a man wants you to admire more than anything else are *his manly qualities*. If you admire only traits which are admirable in both men and women, he will be disappointed. For example, if you admire him because he is kind, thoughtful, helps you with the dishes, is pleasant or well groomed, he may appreciate your praise, but it will do little to stir his feelings for you. *It is his masculinity that he wants noticed and admired.*

What are his masculine qualities? *Physically* they are his large build, his strong muscles, his deep pitched voice, his heavy jaw, his manly beard, his mustache, his heavy

59

walk, his large hands, and anything which distinguishes him as part of the male sex. His sexual function is masculine. We see his manly strength and endurance at work in sports, weight lifting, swimming, lifting heavy objects, managing difficult equipment, sawing logs, taming horses, and even some of the more common things such as mowing the lawn, painting, opening tight jar lids, turning screws or wielding a hammer. Men's clothes are also part of the physical. They are heavier, rougher and more tailored than women's—and therefore more masculine.

Mentally his manliness lies in his achievements, skills and abilities. This is the skill of the carpenter, the mechanic, the salesman, doctor, lawyer or teacher and all of the other fields of work that men engage in. We see manly ability in the man who wins a debate, receives honor for outstanding service or who achieves a difficult objective. The man who faithfully goes to work from day to day to provide for his family, devotedly filling his role as their guide, protector and provider, demonstrates masculinity. Masculine traits are displayed in his *dependability* in his job, his *decisiveness* in making decisions, his *sound judgment*, his *aggressiveness* towards his objectives, and his *determination* and *steadfastness* in the things he sets out to do.

Spiritually his manliness is demonstrated in his sense of honor and duty in men's affairs, his courage and devotion to a cause, his sense of fair play, his noble deeds, his high standards and aspirations or any high ideals which have to do with a man's life. Few men have all of the masculine traits listed, but all men have some of them. These and many more are the masculine traits that men want noticed and admired.

Why is admiration of his masculinity so important to a man? Because it *makes him feel manly*, and this realization of his masculinity is one of the most enjoyable feelings a man can experience. When a woman supplies him with the much needed admiration, she becomes indispensable to his happiness, and he will turn to her again and again for the comfort her companionship gives him—the feeling of manliness he experiences in her presence. Admiring his masculinity is, in fact, one of the keys to winning a man's love and devotion.

Discovering Things to Admire

1. *Think About Him:* Spend less time thinking about your affairs and more about him. Women are inclined to focus their thoughts on their children, household chores, problems and plans. If you will think about him, the things he has said and done in your life, and the things he wants to do, you will find things to admire.

2. *Observe Him:* Keep your eyes open and watch what he does, and you will find things to admire. Every man has either *brains, brawn or skill*—so observe him in these three categories.

3. *Listen To Him Talk:* You will have a great opportunity to admire him when he talks, especially if he talks about subjects he is interested in, about himself or his life away from home. In his work is where he is most apt to show special ability or talent, or display courage or other manly qualities in facing the problems or difficulties of his work. If he does not relate these manly traits to you in conversation, you will not likely know about them.

So encourage him to talk about himself and his life away from home. This is not to suggest that you be prying or overly inquisitive. But ask him leading questions to begin the conversation. Whatever he says be interested. If he can be assured that his masculinity will be fully appreciated, he will be encouraged to confide many things about his life of work. If you will keep such conversations going, you will find many things to admire.

How to Listen to a Man

Follow this rule and you will learn to be a good listener: *Do not listen only to what he is saying, but to the man who is saying it*. Notice how absorbed he is in the subject, how he has mastered the intricate details, what skill and knowledge he has gained, how he has worked out and developed his own ideas, how loyal and devoted he is to them, what mental and moral power he can wield, what a genuine man he is when you stop and appreciate him.

If he is talking about politics, religion or world events, don't follow the conversation so closely that you fail to appreciate the man talking. And don't become so wound up in the subject that you form strong opinions which lead to arguments. Follow the conversation, of course, but follow the man, too. He may display a special knowledge about the subject, a knowledge which comes from intelligence, experience or dedicated study. If his attitude shows impatience with how things are, this may indicate that he has ideas about the subject, ideas that need to be expressed and appreciated. As his ideas unfold, look for idealism and devotion to the things he believes in.

If you cannot comprehend all of what he is saying, do not let this lull you to sleep. Look for traits of his character which you can admire. In fact, if you only follow his subject and appreciate that and not the man who is expressing himself, he will be disappointed. You may rest assured that he is not talking only to have his subject appreciated. He wants admiration to be bestowed upon himself as a man. In fact, you can safely guess that if he deliberately talks "over your head," he is doing so only to arouse your admiration.

A woman need not be well educated or possess high intelligence to follow a clever man's discourse. In his pleasure at having himself admired, the man seldom notices that his conversation is not understood. Even when he does notice it, he relishes it as in the following words by Maeterlinck: "What care I though she appear not to understand. Do you think that it is for a sublime word that I thirst when I feel that a soul is gazing into my soul?"

If you learn to listen to a man correctly, it doesn't matter if the subject is interesting or dull. You can converse on world affairs or on the intricate details of his business career, and you will be able to maintain an interest. You will welcome the most tedious monologue as giving you an opportunity to observe the man's character and to seek out the admirable qualities. The following story is an illustration of the right way to listen:

Alice and Jim

Alice is the perfect listener, with an attentive interest in her husband, Jim. Jim is a man who craves admiration, for out in the world he gets little of it. He is a terrific success in business circles, is highly intellectual and has ingenious ideas, but who cares or bothers to find out about them? If fact, some have implied that only luck is responsible for his success. But at home it is a different story.

No sooner do they have a few minutes together than Alice steers the conversation to his work. She prods him from time to time until he is thoroughly wound up in the subject, and then she listens. If you will observe her carefully, you will find that she listens only casually to what he says, but that she nevertheless finds a great deal to admire. What on earth is it? Not his appearance, because he is just an average looking man; not his language, for hers is just as good as his; and not his ideas, for they are perhaps quite ordinary.

She sees loyalty, courage and idealism. Here is a man whose heart rings true to his ideals, to what he believes fair and square. Whether she agrees with him or not does not matter. So she sits there and admires, not his words, not his ideas, but his manliness. His fervent enthusiasm which might irritate others who do not agree with him is regarded by her as another expression of the steadfast champion that he is. So long as she can watch the rapt animation of his countenance and the unfolding of his admirable character, she asks nothing else. Even his moods of depression arouse admiration in her. Isn't he depressed only because of what he considers the futility of many of his ideas?

What If You Can't Find Any Manly Qualities to Admire

In extreme cases a man may deteriorate to the point that he is really not much of a man—on the surface. His wife may feel at a loss to find anything manly to admire about him and would feel insincere to praise him for qualities that do not exist. In such a case there are two things a woman can do:

1. *Have faith that these manly qualities do exist, as they do in the souls of all men.* In this way you give him an ideal to live up to, or employ the power of positive thinking. The German author Goethe has said, "If you treat a man as he is, he will stay as he is, but if you treat him as if he were what he ought to be, and could be, he will become that bigger and better man."

The woman who has an unwavering faith in a man's better side inspires him to live up to such a conception of his ability. She offers him hope that perhaps he has not appreciated himself at his true value—that courage, steadfastness and nobility really are the underlying traits of his character. Many a girl has transformed a man from an apparently stupid, weak, lazy, cowardly, unrighteous man into a determined, energetic, true and noble one.

Often a man is at heart a stouthearted creature and only needs someone to suggest to him that his life does not do justice to his true character. Once persuaded that he is noble at heart and that you perceive it, he becomes anxious to prove both to himself and to you that there is no mistake about the matter. The turning point of many a man's life comes from just such a revelation of his higher capabilities. Remember, *it is not by push or persuasion that a woman brings out the best in her man and impels him to a more successful and righteous life—but by an unwavering belief in his better side.*

2. *Go Back Into the Past:* If you cannot find anything manly to appreciate in the present, dwell on past experiences. Tell him what first attracted you to him, experiences in early marriage that aroused your admiration, difficult circumstances that he faced with courage and persistence. Express admiration for the diligence he displayed in getting his education or establishing himself in his work. Spend some time thinking about the past, searching for specific instances when he displayed real masculine ability or character.

I instructed one of my students to do this, and she said she remembered the days of the depression, those trying years when her husband lost his job and steady employment was difficult to find. She recalled how her husband walked the shoe leather from the soles of his shoes in his effort to provide for his family. It was only through his persistence that his family continued to enjoy the comforts of life.

Since this time the man had slipped in many ways. He had become difficult to live with, and their marriage had deteriorated. But when she expressed this sincere admiration for his manliness in those early years, he was deeply moved. This was the "bread of life" he needed to make another effort. At that moment a change took place within him and he began to take on a new attitude—a new reason for living and striving. And his feelings for her revived and their marriage has blossomed once again.

How to Express Admiration

1. *Be Sincere:* Never is sincerity more important than when it relates to a man's most sensitive nature—pride in his masculinity. *This is something not to be trifled with by superficial flattery.* Sincere admiration will have to be

cultivated before you can express admiration effectively. If you do not feel any sincere admiration for your husband, even after following the suggestions in this chapter, it is best to forego this part of the subject. Anything you say will easily be detected as insincere, and instead of appreciating your praise, he may even resent it, counting it as manipulation in trying to gain a benefit for yourself.

2. *Be Specific:* When expressing admiration do not talk in generalities. For example, one of my students said to her husband, "My, you are a manly sort of a man!" He turned to her and asked, "Oh, how? In just what way do you mean?" She could not think of a single thing to say and was very embarrassed.

So, be specific, and express admiration for particular manly qualities or incidents when his manly qualities are evident. This is why it is so important to observe him and listen to him so you will be able to see specific manly traits which you can admire. If you can "pin-point" incidents in which his masculine traits are evident, they will be undeniably true, even to him.

You Must Accept Him

Although admiration is all important to a man, it will not be appreciated unless it is accompanied by acceptance. If you admire him in some ways but are critical of him in others, it will be like serving him a piece of moldy pie and trying to disguise it by putting whipped cream on top. You will have to accept the total man before your admiration will be well received.

Rewards

When the wife sincerely admires her husband's masculinity, it can bring significant rewards to both of them. For the man it fills a most important need. It can also be a tremendous motivation to him, causing him to grow in masculinity and in his success in life, therefore bringing fulfillment. Rewards to the woman are equally significant. Her greatest need from him is love. When she gives him admiration, he returns love. This is evident in the following true experiences:

"Trying to tell my husband that I accepted him and that I admired him for standing up and sticking to his convictions was a very hard thing for me to come out with. First of all, I am not the kind of person to say something like this, and secondly, I thought I would start to giggle. I tried three or four times to do my little speech, but always ended up turning and walking out of the room. Finally I was going to do it no matter what kind of mess it turned into. So I walked into the room and started, and once I started I realized that what I was saying was really how I felt. This was one of the main reasons I fell in love with my husband. He did stand up for what he believed in and did not let me get away with walking all over him.

"Well, the look in his eyes was just unbelievable. Never can I remember such a look. He had so much pride in his eyes and it was not for himself, it was for me. About a week later he took me out to dinner and made two comments. One hurt, and the other felt great. He said for the first time he felt I really cared; he had never thought I cared what happened to him. Secondly, that he never loved me more than he did then. What more can a woman ask for? Isn't this what we all really want and makes it all worth it?"

Our Devotion Is Unshakable

"I first became acquainted with Fascinating Womanhood about four years ago through my sister. I was skeptical at first, but finally I was able to set aside my overgrown pride and ask the good Lord to help me in a last desperate attempt to save a failing marriage. I must have read those first four chapters a dozen times, wondering if I could have been guilty of so many wrong attitudes. After gathering up what courage I had, I set out on my own private 'love campaign.' It wasn't easy at first; that female pride kept sneaking back, but two weeks later I put the teachings to practice. I was so frightened! All I could do was to pray for the courage that I seemed to lack.

"He was about three hours late coming home, but I didn't question him or complain. I simply said, 'I know you must have put in a hard day, honey. You deserve some time away from everything. I kept dinner warm so I will bring it right to you.' Suddenly an expression of confused pleasure came over his tired face. After dinner I curled up by his feet on the floor and began. 'Honey, I want you to know that I really appreciate you for the strong man that you are. And I realize that you must say no to me once in awhile for the good of both of us, and I really respect you for it.' (I had been begging, pleading, pouting and crying for a new outfit I'd seen, but couldn't have.) 'I couldn't feel safe or secure with someone who let me push him around. I just want you to know I love you as you are and wouldn't change a single thing about you.'

"Well, I can't even begin to describe the expression that came over his face. I only know it was one with deep warmth and love for me. Then he pulled me close to him and held me for a long time. He actually wept and I wept with him out of happiness for the moment and of real hope for the future. The next day he came in acting rather strange and with a big box, explaining he would have been home sooner but wrapping was a problem. And do you know what he did? He had gone shopping and bought a complete outfit for me and both of the children. It was all there from shoes to hats. I just couldn't believe it. Now it was my turn for tears. I knew then that I was on my way to being a Fascinating Woman.

"That was four years ago, and from time to time he still surprises me with flowers or some little token of his love. And I shed a tear or two. He says it makes him feel great to know he can make me happy. In four years my own success stories have become too numerous to keep track of, but I know that each one of them no matter how big or small is one more block for the strong foundation that now makes our devotion for one another unshakable and our marriage indestructable. I must admit, though, without Fascinating Womanhood we never would have made it. I owe the entire salvation and success of our marriage to the knowledge of Fascinating Womanhood. This whole theory is absolutely beautiful and never stops snowballing into something bigger and better every day."

A New Beginning

"My husband and I had been married thirteen years, most of them unhappy. We had been separated three times, and I had decided to leave him for the last time. I had given up on him. About this time a friend of mine told me about Fascinating Womanhood and tried to encourage me to take the class. I told her that nothing could be done for that stubborn husband of mine and I might as well give up, but she begged me to take it. By then we actually had separated.

"I don't know if you know how a person feels when she is going through a separation, but it is worse than miserable. A numbness went through me. I may as well have been dead. I prayed as I have never prayed before that God would help me through each minute, each hour, and that I would depend entirely upon Him to lead me through this as I didn't know where to turn. I prayed that my husband would want to see me and talk to me. He did.

"At first it was accusations and bitterness, then quiet talking and understanding. I decided to take him back, but I was afraid; how was I to know that it was going to work? I asked him if he cared if I took a course called Fascinating Womanhood. He asked me what it was about. I told him all I knew was that it was supposed to make a marriage happier and a better wife of me. He told me to go ahead, and he was very enthusiastic about it.

"At the first class the teacher told us to compliment our husband on 'his manliness, muscles, etc.' I didn't think I could bring myself to say something like that. Finally, just before the next class, I knew I had to do something because the teacher would ask us about it. So I waited until we were in bed and the lights were out. I thought I would faint. Finally I told him what beautiful muscles he had. After I said it he took me in his arms and kissed me over and over. This is when our new marriage began. I was told not to expect material rewards, but a happy marriage. I received both. Some of the things my husband has bought me without my asking are: a beautiful nightie, typewriter, trip to Hawaii, kitchen stove, table and chairs, couch and chair recovered, bedroom carpeting, perfume, flowers and others I can't remember."

I Feel Like a Bride Again

"My story is not too spectacular. I have always had a good marriage. I took the course because I felt a need for more self-confidence, but I found I had more problems that I realized. I had always accepted and admired my husband but never told him so, partly because I admired him so much I thought he must know it. It was extremely hard to start saying these things so I started writing notes. When he commented on them I would say 'Well, it's true,' or 'I wanted to be sure you knew how I felt.' Then I progressed to saying complimentary things. His response was so great that I realized his need to hear these things. He started telling me the ways I pleased him and this gave me the self-confidence I have always lacked. His tenderness towards me is fantastic. I feel like a bride again. The greatest thing was when he said with tears, 'I have come to realize that you are the sweetest, the most feminine woman in the world, and I love you so deeply I can't tell you how much. You are my whole life.' "

His Honey-Eyed Girl

"It was final exam week at the university just prior to my husband's graduation. It had taken him seven years to complete college as he had to stop and work full time every so often to support our growing family. He held jobs while attending school also and held positions in church, as well as carrying out home responsibilities. He had had many moments of feeling sad and discouraged. He couldn't see his accomplishments. All he could see was the time it had taken him to get through college. I hadn't helped much. The only time I praised him was when he had problems and then I didn't do it right. I had a very self-righteous attitude. I was handling the finances and trying to push him into greater activity in the church and nagging him to do things for me such as open my car door. I thought I was helping him by pointing out his mistakes.

"Then my sister-in-law enthusiastically told me about Fascinating Womanhood and I started reading it. I was thrilled because it told us exactly how to do it and what to say instead of just lots of dos and don'ts. I read it over and over, and when my husband came home I was all worked up about it yet so nervous I was trembling. I told him I was glad he is the kind of man he is and that I could see I had not understood him in the past, admitting I had made mistakes and that I was glad he hadn't been like putty in my hands, but had had the courage of his convictions. I asked for forgiveness and told him I wanted to prove to him I liked him the way he is.

"It was just like turning on a radio. His expression changed and his whole being seemed to be affected. He started radiating happiness instead of misery. The next day I applied admiration and told him I was proud of him for his courage in completing his education and not giving up as others would have done with the same hardships. I told him how I appreciated how he worked to provide the necessities of life for us. I also explained to him that I realized I had been holding him back by trying to lead and that I really loved him just the way he is and that I would stop trying to change him.

"This seemed to turn the volume up more than it had been the day before. He treated me like a queen. He even started opening the car door for me. He started leading our family with kindness and love and strength that I had never seen in him before. He called family councils regularly, and I felt like we truly had a Celestial marriage. What's even better, the other day he took me to our dream home site and told me what wonderful plans he has for me and our adorable family (five children). He is in summer school now and thought he would be home only twice, but he has made it home every weekend. He sang 'Honey-Eyed Girl' to me and told me I was the loveliest wife in the world."

Rules for Admiration

1. Accept him at face value.
2. Think about his manliness.
3. Observe his manliness.
4. Listen to him talk.
5. Admire his manliness in words.
6. Be sincere.
7. Be specific.

Assignment

1. Admiring Him:
   A. Write down 10 things you admire in your husband. At least half of these should be *masculine things*. The others can be things you *appreciate* which are not particularly masculine.
   B. During the evening ask your husband if he would be willing to participate in a special project. Ask him to write down 10 things he admires or appreciates

about you and you will do the same for him. Going from memory, write down the things you worked out on your list. When you are both finished, read your lists to each other, taking the time to explain *why* you admire these traits. Be sure to discuss what you have written. No fair just handing each other the list. As a result you will have some new things to add to your Angela Human chart of the last lesson and he will have received some admiration for his masculinity as well as appreciation.

C. Observe his reaction. Write down anything loving he says or does in your "Love Booklet."

2. During the coming week observe him. If you see a manly trait in action, express admiration at the moment. Record results.

3. Practice listening to him talk.

5

His Sensitive Pride

Characteristic No. 3

What is a man proud of? He is proud of his *masculine qualities* which we studied about in the last chapter. A man has an inborn pride in his strong muscular body, his manly skills and abilities and his special achievements. He would like for this manly side of him to be noticed and admired, especially by his wife. And if any of these masculine traits are weak or missing, his pride will prompt him to obscure this lack from the world as much as he can.

The most important thing to learn in this chapter is that *masculine pride is very sensitive*. A man cannot stand to have his masculinity *belittled, ridiculed* or treated with *indifference*. Being subjected to this treatment is one of the most painful experiences a man can suffer. Lacking insight into this subject causes untold misunderstandings between men and women. How many times have you made a casual remark to a man, only to have him snap back with a harsh reply or appear distant? Unaware of your mistake, you may have wondered, "Now what did I say wrong?" Understanding these mistakes and the principles to follow in avoiding them should be a part of every woman's education.

What does a man suffer when his pride is hurt? He suffers the *pains of humiliation* which is felt in a variety of sharp, biting or deflating ways. For example, if a man unfolds a high objective he has secretly been toying with and his wife reacts with doubt in his ability to reach it, this will *cut like a knife*. She has touched upon the most sensitive part of his nature. Or, if he happens to be telling her of something of which he is particularly proud, and she makes a casual remark and changes the subject, he will feel like a *deflated balloon*. Or, if she in some way indicates that he is not measuring up to what he should be as a man, he will feel *degraded* and, somehow, *less of a man*. These are some of the things men suffer when their pride is hurt. Now, let's take a closer look at the mistakes women make which cause this pain:

Mistakes Women Make

Do not think that women would be so cruel as to deliberately hurt a man's pride. Most wounding goes on in innocence, which is why the woman fails to see she has done anything wrong and continues her mistakes time and time again. The following are some true experiences in which women blindly wounded masculine pride:

1. *Belittled:* A young man and woman were engaged to each other several times, but each time as marriage plans were about to materialize the man backed out. Finally he broke their engagement and married someone else. For years this was a mystery to those who knew them. He appeared to love her dearly. She seemed to have the qualities that ought to please a man. They appeared to have everything in common and would prove to be the ideal couple.

Many years later the truth was discovered. She lost him because *she belittled him.* She laughed at his big ideas (which he had many of); she made fun of his actions on the basketball court; and she joked about his performances in plays. Who knows how many other things she downgraded. The tragedy is that the girl really admired the man and made these mistakes in innocence. Her remarks, which were only made in jest, were such a constant eroding of his pride that it was more than he could stand. Regardless of his fond affection for her, he could not accept a permanent relationship.

2. *Ridiculed:* A man presented an idea to his wife for a business investment which would require considerable money. Although there was risk involved, returns were to be high. The man thought the proposition through carefully and, acting upon his best judgment, decided to go ahead. He then turned to his wife for approval. She heard his plan in detail then said, "Well, if you want to lose all your money, go ahead." His explosive reaction was puzzling to her. "I may have been blunt," she pondered, "but how could I have said anything that wrong?" It is not required of women to be dishonest and support an idea that they disagree with, but opposition can be presented *without injuring masculine pride.* She could have said, "I

will think about it," and then could have presented her viewpoint in a feminine way, a way which I will explain in a later chapter.

3. *Belittled:* There is a "cold water" method that some women use in dealing with men. In this case the wife does not openly disagree with her husband, she just quietly pours "cold water" on his ideas and especially on his enthusiasm for these ideas. One such experience that comes to mind is of a man who had an interesting and new idea for sports equipment. When he enthusiastically explained the device to his wife one night, she looked at him like *a wise old owl* and said, "Why don't we consider the pros and cons of this?" Some other "cold water" expressions are "Let's be practical," or "Let's be sensible!" Here, again, it is not necessary to support an idea that you lack confidence in; but remember, if you diminish masculine enthusiasm, you also diminish masculine pride.

4. *Belittled:* A woman wrote to me the following experience: "My husband taught a Sunday School class and he did it very well. One day I suggested that he ask our son to give part of the lesson in the form of visual aids. With an aggravated tone in his voice, my husband looked at me and said, 'What's the matter. Don't you like the way I do it?' 'Well, you could do better,' I said. He became violently angry, raised his voice and said that I had never appreciated him, that I had depreciated him in the eyes of his children and that he had about had enough. He rushed out of the house, slammed the door, and was gone for several hours." It would be particularly humiliating for a man to have to rely upon his son to help him give an adequate performance.

5. *Indifference:* A woman was stirring gravy on the stove. When her husband arrived, he came into the kitchen and began talking to her, telling her of an incident that happened while he was at work. With enthusiasm he told how his boss, who rarely gives compliments, had commended him for his performance on his job. The wife responded with, "Well, isn't that wonderful! Jimmy, go out and turn off the water," then gave full attention to other details of the meal. Once again he tried to win her attention, but she said, "Go tell the girls to wash for dinner." Remember, ladies, the way to a man's heart is not through his stomach; it is through your interest and appreciation for him *as a man.*

6. *Belittled:* A man was very despondent over prob-

lems in his business. With loving affection, his wife tried to cheer him up. As he unfolded his problem, she could see clearly that he was faced with a possible failure in his business. Eager to play the part of the perfect wife, she courageously said, "Honey, don't worry. If you fail in your business, it won't matter. I will be content if you merely run a small grocery store." But her self-sacrificing attitude was not met with appreciation. The man snapped back harshly, "Sometimes you say just the wrong things."

What did she say wrong? It was this: She projected him as a failure—a failure which would be a *permanent* situation. He had always had high hopes for himself, but according to her he would have to settle for less. Although a man must know that a woman will accept failure, and cheerfully adjust to humble circumstances, *he would like to feel her confidence in his ultimate success.*

What should she have said? She should have assured him that if he was to fail, it would be only *temporary.* She could have said, "These are discouraging days for you, but they are part of being a success, as is evident in the lives of all successful men." But a woman should not say "You will not fail." This would be unrealistic, would be expecting too much of a man and again would be the wrong thing to say. But a woman should talk of *ultimate success,* and not *permanent failure.*

Some women instinctively know the right thing to say. For example, years ago I knew a lady whose husband was faced with a possible failure in a professional college. At a time when he was painfully discouraged and she could see the probability of his failure, she said to him, "Why, George, if you fail you will probably be a bigger and better man than if you don't." This came as a great relief to the man and probably was the means of easing his tension so that in spite of great odds he did pass.

Another lady had a similar circumstance in that her husband had been fired as manager of his company. She said to him, "Henry, this may be the door to opportunity, a stepping-stone to greater success." The man was so relieved he almost cried. And it was the door to opportunity, for he became more successful ten times over than when manager of the small company. The main point is this: The first lady projected her husband as small in the face of failure. The second and third ladies projected their husbands as bigger and better. And I would like to add this: When a man is discouraged, whatever a woman says, it should be mixed with a genuine sympathy for his suffering. How to go about this will be taught in the next chapter.

7. *Indifference.* A drama teacher of a college began the production of a play. He seldom asked his wife for help, but this time he asked her to be in charge of making the costumes. With pride in her work, she worked long hours—and they were beautiful. She had hoped he would be proud of her, but instead she noticed a growing antagonism. One evening he said, "You're not interested in me. You're only interested in those costumes." She was surprised and hurt and could not understand his lack of appreciation.

Her failure was in her all-consuming interest in the costumes instead of her husband. Being involved in the production, she had a wonderful opportunity to observe her husband's talents first-hand, talents as a director, an organizer and a teacher, qualities she could never appreciate from an audience. He wanted her to appreciate him and the traits of his character which were responsible for his success.

She, however, felt that he only needed her assistance with the costumes, and thus she buried herself in this responsibility. She also felt that a great part of the success of the play rested on her shoulders—that he could not make it without her. And such is the great misunderstanding that often arises between men and women.

The Working World

Difficult as it is to believe, *other men* also wound masculine pride. In the working world a man's pride is often brutally cut down. His ability may be questioned. In some companies backbiting is common. Some sadistic employers deliberately undermine an employee. In the struggle for position men sometimes discredit one another. Often a creditor or customer offers cutting remarks. Some workers are derided by their superiors. In professional schools the policy is frequently—cut down their pride and undermine their confidence to weed out the weak ones. The same policy is found in some branches of the armed forces training programs. If a man is fortunate enough to come home to a woman who will heal his wounds, he can withstand permanent damage; but if he comes home to further humiliation, his total personality can suffer.

In His Background

Undermining of pride may have begun in his earlier years. As a young man, the first sign of a beard may have brought ridicule from his brothers and sisters. Even his mother may have viewed it with indifference. His ideas and achievements are often passed over lightly. Belittling is most severe in the school environment where young people are anxious to elevate themselves by cutting down someone else. Teachers, too, are sometimes guilty of belittling remarks. Now, in addition to the pains of humiliation, there are three other problems a man suffers in connection with his pride. They are reserve, a numbing effect and dishonesty, as I will now explain:

Reserve

By reserve we do not mean bashfulness or timidity. The latter peculiarities apply to comparatively few men. Reserve, on the other hand, is an attribute of all. Reserve is a wall a man tends to build around himself, caused by the fear of humiliation. Although he longs to confide, to reveal his secret hopes and dreams with the hope of receiving admiration, he is reluctant to do so. He hesitates to expose his ideas to the possibility of indifference and antagonism. Nothing is so frightening to a man as the horror of making a fool of himself. He therefore subdues the impulse to seek admiration. Nothing but the absolute certainty that his ideas will be met with appreciation rather than contempt or indifference will induce him to throw off his armor of reserve and reveal to others the things that mean the most to him. And even if he does, the slightest hint of misunderstanding or disrespect will shatter the illusion and drive him behind his wall of reserve again.

To understand the nature of this reserve, take an example of a young girl who has won a young man's confidence so that he is unfolding his secret hopes and dreams to her. As he begins to reveal the finer traits of his character, she has a most wonderful opportunity to acknowledge his manly qualities. But, let her but indicate by a yawn or a glance out the window that she is not the least bit interested, and the poor man will *wince as if struck by a lash*. It may be the first time in his life he has ventured to express such feelings. If the girl acts indifferently at such a crisis and fails to recognize its significance to him, she has,

77

so far as he is concerned, *a heart of stone*. Therefore, no matter where or when he meets her in the future, he will not again risk a similar rebuff. He will be behind his protective wall of reserve.

Such is the case with every man. His longing for understanding, great as it is, is not sufficient to make him throw off his habitual cloak of reserve except in rare instances. And even then he will quickly resume it unless he can bask in the full glow of an all-comprehending sympathy. The one characteristic, therefore, seems to be diametrically opposed to the other. Together they constitute a problem difficult enough to tax any woman's wits.

The main point I wish to emphasize about reserve is this: When a man's pride has been wounded frequently, he tends to build a *tight* wall of reserve around himself which is a real problem in marriage. When this occurs, he appears distant. He may talk, but does so cautiously. You cannot tell his innermost feelings, for he does not expose them, although you may sense his longing to do so. He tells little of his accomplishments away from home, or his problems or dreams. Through all of this you can detect an unhappy feeling.

Occasionally a man will clam up and not talk at all. This is called "going into his shell." He acts as though he has climbed inside himself, locked the door and pulled down the blinds, making it impossible to get next to him. This tendency for a man to go into his shell is common. The higher the caliber of the man the more he tends to draw into himself when his pride is hurt.

There should be no wall of reserve in the ideal marriage. A man should always be able to express himself freely and completely without fear of humiliation. He should, in fact, feel absolute confidence that his conversation will always be met with the most sincere respect, and receive in full the admiration that he needs. So, if you can sense this reserve in your husband, take the necessary steps to eliminate it. If you do not, he will be much more tempted to seek the company of another woman who can fill this important need in his life.

How to Break Down the Wall of Reserve

When a man is withdrawn behind his wall of reserve, you cannot *pull him out* by insisting he talk. Nor can you *compel* him by making him feel ashamed of his peculiar behavior, saying such things as "Why are you so quiet?" or "Why don't you ever tell me anything?" Nor can you *invite* him out by saying, "Did I do anything wrong?" Perhaps you did, but whether it was you or someone else that let him down, he will have too much pride to say, "Look, I needed my ego boosted but instead I got a rebuff." Admiration isn't anything a man will ask for. The only thing you can do when a man is reserved is to be loving and reassuring and try to break down his wall by doing the following:

1. *Accept Him At Face Value:* This again is the first step. If you overlook his faults and look to his better side, he will be more confident and trusting and can more easily confide his innermost feelings to you.

2. *Don't Belittle Him:* Make sure you do not make mistakes that only strengthen the reserve he already has. You will have to completely eliminate any belittling remarks or forms of indifference, or his reserve will be a permanent problem.

3. *Admire Him:* Your generous and sincere admiration will do more than any other measure to win his confidence and break down his wall of reserve.

4. *Don't Be Critical Of Others:* If you are fault-finding, with an eye open to every fault you can find in those around you, he will be afraid to expose his intimate feelings to your criticism and contempt. You must not tell him of your poor opinion of this person or that, or betray the faults of envy, jealousy or contempt. You must not make light of anyone. Even when you cannot approve of what someone says, you must show appreciation for his motives or basic character. The more ability you manifest as a critic, the less inclined he will be to expose himself to your criticism. He must be assured that his confidences will be met with an admiring interpretation and not with a faultfinding one.

5. *Appreciate The Good In Others:* If you appreciate the good in others, he will be assured that you will see the finer side in him, also. He will not fear ridicule and indifference when he confides his ideals and ambitions to you. Search for the good in everyone you meet and express your appreciation for them. This is the easiest way to develop a confidence-inspiring character that will encourage a man to lay down his reserve.

6. *Hold Confidences Sacred:* Never repeat to others things which have been told to you in confidence. If you

79

disclose the secrets of others, he will take it for granted that you will disclose his also, and thus subject him to the same misunderstanding, ridicule and indifference that he hopes to avoid. Unless he thinks that he is confiding his innermost hopes and ambitions to one who will not betray them to others, he will not confide them to you no matter how sure he is of your personal admiration of him. Even though he knows *you* admire him, how does he know others will. They might ridicule the things you admire. He cannot risk contempt from anyone.

When his reserve seems to be disappearing and he begins to disclose things about himself which you can admire, do not imagine that his reserve has disappeared altogether. You will need to further eliminate it by devotedly following the six steps suggested. And during this time, make certain that everything he does confide to you is met with understanding. Otherwise, his first confidences will never be followed by another. If your response is always appreciative, he will add another confidence and another until at last, if your reaction is never disappointing, he will lay bare before you every motive, ideal and hope that stirs within him. Admiration is too important for him to deny himself, once he has had the full enjoyment of it.

Remember, however, that underlying the desire for admiration his reserve is always waiting in the background, ready to appear at the first sign of indifference or criticism, even when the criticism is only apparent in the woman's attitude towards other people. You can therefore understand how difficult it is for a woman with a weak, faultfinding, and indifferent character to keep the reserve in the background long enough for the man to express himself.

If a woman has seriously trampled on her husband's pride, she will have to be extremely patient in eliminating his reserve. Until she has consistently demonstrated her full respect for her husband's manliness for a sufficient time to assure him of her dependability, he will be cautious about disclosing his innermost feelings. He will be fearful of a repeat of those painful experiences of the past.

The Numbing Effect

When a man's pride has been injured over a long period of time, he learns to protect himself from the hurt by hardening himself against it. He learns not to care. His senses become dulled or numb. In Dr. Edrita Fried's book *The Ego in Love and Sexuality,* she speaks of this numbing effect. But Dr. Fried points out that the great danger is this: *When we become numb to pain, we become numb to pleasure as well.* "We pay dearly for the self-induced numbness, for while it relieves pain, it also reduces our ability to experience pleasant emotions and respond to pleasant stimulation. Unresponsiveness, like an indiscriminate scythe, mows down the flowers with the weeds."

The man who has become dull to the constant pain of humiliation has also separated himself from pleasure. He no longer experiences the hurt, but neither does he see the beauty of a summer day, delight in the laughter of his children, or respond to the love that his wife offers. His sexual feelings may diminish, and he can even become impotent.

Dishonesty

A man with a sensitive pride may, in certain circumstances, resort to dishonesty in an effort to protect his pride. For example, when a man faces failure or defeat, his fear of humiliation can cause him to try to hide his mistakes. This is a time when he may keep important facts from his wife and may be tempted to make dishonest statements. This can lead to serious problems, since the lack of facts can be confusing, especially to the wife.

I know of a situation of this kind when a man was faced with a business failure. Because of masculine pride, he was afraid to tell his wife the full truth, because of the poor opinion she would have of him. Because he withheld important facts, she mistakenly believed her husband to be innocent and that others were to blame for the failure. She took the initiative to demand restitution of the other parties involved and placed her husband in a very embarrassing position. In this case, the man did not dread so much to have his wife know of his failure as he dreaded what she would think of him. And, although all human beings try to avoid a disclosure of their failures, when masculine pride is at stake, the problem is painfully acute.

Now, if a man is unable to obscure the truth, he has a tendency to be defensive about his mistakes. He may blame circumstances, or others or just fate. He will sometimes even blame his wife for how things turned out. A man will sometimes put up quite a tough argument in an effort to preserve his image in the eyes of his wife. But the more he tries to conceal the truth, the more confusing it can become to his wife, for what he says may be in contradiction to what appears to be the true facts.

A woman can help if she will try to understand the man's desperate effort to protect his pride. Although his dishonesty is never justified, she should not condemn him. Keeping in mind that "what she thinks of him" is uppermost in his mind, she can assure him that she will always uphold him and admire him even in the most trying circumstances. With her complete trust in his manliness, he will be less afraid to expose the hard truth to her.

Sometimes a man will *belittle himself*, which may be puzzling to his wife. In this case he urgently needs the support of her admiration but is too proud to ask. The only means he knows to bolster his ego is to belittle himself with the hope that she will quickly disagree with him and offer praise instead. If this is a problem, the woman can reduce this tendency by seeking her own opportunity to admire him when he does not expect it. It will be best to not supply lavish admiration when a man belittles himself, since it would encourage a habit.

A Woman's Responsibility

A woman has a double responsibility to a man in regard to his pride—first, to not injure the man's pride herself and second, to heal the wounds that others inflict. If she can be his refuge in times of trouble and defeat, he will turn to her in full confidence for a restitution of his feeling of manliness. She then becomes indispensable to his happiness and contributes greatly to his overall success in life.

On the other hand, if she fails him on both counts, if he returns from the battlegrounds of life and, instead of receiving understanding and reassurance, is subjected to further contempt or indifference, the effect upon his personality can be serious as it is on his total success in life. And even more serious is his altered feeling towards her for having so let him down. So a woman is in a precarious position—*she can either build or destroy a man*, depending on how she deals with his sensitive pride.

When we see the sensitivity of a man's nature, we can realize how careful a woman must be in her relationship with him. She cannot permit herself to have an "unbridled tongue" in which she says anything she pleases. She cannot "pour out her heart to him" as she would to a *buddy*. Because of this, a woman is required to withhold many of her feelings since her confessions may wound the man's pride. Now, this does not mean a man cannot be a woman's friend. After she is fully aware of the man's sensitive nature, she can carry on intimate conversations with him and turn to him in times of difficulty. And if she will give herself completely and unselfishly to being a wonderful wife, she will feel a closeness to her husband that will be "bone of his bone and flesh of his flesh." But a man is never a friend to a woman in the same sense that another woman is, or that a parent is. And this is because of the unique relationship between men and women.

And now I would like to relate a true experience about how injured pride and a feeling of not being accepted caused a wall of reserve to appear in a man:

The Great Wall of Reserve

"I was feeling very depressed and discouraged with life. There seemed no purpose or reward, and I seemed to myself a very unimportant 'thing.' I would try to pull myself out of this by saying, you are the mother of two children, so therefore you do have at least an obligation to raise them to be good citizens. The things I had always enjoyed, held no joy anymore. I would sit and knit or sew and strive for that ounce of pleasure I was sure it would bring. But nothing—I was empty.

"I can look back now and see where my trouble started, but at the time I was lost. My husband and I had been married ten years before we had any children. Our marriage was average; really no troubles or problems were insurmountable. I worked most of those years and was content. Then two children later and in the midst of building our dream house. I started becoming ill. I experienced a dreadful 'anxious' feeling that I was to be tortured with for eighteen months. It was an endless round of doctors whom I tried to convince that 'something was wrong with me.' They could find nothing.

"Finally in desperation, convinced that my sanity was leaving, I went for psychiatric treatment for three months.

83

I learned that I was emotionally mixed up. In the course of the sessions the doctor managed to convince me that I was married to an immature, selfish tyrant (which is not the case at all). He convinced me that I was right and my husband wrong. Well, I thought I had problems before, but now I set about to change my husband. I managed to do it, all right. I changed him from a loving, tender and very understanding man to a violent, uncommunicative, withdrawn tyrant who did things so out of his character that even he could not account for them. Bit by bit, nag by nag, accusation by accusation, I built the biggest and most insurmountable wall of reserve in my marriage anyone ever saw. It made the great Wall of China look like a child's toy.

"Once the wall was up, I tried to climb the wall by tearing down my husband, instead of the wall. In return I received threats of desertion, violent outbursts, saw a happy man retreat into such deep depressions that I feared at times he might take his own life. Of course, I was all right. I even told him it was a phase he was going through and I wished he would hurry up. I used to ask him why he didn't appreciate me. I was everything a wife should be. Ha! Oh, yes, I kept the house clean, the children clean, and I couldn't help it if I was moody and depressed and didn't ever feel good. Anyone who tried as hard at marriage as I did and sacrificed so much just trying to win my husband's approval had a right to feel like me.

"One day when I was reciting my usual tale of woe and misery to a friend, she gave me *Fascinating Womanhood* and said, 'Please read this and pay careful attention to Inner Happiness and Worthy Character.' I read it and it seemed too deep for me. I thought I will never be able to be like that. I will try, but I just don't think I can. And I can say here and now that I never would have been able to without the help of my Fascinating Womanhood teacher. She was a magnificent inspiration. I began to live Fascinating Womanhood, and the walls of reserve soon came down. Fascinating Womanhood has saved my marriage and made my husband happy once again. I am now enjoying the flowers and trying very hard to remember Fascinating Womanhood every day."

Problems a Man Suffers Because of Masculine Pride

1. The pains of humiliation.
2. The wall of reserve.
3. The numbing effect.
4. Dishonesty.

How to Break Down His Wall of Reserve

1. Accept him at face value.
2. Admire his masculinity.
3. Don't belittle him or show indifference to his masculinity.
4. Don't be critical of others.
5. Appreciate the good in others.
6. Hold confidences sacred.

Assignment

1. Don't belittle him or show indifference to his manliness.
2. If your husband has a wall of reserve, take the necessary steps to break it down.

6

Sympathetic
Understanding

Characteristic No. 4

A man needs sympathetic understanding for 1) his pressing and constant responsibility to provide the living for his family; 2) his inborn desire for status, position or acclaim. We will now devote ourselves to a study of this subject and how a woman can successfully give a man the sympathy he so urgently needs:

1. His Responsibility to Provide the Living

A woman needs to understand *with an all-comprehending sympathy* what a man faces in providing the living. An excellent description of this part of the masculine role is found in Dr. Marie Robinson's book *The Power of Sexual Surrender*, from which I quote:

"For the majority of men, when they come of age and marry, take on an enormous burden which they may not lay down with any conscience this side of the grave. Quietly, and without histrionics, they put aside, in the name of love, most of their vaunted freedom and contract to take upon their shoulders full social and economic responsibility for their wives and children.

"As a woman, consider for a moment how you would feel if your child should be deprived of the good things of life; proper housing, clothing, education. Consider how you would feel if he should go hungry. Perhaps such ideas have occurred to you and have given you a bad turn momentarily. But they are passing thoughts: a woman does not give them much credence; they are not her direct responsibility; certainly she does not worry about them for long.

"But such thoughts, conscious or unconscious, are her husband's daily fare. He knows and he takes the carking

86

thought to work with him each morning (and every morning) and to bed with him at night, that upon the success or failure of his efforts rest the happiness, health, indeed the very lives of his wife and children. In the ultimate he senses he alone must take full responsibility for them.

"I do not think it is possible to exaggerate how seriously men take this responsibility; how much they worry about it. Women, unless they are very close to their men, rarely know how heavily the burden weighs sometimes, for men talk about it very little. They do not want their loved ones to worry.

"Men have been shouldering the entire responsibility for their family group since earliest times. I often think, however, when I see the stresses and strains of today's market place, that civilized man has much harder going, psychologically speaking, than his primitive forefathers.

"In the first place, the competition creates a terrible strain on the individual male. This competition is not only for preferment and advancement, it is often for his very job itself. Every man knows that if he falters, lets up his ceaseless drive, he can and will be easily replaced.

"No level of employment is really free of this endless pressure. The executive must meet and exceed his last year's quota or the quota of his competitors. Those under him must see that he does it, and he scrutinizes their performance most severely, and therefore constantly.

"Professional men—doctors, lawyers, professors—are under no less pressure for the most part. If the lawyer is self-employed he must constantly seek new clients; if he works for an organization he must exert himself endlessly to avoid being superseded by ambitious peers or by pushing young particles just out of law school and filled with the raw energy of youth. A score of unhappy contingencies can ruin or seriously threaten a doctor's practice, not the least of which is a possible breakdown in his ability to practice. A teacher must work long hours on publishable projects outside of his arduous teaching assignments if he is to advance or even hold his ground.

"There is no field of endeavor that a man may enter where he can count on complete economic safety; competition, the need for unremitting year-in year-out performance is his life's lot. Over all this he knows, too, stands a separate spectre upon which he can exert only the remotest control. It is the joblessness which may be caused by the cyclical depressions and recessions that characterize our economy."

The man's feeling of responsibility to provide for his family is *inborn*. He instinctively knows that he cannot turn aside from this financial obligation with clear conscience. His wife may work but may resign her job at any time without a feeling of guilt. Economic problems may result, but she will not have a lower opinion of herself or be disgraced in the public eye. In contrast, the man cannot stop working without injuring his feeling of self-worth and his image in the public. He, and everyone else would consider him a failure if he neglected this important function.

How a Woman Can Help

This description of a man's life cannot help but awaken our deepest sympathy, motivating us to want to do something to relieve our husband's strain and make his life easier. Some women feel impelled to seek employment or even assist their husband in his work, but these solutions are too wrought with problems to be the answer. There are, however, things a woman can do to help immeasurably, such as the following:

1. *Reduce Expenses:* One of the most important ways a woman can help is by minimizing her desire for material goods, cutting expenses and living well within her husband's income. This, however, is not easy for women to do. Modern America is wrought with excessive materialism. Clever advertisements cultivate a desire in all of us for the latest models in household equipment, new carpeting, draperies, furnishings and even a bigger and better house. The desire for these material comforts is enhanced by an awareness that "other families have them." It takes a remaking of our philosophy of life to make any real change in our values. But, it can be done when we gain a real sympathy for the man's responsibilities.

2. *Reduce Demands on His Time:* She can further help by understanding her husband's objectives and his particular job situation and then adjusting her demands on his time around it. He may need to work long hours, or give himself devotedly to his work. When he comes home he may need time to relax and recover from the day's work. She may have to forego places she would like to go,

or things she had planned for him to do and adjust her life to his.

3. *Live Feminine Roles:* A woman can help if she, instead of trying to lift her husband's load, will successfully live her own feminine role and be all that a woman should be. This means to keep the home intact, be feminine, cheerful and do all she can to put a proper spirit in the home.

4. *Make Allowances for His Bad Behavior:* The man who is under a strain in his work may have difficulty being his best when at home. The wife can help by understanding his world of responsibility and making allowances for his negative behavior, as I will now explain:

Why Men Let Down at Home

The struggle to provide the living helps to explain why men so often let down at home—why they become cross, impatient and negligent of wives and children. This can explain why a man may fail to fix the roof or mow the lawn. The duties seem unimportant to him in comparison to the demands of his work. Or, it explains why a man will completely ignore his children or is just plain irritable or difficult to live with. Women have said, "My husband doesn't treat his family as well as he does total strangers." Well, the truth is, ladies, that when a man comes home, he is often tired of being his best for total strangers and would like to relax and be his worst for his family, hoping that they will overlook this lesser side of him. In Florida Scott Maxwell's book *Women and Sometimes Men*, she explains this tendency of man to show his inferior side:

"One of the poignant paradoxes in the life of a woman is that when a man comes to her, he so often comes to recover his simple humanity, and to rest from being at his best. So a woman frequently has to forego his better side, taking it on trust as a matter of hearsay, and she accepts his lesser side as her usual experience of him. . . . While she wishes to admire him she may lack the knowledge, and perhaps the intelligence to understand the side by which he wins acclaim. She sees him collapse into his home, accepts his need of collapse, indeed receives him with every antenna alert, yet she may forego his superiority with regret. She longs to see his greatness, but has to meet the claim of his smallness."

89

The following are some of the ways women show a lack of sympathy for their husbands:

1. *Late For Dinner:* A common complaint among women is the husband who is late for dinner. Often he doesn't even call. The wife waits impatiently and when he finally arrives, both the dinner and the wife are cold. This impatient attitude of the wife demonstrates a lack of understanding for his life away from home. She only sees her side of the picture and fails to see his demands, pressures and unforeseen circumstances which have caused his delay.

2. *Neglected:* Another complaint is the husband who neglects wife and children. He never takes the wife anyplace, and when he is home he sometimes shuts himself in his den and completely ignores his children. Here, again, the wife may fail to understand her husband's work and the priorities which he must put ahead of her and the children if he is to succeed. The pressures of his work may have so washed him out that he feels it is all he can do to recover from the day's work.

3. *Neglect Of Home Duties:* This complaint is of the man who will not mow the lawn, do repair jobs or painting or other home duties. He may or may not be justified for his negligence, but his wife's attitude shows a lack of understanding for the common pressures of his life.

4. *When He Arrives Home:* Women who lack sympathy greet their husbands at the door with problems and allow their children to rush in with their share of complaints. Rather than the man receiving warmth and comfort, the very thing he needs to relieve his pressures of the day, he is faced with a dose of unpleasantness that adds to his burdens.

5. *Investments:* Women who fail to understand the man's struggle to provide often fight against their husband's plan to invest, expand their business or change occupations. Often the comment is "Oh, we have everything we need now. We have a home almost paid for, a nice car, a nice income and money in the bank. Why are you dissatisfied? Why do you want more?"

She fails to see into the future, to visualize additional children, college educations, more expensive clothes as the children mature, and even the decline of her husband's productivity as the provider. But the husband may have this vision, knows he must make it now so he will have money to meet these expenses.

I knew a woman who complained that her husband spent most of his time away from home. They have several children whom she felt she was raising almost alone. The children seldom ever saw their father. But in checking into the matter I found that the husband spent most of his time away from home *working*. He and his wife wanted to have several more children and were planning expensive educations and other high goals for them. He felt it was essential for him to earn a large income by working long hours and seeking every opportunity for advancement in his field. She showed a serious lack of appreciation and sympathy for his motives.

Another woman complained to me that her husband held down two jobs. He was also away from home most of the time. One day she said to him, "You are nothing but a pay check to me." The man was crushed. She failed to realize that he was working double time to solve some difficult financial problems. Although she had been informed, she did not have the depth of sympathy to understand completely.

Another woman wrote the following letter: "We live in a peculiar area where most of the men work for the government in highly skilled jobs, most of them experimental. The mental challenge is extremely keen, the competition great, and the personal satisfaction tremendous. But the children don't have a father and the wives a husband. The short time my husband is home we are happy, but the job has his heart and soul."

My comment is this: Men who lose themselves in their work have to neglect wives and children to some extent. They are the men, however, that make the most notable contributions to society. Our world could not exist as it does now if it were not for such men. Those men who have been fortunate enough to have wives who have understood and given them loyal support have been blessed and have been able to reach their goals much easier. It would be well for all women to realize that *it is better to have ten percent of a hundred percent man, than one hundred percent of a ten percent man.*

The Sympathetic Wife

Let me portray a picture of the sympathetic wife who truly understands her husband's world of work. When he is cross or irritable, she peeks into his world and tries to understand what he may have put up with that day. Her sympathy makes her *forgiving* of his bad behavior. If he is late for dinner, she measures her own inconvenience against what may have been required of him and counts her problem as nothing significant. Her husband, instead of coming home to more problems, has come home to a haven of rest and comfort.

When he comes home each day, he is always greeted with a warm smile, and never problems. She does not let the children rush in the climb on him, or offer their complaints. After they greet their father, she leads him into the bedroom where she can make him comfortable. She arranges his pillows, takes off his shoes and encourages him to relax. She allows him this time of peace before exposing him to the rest of the family. He works to protect and shelter her, and this is her way of protecting him.

If her husband does not get around to repairing the fence or painting the kitchen, she tries to understand that although these jobs seem important to her, they may seem insignificant to him in comparison with his heavy responsibility of work. And she also understands that when he comes home, he often must regain something of himself for the next day's work. These minor repair jobs seem secondary to his rejuvenation of body and spirit. Her sympathetic attitude makes her *patient* with his neglect of home duties.

If he does not take her out to dinner or other social events, she understands this neglect, also. She, of course, has been home all day and needs the diversion. But he, on the other hand, has a greater need which supersedes hers—the need to recuperate from his strenuous life. Taking her out would only add to his burdens, or so he feels. In weighing out both of their needs, she foregoes her own in preference to his greater need to unwind.

She may have a desire for a few additional home furnishings which would make their home life more enjoyable. But, she asks for only those things they can well afford. Much as these things mean to her, her husband's health means even more.

The sympathetic wife is not jolted when her husband wants to invest their money—just to make more money. She has a genuine sympathy for the man's motives, for his desire to get ahead and plan for future years when he may have added financial burdens or may decline in his capacity to earn the living. And if she offers any opposition to his plans, it is softened by her sympathy for the man's reasons.

A challenging problem is when the husband spends a great amount of time away from home striving for success. He may neglect his wife and children, so that much of the training and care of the family is left up to the wife. The wife and even the children may interpret this as a lack of interest in their welfare, and even a lack of love. The home and family life, which is the very center of their existence, seems only secondary to the father. But the sympathetic wife does not look at it this way. She understands that her husband's motives are not due to lack of interest, but *because of* a genuine love and concern for them. He is thoughtful of their needs now and in the future and wants to provide opportunities for their welfare.

The woman with this attitude does not feel neglected, nor does she feel her children are neglected. Therefore, the children themselves do not feel neglected. Children are inclined to take the attitude of the mother, so she greatly benefits them by her sympathy for her husband's goals and problems. With such a family atmosphere, the husband is greatly aided towards success. He has the comfort and assurance that he needs to function at his full capacity. And if he is always met with the comfort of understanding, you can count on it that he will always be home as often as possible. This is the way to bring a man home to your side, not by force of an unwholesome obligation.

Sometimes a man spends much time away from home for a different reason. Instead of working for the welfare of the family, his time is spent in pleasures—sporting events, time with the boys and other activities. In this case the man's neglect seems without justification. But the sympathetic wife will not condemn the man. She will look to herself for the answers, will ask herself if she may have driven him away by an unsympathetic attitude of the past. If she resolves to always give him the sympathy he needs, he will probably lose his other interests and will begin to realize that his greatest pleasure is his family. Here, again, the wife does not bring him home by force, but by building a home life which he will seek of his own free will.

2. His Desire for Status

Parallel to the man's struggle to provide is his *struggle for status*. This driving desire is noticeable in all male members of the animal kingdom. Robert Ardrey, in his book *African Genesis*, states that in the animal world the instinct for status, for the acquisition and defense of territory are more compelling for the male than is the sex instinct. The pecking order in the barnyard, the formation in which a flock of wild geese will fly, the hierarchy in a colony of baboons, and the ranking within a herd of elephants is a more driving force for the male than is the sex function.

The drive for position is evident in the human male. This explains why men will work so diligently for advancement or higher rank in their work. Do not think that their sole motivation is money. Although it must be recognized that money is a strong incentive for dedicated efforts, the desire for position is also a factor. This fact is manifest in the many men who do not need more money but nevertheless drive on for a higher position.

This desire to excel other men is noticeable even if the man is only trying to win a game or toss a better basketball than another man. But sometimes his drive for status impels him to higher heights—the championship cup, the gold medal of achievement, or president of his company and along with this, the acclaim and recognition which comes with an honored position. I wish to stress that this is a *masculine trait*. Feminine women are noticeably lacking in the drive for position. They may desire some acclaim for talents or achievements, but seldom have tendencies to gain superiority over one another. The man, on the other hand, desires to shine out brightly, *to seek an honored place in the world of men*.

Now, it must be recognized that both men and women may strive for *excellence in their work* for a different reason than status. They are motivated by a feeling of satisfaction and self-worth which good works can bring. This is the joy of the artist, the carpenter or the swimmer who finds rewards in his own feeling of achievement. But, even in this case, both men and women desire appreciation for excellent work. But a man may also desire recognition, acclaim and honor for his excellent work, for the feeling of status it brings. The desire for acclaim is much stronger in men than in women.

To some extent, the desire for status is a negative trait. It would be better if men were moved to action only by love or a desire to serve humanity. But we must realize that men are human and that this trait is not without some merit. The drive for status, if not mixed with greed and a lust for power, can cause men to strive earnestly to prepare themselves for a worthwhile life and to bring themselves out of obscurity where they can more adequately influence and serve mankind.

What should a woman do if she recognizes an intense desire for status in her husband? She should first be sympathetic with his desire and give him the freedom to "reach for the stars" if he so desires. Then she must realize that in attaining the position he seeks, his life will not be easy. He will probably have to work long hours and give himself wholeheartedly to his work. He will have *mountains to climb, rivers to cross* and *battles to win*. She will have to make allowances for neglect, bad behavior and again be the sympathetic wife I have just described.

Status with His Wife

When a man has achieved an honored position, it may be heartwarming to him to receive the acclaim of the world, but greater is his satisfaction in receiving the *acclaim of his wife*. Although he would like to be a hero to his friends and colleagues, his greatest joy is in being a hero to the woman he loves. This is all important to him in so much that if he does not receive her praise, he can be painfully disappointed.

And yet how many heroes have been honored everywhere except at home? A man may work for years to earn an educational degree only to have his wife fail to comment, or if she does, it is more with the attitude "it's about time." Or, if she receives the news that her husband has received an award for meritorious service, she acts as though any other man could have done as well. Or imagine how painful to her to esteem some other man as a hero, such as a brother, father, or man in the community. Although modest comments about other men are proper, it would be a mistake for a woman to be overly enthusiastic about another man's accomplishments.

There are other women who actually have a great appreciation for their husbands' achievements but deliberately withhold praise for what they feel is the man's own good. The wife may fear that too much praise will make her husband arrogant or unprepared for a possible defeat. Thus, she feels it her duty to "keep his feet on the ground" by being lukewarm about his achievements. One such situation was written to me in the following words:

And Touch a Star

"I sat in Fascinating Womanhood class and listened while another wife told how in the past she had always pointed out her husband's flaws to prevent his ego from being inflated. Until Fascinating Womanhood, she said, she clearly saw it as her duty. Somewhere, deep inside of me, an alarm went off. Why were those words so familiar? Suddenly I knew. They were echoes of words I had probably never said out loud, but I had surely thought a thousand times and worse, believed them to be true. 'I saw it clearly as my duty. . . .'

"My husband, Bob, is a successful and well known writer of songs and scripts for movies. He is like most creative men, a dreamer of dreams, his eyes on the stars. He expects each new project to be a great and wonderful success. Now I, on the other hand, am a realist. Nothing is perfect . . . everything cannot be great . . . there are degrees to success, I would point out. There is always another picture which gets better reviews, other songs getting more play, other writers getting more recognition. Clearly it was my duty to point this out and more.

"Please understand, I never meant to be unkind. Indeed, wasn't it kindness to show Bob reality? If the balloon doesn't go too high, would it then, not have so far to fall? Was I not his anchor? Surely I was helping my love to see the pitfalls on the ground by forcing his eyes off the stars. Until now, I believed that . . . but now that alarm was ringing in my head. I knew now what a terrible thing I had been doing to the man I loved and who loved me. An anchor? An anchor is a dead weight which keeps the boat from moving. I would not be that again! There are plenty of people to help keep Bob's feet on the ground—critics who are paid to judge his creative talents to others, producers who know if his product is good or bad, and of course, the audience, who ultimately applauds or not. There is no excuse for him to be criticized by me, the one person from whom he needs approval and admiration.

"Later that week we went to a screening of his new picture. He watched my reactions throughout the movie. Even before it ended I told him how really good it was—how proud I was of him. He glowed with pride. Later, when we returned home our children asked, 'How did it go?' He looked over their heads and into my eyes and said, 'It must have been a masterpiece, your mother loved it.'

"Let others criticize—my husband still dreams his perfect dreams. The only difference is that he has a wife who now understands that a creative man cannot touch the stars unless he reaches out for them without concerning himself too much with the pitfalls on the ground."

—Beverly Hills, California

Another thing a woman must guard against is being a competition to the man's feeling of status herself. A woman should never excel her husband in a field in which he is trying to win acclaim, or win an honor which would overshadow his success. If you are the one who has won honor and acclaim, this would threaten his own position. This problem is apparent with many famous women, especially movie and stage actresses. If they marry men who can outdo them, then there is no problem; but if the man simply cannot meet the competition of his wife's acclaim, it can defeat the man's struggle for status. How can he impress her or anyone else with his meager efforts if she has already won the honors of earth?

Sympathy for the Discouraged Man

A man has a special need for sympathy when he is discouraged. This tendency to be depressed is common among men. Whether rich or poor, learned or unlearned, few men escape this unpleasant experience. In fact, the more learned, talented and aggressive men tend to have the most intense suffering. Abraham Lincoln had periods of depression in which he merely sat and brooded or read the newspapers. At one time he wrote, "I am now the most miserable man alive." Most men of great responsibility have periods of real discouragement. But all men, both young and old, have times when they are depressed, times that need to be understood.

Realizing the nature of man in today's world, it is easy to see why they become discouraged. It is a world

97

with many demands and little real security. A man has many worries—money, success, his children, and the future. In striving for status, he may have lost rather than won the position he had been seeking. Then, his sensitive pride is always at stake, subject to insults, ridicule, and the keen competition of his associates. Or he may be depressed because too much is expected of him, there are demands he cannot meet, or problems he cannot find solutions to. Or, it may be just a bad day for him.

A woman has the power to break this spell of gloom and bring her husband to his good spirits again. But it is a delicate situation in which she must be guided by knowledge of what to do, and especially *what not to do*. If she succeeds, she can be of service to her husband in a most important way. Remember, one of the functions of a woman is to "shed joy around, and cast light upon dark days . . . is not this to render a service?"

How to Give True Sympathy

Many women do not know the art of giving true sympathy. It is not that they do not try, but that they do not know how. They make all kinds of mistakes, saying just the wrong things and often none of the right things. To understand this subject, let me start with the negative:

1. *Do not try to help him solve his problems:* This means to not offer too many suggestions or offer to help him in any way. This may be appreciated but it is not sympathy and is not what a man really needs from a woman. What he does need is *sympathy for his feelings and a reassurance of your confidence in him.*

2. *Do not minimize his problems:* Do not say, for example, "You worry too much," or "Your problems are just in your imagination," or "Life is not as tough as you think." These attitudes show a lack of sympathy and are belittling to masculine pride. If you, a timid woman, can be so fearless in the face of difficulty, how does it make him feel as a man?

3. *Do not advise him to count his blessings:* If he thinks of this idea himself, it may help; but if you remind him that he has every reason to be happy, he will feel *ashamed* for letting life get him down and *his worries will seem inexcusable*. Not only will he feel a lack of sympathy from you, but he will feel humiliated. The fact that he has "blessings" can make his discouragement worse.

98

It is interesting to note that when a woman is discouraged, she is different. She, of course, wants sympathy for her feelings, but she wants more than this from a man. She looks to him for help and guidance in times of trouble. She wants his suggestions and his help in solving problems. The man is her protector and her guide, and she leans on him for helpful advice because she is a woman. But do not expect that men are like we are. They have a sensitive masculine pride. Having a woman solve their difficult problems only makes them feel ineffectual and incomplete as a man. This does not mean that a woman cannot offer suggestions to a man when he asks for them. But when she does give advice, it must be given in a feminine manner as I will explain in another chapter. The main thing he seeks when he is discouraged, however, is not her advice, no matter how great it is or how much he may need it. He seeks her sympathy and comfort and a restoration of his confidence in himself.

4. *Suffer with him:* Feel with him. Try to understand what he is going through. Have an *empathy* in which you *share feelings* or *suffer with him*. It is not necessary to understand the cause of his problems but it is important to understand his pain and to express sympathy for that pain.

5. *Some things to say:* "Life is so tough, I don't see how you men put up with it." "You poor dear. I know how you are suffering." "You have every reason to be discouraged." "You are doing fine, considering the problems you have to face." "This is a dark hour that will pass."

6. *Don't let his gloom rub off on you:* In your sympathy, don't become depressed along with him. Maintain a cheerful attitude, and especially optimism. But, do not make the mistake of being overly exuberant or light hearted when he is depressed. This would cause him to feel that you lack sympathy. He wants you to feel *with him*.

7. *Display confidence in him:* Let him know that no matter what the situation you still believe in him and his ability.

8. *Restore confidence in himself:* Do this by pointing out his better side and especially his manly qualities.

9. *Allow time for his spirits to lift:* Often it takes time for a man to "snap out of it." If he needs this time you will have to extend it to him. In the meantime continue to show sympathy when he appears to need it.

10. *Have faith that your sympathy helps:* If a man's spirits do not lift immediately a woman often feels that she has done him little good. Be assured that your sympathy has been appreciated and helpful even though he does not appear to respond.

The quality of sympathy is rare in women. Because of this, a man often learns to do without it—learns to withstand alone the buffetings of time and circumstance. His masculine pride would prevent him from asking for sympathy. And it is only of value when it comes from the heart in a moment of real need. But there is a deep need that stirs within every man for a genuine sympathy for the problems he faces, and great is his joy when his wife can fill this need. One woman who worked diligently on the three points in this chapter, said that one night her husband smiled directly at her and said, "Sweetheart, for the first time in almost seven years I get butterflies in my stomach when I think of coming home to you."

When a Man Has Failed

As we conclude this chapter, I would like to refer to a particular time a man needs sympathy—*when he faces failure*. This is a time of agony for a man, not so much for the failure itself as the fear of what his wife will think of him. When we understand the man's sensitive pride and his desire for status, especially in the eyes of his wife, we can understand the pain of his humiliation.

If the failure is financial and he must lower his standard of living, he can suffer even more acutely. This is caused by his protective feeling for his family, his desire to provide for them adequately, realizing that he must now subject them to inconveniences and discomfort. The wife who can understand these bitter moments and has the fineness of character to adapt to her circumstances cheerfully, meets a need in a man's life that nothing can equal. He may never have fully appreciated her until she was put to such a test. Defeat is really a woman's most golden opportunity to show her true worth. But if a woman lets a man down at these moments, his feeling for her would be difficult to recapture. An illustration of a man's agony in his failure and how it is met by the perfect wife is found in Washington Irving's essay "The Wife," from which I will quote:

"My intimate friend Leslie had married a beautiful and accomplished girl, who had been brought up in the midst of fashionable life. She had, it is true, no fortune; but that of my friend was ample, and he delighted in the anticipation of indulging her in every elegant pursuit and administering to those delicate tastes and fancies that spread a kind of witchery about the sex. 'Her life,' said he, 'shall be like a fairy tale.'

"The very difference in their characters produced a harmonious combination—he was of a romantic and somewhat serious cast; she was all life and gladness. I have often noticed the mute rapture with which he would gaze upon her in company, of which her sprightly powers made her his delight; and how, in the midst of applause, her eye would still turn to him as if there alone she sought favor and acceptance.

"When leaning on his arm, her slender form contrasted finely with his tall, manly person. The fond, confiding air with which she looked up to him seemed to call forth a flush of triumphant pride and cherishing tenderness as if he doted on his lovely burden for its very helplessness. Never did a couple set forward on the flowery path of early and well-suited marriage with a fairer prospect of felicity.

"It was the misfortune of my friend, however, to have embarked his property in large speculations; and he had not been married many months, when, by a succession of sudden disasters, it was swept from him, and he found himself reduced almost to penury. For a time he kept his situation to himself and went about with a haggard countenance and a breaking heart. His life was but a protracted agony; and what rendered it more unsupportable was the necessity of keeping up a smile in the presence of his wife; for he could not bring himself to overwhelm her with the news.

"She saw, however, with the quick eyes of affection, that all was not well with him. She marked his altered looks and stifled sighs and was not to be deceived by his sickly and vapid attempts at cheerfulness. She tasked all her sprightly powers and tender blandishments to win him back to happiness; but she only drove the arrow deeper into his soul. The more he saw cause to love her, the more torturing was the thought that he was soon to make her wretched.

"A little while, thought he, and the smile will vanish from that cheek—the song will die away from those lips—the luster of those eyes will be quenched with sorrow; and the happy heart which nows beats lightly in that bosom will be weighed down like mine, with the cares and miseries of the world. At length he came to me, one day, and related his whole situation, in a tone of the deepest despair.

"When I had heard him through I inquired, 'Does your wife know all this?' At the question he burst into an agony of tears. 'For God's sake!' cried he, 'if you have any pity on me, don't mention my wife; it is the thought of her that drives me almost to madness!' 'And why not?' said I. 'She must know it sooner or later; you can not keep it long from her, and the intelligence may break upon her in a more startling manner than if imparted by yourself; for the accents of those we love soften the harshest tidings.

" 'Besides, you are depriving yourself of the comforts of her sympathy; and not merely that, but also endangering the only bond that can keep hearts together—unreserved community of thought and feeling. She will soon perceive that something is secretly preying upon your mind; and true love will not brook reserve; it feels undervalued and outraged when even the sorrows of those it loves are concealed from it.'

" 'Oh, but my friend! to think what a blow I am to give to all her future prospects—how I am to strike her very soul to the earth, by telling her that her husband is a beggar! that she is to forego all the elegances of life—all the pleasures of society—to shrink with me into indigence and obscurity! To tell her that I have dragged her down from the sphere in which she might have continued to move in constant brightness, the light of every eye, the admiration of every heart! How can she bear poverty? She has been brought up in all the refinements of opulence. How can she bear neglect? She has been the idol of society. Oh! it will break her heart—it will break her heart!'

"After additional patience, the friend finally persuaded Leslie to go home and unburden his sad heart to his wife. The next morning the friend was eager to know the results. In inquiring, he found that Leslie had made the disclosure.

"'And how did she bear it?' 'Like an angel! It seemed rather to be a relief to her mind, for she threw her arms round my neck, and asked if this was all that had lately made me unhappy. But, poor girl!' added he, 'she can not realize the change we must undergo. She has no idea of poverty but in the abstract; she has only read of it in poetry, where it is allied to love.

"'She feels yet no privation; she suffers no loss of accustomed conveniences nor elegances. When we come practically to experience its sordid cares, its paltry wants, its petty humiliations, then will be the real trial.'

"Some days afterward he called upon me in the evening. He had disposed of his dwelling house, and taken a small cottage in the country, a few miles from town. He had been busied all day in sending out furniture. The new establishment required few articles, and those of the simplest kind.

"He was going out to the cottage where his wife had been all day superintending its arrangement. My feelings had become strongly interested in the progress of the family story, and as it was evening, I offered to accompany him. He was wearied with the fatigues of the day, and as he walked out, fell into a fit of gloomy musing.

"'Poor Mary!' at length broke, with a heavy sigh from his lips. 'And what of her?' asked I; 'has anything happened to her?' 'What!' said he, darting an impatient glance; 'is it nothing to be reduced to this paltry situation—to be caged in a miserable cottage—to be obliged to toil almost in the menial concerns of her wretched habitation?'

"'Has she, then, repined at the change?' 'Repined! She has been nothing but sweetness and good-humor. Indeed, she seems in better spirits than I have ever known her; she has been to me all love and tenderness and comfort!' 'Admirable girl!' exclaimed I. 'You call yourself poor, my friend, you never were so rich—you never knew the boundless treasures of excellence you possess in that woman.'

"'Oh! but, my friend, if this, our first meeting at the cottage were over, I think I could then be comfortable. But this is her first day of real experience; she has been introduced into a humble dwelling; she has been employed all day in arranging its miserable equipments; she has for the first time, known fatigues of domestic employment; she has, for the first time looked around her on a home destitute of everything elegant—almost everything convenient; and now may be sitting down exhausted and spiritless, brooding over a prospect of future poverty.'

"There was a degree of probability in this picture that I could not gainsay; so we walked on in silence. After turning from the main road up a narrow lane, so thickly shaded with forest trees as to give it a complete air of seclusion, we came in sight of the cottage. It was humble enough in its appearance for the most pastoral poet; and yet it had a pleasuring rural look. A wild vine had overrun one end with a profusion of foliage; a few trees threw their branches gracefully over it; and I observed several pots of flowers tastefully disposed about the door, and on the grass-plot in front.

"A small wicket gate opened upon a foot-path that wound through some shrubbery to the door. Just as we approached, we heard the sound of music. Leslie grabbed my arm, we paused and listened. It was Mary's voice, singing in a style of the most touching simplicity, a little air of which her husband was peculiarly fond. I felt Leslie's hand tremble on my arm. He stepped forward, to hear more distinctly. His step made a noise on the gravel-walk.

"A bright, beautiful face glanced out of the window and vanished, a light footstep was heard, and Mary came tripping forth to meet us. She was in a pretty rural dress of white; a few wild-flowers were twisted in her fine hair; a fresh bloom was on her cheek; her whole countenance beamed with smiles—I had never seen her look so lovely.

" 'My dear Leslie,' cried she, 'I am so glad you are come! I have been watching and watching for you; and running down the lane, and looking for you. I've set out a table under a beautiful tree behind the cottage; and I've been gathering some of the most delicious strawberries, for I know you are fond of them—and we have such excellent cream—and everything is so sweet and still here! Oh!' said she, putting her arm within his, and looking up brightly in his face—'oh, we shall be so happy.'

"Poor Leslie was overcome. He caught her to his bosom, he folded his arms around her, he kissed her again and again, he could not speak, but the tears gushed into his eyes; and he has often assured me that, though the world has since gone prosperously with him, and his life has, indeed, been a happy one, yet never has he experienced a moment of more exquisite felicity."

This account of Irving's is a perfect example of a man's experience with failure and how a woman can meet this test. Mary's response is an illustration of our ideal of Angela Human. In making application of this story, however, remember that a woman may be required to adapt to circumstances less attractive than a cottage in the woods. It could be an unattractive house in a crowded city, or a modest home in a dry desert country. But, adapting to these dreary situations cheerfully could be counted as opportunities to show true worth, and thus deepen the man's appreciation of his wife.

Assignment

1. Say something like this: "I am beginning to understand the heavy responsibility you have to provide for me and the children. I want you to know how much I appreciate it, and I am sorry if I have not done so enough in the past."
2. If he is discouraged or depressed, follow the suggestions I have given in "How To Give True Sympathy."

7

Make Him No. 1

Characteristic No. 5

A man wants a woman who will place him at the top of her priority list—not second, but first. He wants to be the king-pin around which all other activities of her life revolve. He does not want to be the background music to her other interests and dreams. This desire is not necessarily a conscious one, but an *inner need* which surfaces violently when not adquately met—when the wife places other things first such as the children, homemaking or a career. Being placed in this inferior position can cause the man to form bitter resentments towards his wife and even his children.

A man does not expect his wife to neglect important duty in his behalf. He realizes the demands of her life and expects her to give each responsibility the attention it requires. He certainly would not want his children to suffer neglect. And he knows that she is entitled to other interests and diversions. But he does not want to be *less important*. And he does not want to be looked upon as a convenience, a paycheck, an escort, a social asset, a ticket to security, or even just a sex partner. He would like to feel that she married him for *him* and not as a means of filling her needs or reaching her objectives.

There is a tendency for women to fail in this respect, to place other things ahead of their husband. This tendency began in early childhood and was clearly evident in our world of dreams. When we were little girls, if we were typical, we dreamed of a little vine-covered cottage with roses blooming around the door. Children were playing on the floor; there were pots and pans in the cupboard and frilly tie-back curtains. Everything was typical of the perfect home scene except that there was *no husband present*. (This was some time before we dreamed of a handsome prince sweeping us off from our feet.) There is a little poem found in an early edition of Childcraft Books which so well describes this childhood scene minus the husband:

The Shiny Little House

I wish, how I wish, that I had a little house,
With a mat for the cat and a hole for the mouse,
And a clock going "tock" in the corner of the room
And a kettle, and a cupboard, and a big birch broom.

To school in the morning the children off would run,
And I'd given them a kiss and a penny and a bun.
But directly they had gone from this little house of mine,
I'd clap my hands and snatch a cloth and shine, shine,
    shine.

I'd shine all the knives, all the windows and the floors,
All the grates, all the plates, all the handles on the doors,
Every fork, every spoon, every lid and every tin,
Till Everything was shining like a new bright pin.

At night by the fire, when the children were in bed,
I'd sit and I'd knit, with a cap upon my head,
And the kettles, and the saucepans they would shine, shine,
    shine,
In this tweeny little, cozy little, house of mine!

(Originally appeared in *The Land of Poetry*, Book 2, 1930.)

NANCY M. HAYES

As you can see, no mention was made of a husband in this little girl's dream of domestic perfection. Her focus was on the children and homemaking joys. Little girls also dream of the splendor of the wedding—the white dress of satin and lace, the tiered wedding cake, candles, ribbons and bells—everything except the groom. He just does not come into the picture at this point. But later on, as the little girl reaches puberty, the handsome prince charming at last comes into the scene.

The tragedy is that after the girl wins her husband, she often reverts back to the earlier dream. At last she has her little cottage, children, and all the domestic comforts and joys she looked forward to. Her husband has only been a means to this end. As she devotes herself to the home scene, her husband drops into the background. Then, as life progresses, she has added responsibility of family life and other demands and pressures. She may also include other interests, to keep life more meaningful. If time permits, she may even turn to a career. All of these things tend to push the man further into the background. Now, let's take a close look at the things women tend to place ahead of their husbands:

1. The Children

Most women feel a sacred responsibility for their role as mother, an obligation to nurture their offspring in body and spirit, and to provide them with every opportunity to grow to their highest potential. This noble feeling of motherly devotion, when moved by a strong feeling of mother love, can cause a woman to so focus on the care and training of her children that she automatically places them as prime importance in her life.

An example of this is a woman I knew years ago whom I shall call Clara. Clara was the perfect mother, all kindness, patience and love. She usually wore a kindly smile and talked with a gentle tone in her voice when speaking to her children. But she was firm, too. She had studied books on the subject of training children so was not without the strength needed to be a good mother. Clara was a model of unselfish devotion. I remember her sitting by her children's side, helping them practice the piano or helping them with their homework. She kept extensive scrapbooks for each child and gave them the most lavish birthday parties in the neighborhood and everything which delights little children. Her children were the center of her life. I have never seen a finer example of mother love and sacrifice and a higher goal of perfection in duty. I admired Clara and for a long while wanted to be like her—up until the time I realized what problems her devotion had caused.

Her husband was the unhappy second fiddle to all of this—merely an appendage to the family scene. He was the father and the provider, but he was not the king. I think Clara really loved her husband and treated him well enough, but he was obviously second place to his children. And what was the result? The man bitterly resented this excessive devotion to his children and the inferior position it placed him in. In earlier years he had been a gentle type man, but this situation brought out an ugliness to his personality that was unknown before—a sort of meanness in temperament that was a surprise to some who had known him. Not only did he resent his wife but also his children and, as a result, found it difficult to be a good father to them. He would often leave home for long periods of time to get away from it all, but would be just as hard to live with when he returned.

This inferior position can cause a man to resist the birth of more children. He may only subconsciously realize it, but more children means more motherly demands and will only intensify his problem of feeling neglected. Or, if a new baby does arrive, he may resent the child. Or he may ignore it. The father may struggle with a feeling of guilt for this lack of love for his own baby, without realizing it is caused by his own feeling of neglect.

Placing her husband No. 1 does not diminish a woman's sacred responsibility to her children nor is it an indication of lesser love for them. A woman can serve both husband and children without conflict. Actually, a man does not want his wife to neglect his children. He is just as interested in their care and training as she is, but he would like the assurance that her love and devotion to them does not supersede her dedication to him. Children miss nothing when the father comes first. They feel *more* secure and happy. This is because when the wife makes her husband No. 1, she builds a happier relationship with him. This happy marriage will be the center of a happy home in which the entire family benefits.

The tendency to place children in priority over husbands is common and difficult to guard against. In the first place, if we are to succeed in the role of motherhood, it requires a wholehearted effort. So it is hard to draw the line between *adequate* attention to children and *excessive devotion* to them. But if we are to attain happiness in marriage, we must work out a proper balance between devotion to children and devotion to husband, and often this means choices. Let us review some situations in which these choices occur, situations in which the wife may be tempted to put the children in priority.

1. *A Place of Residence:* Sometimes a man finds it important to move his business to a new community. The new job may bring in more money or provide greater opportunity for success in the future or other advantages. If his wife is overly protective of their children, she may

feel they will be put to some disadvantages and may stubbornly refuse to move on this account. In so doing she disregards her husband's welfare in preference to benefits to her children.

If a man is overlooking serious disadvantages to his children so that a move would be an injustice to them, the wife should make an appeal to her husband to more seriously consider their welfare. But, usually children will not suffer seriously. A good family can be happy anywhere and is usually strengthened by adversity. This is especially true if the wife is devoted to her husband and close to her children.

If the man's reasons for a move are selfish or without justification the wife should make an appeal to her husband to consider the more important values. But in this case he would not feel in a secondary position, since the wife has not disregarded his welfare in preference to the children.

When buying a house, sometimes the wife will consider advantages to her children and ignore her husband's needs or requests. She may press to buy a house that is beyond his means, feeling it will benefit the children. Or she may ignore a particular feature in a house that pleases him, while concentrating on the whims of her children. He may have always wanted a view, a deck, a pool or a private study. He may be willing to forego these in preference to his wife's desires, but he is not inclined to feel it is required of him to place his *children's* wishes ahead of his own.

2. *Time and Attention:* Sometimes a man will have to compete with his children for his wife's time and attention. She may be so busily occupied with attending to her children that she seldom has a moment to give him undivided attention. Or if he does demand her time for a few minutes, she acts uneasy in her feeling of duty to the children. There are times, of course, when family demands cannot be put aside, but often it is a case of excessive devotion. The man can detect this reasoning and will count it as placing the children ahead of him in importance.

There are women who express good fortune in having a husband who is a salesman or in a profession which takes him away from home a great amount of time. They have considered it an advantage so they could concentrate on raising their children more devotedly. They completely disregard their husband's needs for time and attention.

3. *Money and Things:* There is a tendency for women to pamper their children, giving them every little thing their hearts desire. An entire chapter could be written about the harm to children by over-indulgent mothers, but the point here is not harm to children, but to fathers. If the man can well afford these things, then there is no problem to him personally; but if the wife indulges her children at her husband's expense, buying them things he cannot afford, she places an added strain upon his life. Her extravagances are a serious indicaton of her preferment of her children over the welfare of her husband. She is placing their wants ahead of his basic needs.

4. *Interest and Thought:* Sometimes a wife is just more *interested* in her children than her husband. The children are always uppermost in her mind, so that she focuses all thought on them. She seldom thinks of her husband and his problems, how she may be a comfort to him or serve him in this way or that. She fails to remember the small requests he makes, what he likes for dinner, how he would like to spend the evening or what is important to him. Yet she is overly attentive to her children's requests because she is always thinking about them. These are only a few of the ways that women tend to put their children ahead of their husbands in importance.

2. Homemaking

Most men really appreciate a clean, orderly home, made comfortable and "homey" by the touch of a woman's hand. They would consider it a miserable disadvantage if the wife were to fail in this important function. However, a man does not want the homemaking to become more important than he is. A house is made to serve the family, not the family to serve the house. He would like to feel that his wife's efforts are mostly for his benefit, not for some personal pride she may feel in the perfection of homemaking.

There is a tendency for women who are excellent homemakers to go "overboard" in their aims for perfection. Their motive, however, is not so much to please their husband and family as it is to *please themselves* or *impress others.* An excellent example of this is found in the old movie "Craig's Wife." Craig's wife always had a scrutinizing eye on the servants to see that they overlooked nothing in the polished perfection of the house. She would not let her husband sit on his own bed because it would wrinkle the beautiful bedspread. She did not like fresh flowers in the house because the petals dropped off and cluttered the tables. Her husband soon realized that she adored the house more than him, so he left. As the trucking company came for his things and was moving a large trunk down the hall, it scraped the highly polished floor, leaving a deep scratch. Craig's wife sat on the floor and wept—not because her husband was leaving her, but because of the scratch in her beautiful floor. In the end she suffered a terrible empty feeling for having been such a fool as to worship a house and in so doing lose a husband.

The main points to remember are these: Although good homemaking is a most admirable virtue, *it can be overdone.* And, although we should keep house as a matter of principle, if we strive to please anyone, it should be our husband and family, and not ourselves or other people. The goal should be a *home,* not a *showplace.* And, although a man appreciates efforts to keep the house beautiful for him, he does not want homemaking placed in priority over him, or things which are more important to him. *The castle is not more important than the king who dwells therein.*

3. Appearance

All human beings should have a certain pride in their appearance which prompts them to be well groomed and well dressed as a matter of principle. Even if we were to be far removed from civilization, we should strive for a proper appearance for our own feeling of self-esteem. But, when too much attention is placed on appearance, one has to stop and question the motive. If the effort is to please our husband, he may well appreciate it. If, however, we spend endless hours shopping, sewing, and grooming and in so doing, *neglect* our husband, it can give him the impression that it is *others* we are trying to impress. He can feel second place to the public we dress for. This is another way a woman can fail to put a man Number One in her life.

4. The Wife's Parents

Some women feel a strong love and attachment for their parents which exceeds the feelings they have for their husband. They are overjoyed at the prospects of returning home, seek excuses to be with their parents again and again or to spend excessive time with them. Although the love between parent and child is a very fine thing, if a woman does not transfer her major attachment to her husband after marriage, it can cause her husband to feel second place to her parents. This in turn can cause the husband to resent his wife's parents, since they are a competition to him.

5. Money and Success

Sometimes money and the man's success become more important than the *man himself*. I can explain this by giving the following example: A woman I knew was married to a man of rather low economic status. The man was satisfied with his station in life, but his wife wanted more money and prestige. She suggested to him that he return to school and become a surgeon. The man was rather quiet about the idea at first, but eventually began to lay plans in that direction. It did not work out, however, due to the man's own lack of interest and initiative. Her attitude quite injured the man, as you can well imagine. He had been content with his life and felt his wife's desire for his greater success was more important to her than him and his own feelings.

Another lady had an almost opposite situation. Her husband *wanted* to get ahead by expanding his business. This would make it necessary for him to sell their home and move his family into an apartment temporarily. His wife "put her foot down" and refused to move. "I did not mind the inconvenience," she told me, "for I have lived in lesser circumstances but I was afraid we would lose our money." In this case, regardless of how much the man wanted to pursue his plans for success his wife felt security was more important. Here, money and security were more important than the man. We can see from these two illustrations that when we make a man Number One in our life, we must also make his interests, desires and responsibilities Number One.

One of the greatest threats to a man's position of No. 1 is when his wife earnestly pursues a career. The dedication and drive required for success tends to push the man into the background. And if she finally reaches a pinnacle of success, she overshadows her husband and makes him feel relatively unimportant. This is a serious problem with famous women. The greater their success, the less important the man becomes, at least in his opinion. He is just automatically placed in a secondary position. This is a challenging problem to the wife, but not without a solution. When she realizes the importance of making her husband No. 1, she can strive to keep her priorities straight and let her husband know that he is always in the first position. But, even if the wife is not pursuing a career—if she is just working—the demands of her work in order to hold her job can cause her husband to feel less important.

Another threat to the man's position occurs when a woman pursues other interests such as the development of talents. Men, generally, would like to extend women the freedom to develop talents and pursue interests, and often encourage them to do so for their own personal development. If the wife works at her talent earnestly, it can be a very fine thing and bring her more fulfillment in life. But, if she pursues a talent with such great dedication and enthusiasm that it overshadows her husband, it can cause him to feel "second fiddle" to her other interests. This is the reason a man may say "no" when his wife wishes to divert her attention from domestic duties. However, if a woman is always careful to keep a man in the Number One position and let him know it, she can usually win his cooperation in devoting a reasonable amount of time to outside activities.

Should a Man Make His Wife No. 1?

Although a man may love his wife devotedly, it is not always possible or even right for him to make her Number One, and this is because of the nature of his life. A man's Number One responsibility is to provide the living for his family. Often his work and life away from home are so demanding that it must take priority over all else if he is to succeed. This often means that he must neglect his family in the responsibility he feels in his work. In reality, he *is* putting his wife and family both Number One, but women often fail to interpret it this way.

In addition to making the living, men have always shouldered the responsibility to make the world a better place. They have largely been the builders of society— have solved world problems and developed new ideas for the benefit of all. This challenging role of public servant is not easy and also demands the man's attention away from his family.

If you will examine the lives of these noble public servants, you will usually find a wife who was willing to put the man *and his work* Number One and be content to take a second place. President and Mrs. Dwight D. Eisenhower are a good example of this. Mrs. Eisenhower recalls that during the first two weeks of their 53-year-long marriage, her husband drew her aside one evening and said, "Mamie, I have to tell you something ... My country comes first and you second." Mamie accepted this, and that is the way they lived. So, when you make a man Number One, you also make his work and outside responsibility Number One. But when the wife takes a second place to the man and his world, she loses nothing. The tender love he returns for her cooperation is more than a compensating reward.

When a woman fails to fill the man's need to be Number One, when she puts her children, homemaking, career or other interests first, he can suffer a tremendous lack. This is often the very reason a man is driven to another woman. In fact, it is a well known fact that men are seldom driven to a mistress because of sex passions. It is usually her ability to fill an emotional need, to make him feel appreciated and important in her life. The following experience is an illustration of how sex failed to keep a man home, and his emotional needs drove him to other women. I quote from a letter I received:

It Wasn't Sex that Drove Him to Other Women

"Our sex life was good, the only good part of our marriage it seemed. I told my husband so and complimented him on being such a wonderful lover, but the trouble was, that was the only thing I complimented him for or admired him for. I found nothing to praise in him; I certainly didn't accept him, and he was never treated as

115

Number One. In other words, I counted him as good for nothing except as a sex partner.

"Because of this, he turned to other women who made him feel Number One and admired his manly attributes; he turned to women who would listen to his stories and give him the time and attention every man needs. Of course, I hated him for having other women. I couldn't understand why he wasn't satisfied with the sex I gave him. But after Fascinating Womanhood, I could see that it wasn't sex he needed from these other women but acceptance, admiration and being Number One. By withholding these things from him, I had driven him to unfaithfulness. But I have no fears now that he will ever have another escapade, because I know what kind of a woman a man wants."

And now, I would like to add the following success experiences which are typical of the rewards which come when you place a man Number One:

My Children had Been No. 1

"I have long admired the marriage of a certain couple I know. In over 65 years of married life, they are loving and devoted, each idolizing the other. I thought about them often and wished and hoped my marriage would become as theirs and prayed that it would. During our 19 years of happily married life, we've become the parents of eight lovely children. I worked hard at being a good mother— my children had been the No. 1 thing in my life. I was really jolted when I learned through Fascinating Womanhood that the husband is supposed to be No. 1. It took me awhile to accept this idea. As I'm learning to practice this principle, I'm learning to have the kind of marriage I have wished for. I'm learning to give him more of the attention he needs and deserves. In return, he is more attentive to me and we have more harmony in our home and more fun in life."

My Husband Was a Second Class Citizen

"Our three children were born bright, healthy and beautiful. I was awed by them and apologetic about the world into which we had brought them. I mistakenly thought I could make up for the inevitable hardships they would face by devoting myself to them. For five years I put them ahead of everything and everyone. I spared no expense buying baby pictures, toys, clothes, etc. I felt no one could care for my children as good as I could and got baby sitters only when they were asleep. I felt personally responsible for their happiness and was miserable carrying this burden on my shoulders. My husband, naturally, was a second class citizen in our home. He had to compete for my time and attention. I even made him be quiet when the children wanted to talk at the same time he did.

"Then my husband had a serious accident, and for a time we thought he might die. As I sat in the intensive care unit waiting room, I was filled with such guilt that I was physically sick. I thought of my husband's status in our family unit. I thought of how much he had wanted a swimming pool and of how much I had made him do without so we could buy a larger house someday. When I thought I was losing him forever, I realized how much he meant to me. I realized that our children would leave home someday and that my husband was my life partner. Our friends and families had lives of their own. I was the one who had the most to lose. I prayed and prayed for another chance.

"God did give us another chance. We put in that swimming pool as soon as he got home from the hospital. My husband thrives on being Number One in our home. The children have responded and are becoming less selfish and self-centered. I have given them the responsibility for finding their own happiness and this has let me be more free. Because they no longer feel "the sun rises and sets" on them, I feel they will be better prepared to face maturity. Had we not had this great warning and fear, I feel that by now my husband and I would not be living together. I would be living through my children, resentful, tied down, and envying my husband's freedom. I now feel we are both free, free to love each other and our children."

Assignment

Tell your husband that he is the most important person in your life and then prove by your actions that this is true.

8

Man's Role in Life

Characteristic No. 6: The Man's Need to Function in His Masculine Role, to Feel Needed in This Role and to Excel Women in His Masculine Responsibility

What is the Role of Man? It is to be the *guide, protector* and *provider* for his wife and children. This role is not merely a result of custom or tradition, but is of divine origin. It was God who placed the man at the head of the family and commanded him to earn the bread. Women were given a different assignment—that of *wife, mother* and *homemaker*. The masculine and the feminine roles are complimentary to each other. Marriage is a partnership, but it is not an *equal* partnership. The masculine and feminine roles are equal in *importance*, but they are not equal in *responsibility*.

In Henry A. Bowman's book *Marriage for Moderns*, he compares the partnership of marriage to a lock and a key which join together to form a functioning unit. "Together they can accomplish something that neither acting alone can accomplish. Nor can it be accomplished by two locks and two keys. Each is distinct, yet neither is complete in and of itself. Their roles are neither identical nor interchangeable. Neither is superior to the other, since both are necessary. They are equally important. Each must be judged in terms of its own function. They are complimentary."

There are three important parts to Characteristic No. 6. First, *the normal man has a great need to function fully in his role as the guide, protector and provider*. This means that he would like to take his place at the head of the family, to have his family honor him in this position and do those things which make it easier for him to serve in this capacity. He would like to succeed in earning the living, in meeting his family's essential needs and to do so independently, without the help of others. He would like to serve as the protector, sheltering his family from danger, harm or want. He does not want his wife to share his masculine burdens or to deliberately step over into his role, but prefers for her to devote herself fully to making a success of her career in the home.

The second part of Characteristic No. 6 is this: *A man wants to feel needed, that his family depends upon him for guidance, care and financial support*. When a woman becomes totally capable of providing for herself and is able to make her own way in the world, independent of the help of her husband, in a very real sense she loses her need for him. This can cause great losses in her husband. So deep is his need to feel needed as a man, and to serve as a man, that when he is no longer needed he may question his own usefulness or his reason for existence. Being deprived of functioning in this area can cause a loss of feeling of personal worth, a loss of masculinity. This will greatly affect his tender feelings towards his wife, since romantic love is based largely on a man's protective feelings for his wife and her ability to make him feel masculine.

The third part of Characteristic No. 6 is this: *As the man functions as the guide, protector and provider, he would like to do so with greater efficiency and skill than women do, or could do*. He would like to be a more competent leader, a stronger protector and a more successful provider than she is or could be. He does not desire to excel her in her own domestic duties, her role as a mother, or any of the feminine arts. He only wants to excel her in anything which requires masculine strength, skill competence or ability. I would like to point out emphatically that a man does not desire to excel a woman as a person, or to be more respected or honored than she. He only wants to feel superior in his own masculine fulfillment. This need is inborn and a part of masculine pride. It would be humiliating to him if a woman were to beat him in his own field.

In summary, Characteristic No. 6 means: *A man has a need to function fully in his masculine role, to feel needed in this role and to do so with greater competence and ability than women do, or could do*. Unfortunately we see this principle violated on every turn in modern life. Women have invaded all phases of a man's world. Not only do we have a generation of working mothers, but they are competing with men for greater achievement, the more honored position or a bigger paycheck. At home the wife

119

tries to take over the reins of the family and run things her way. This is an age of dominating women who are stepping into the masculine position. Disappearing is the trusting wife who looked to her husband for strong guidance—a solid arm to lean on. The masculine arm may be there, but she is not leaning on it. The independence of women is making masculine care and protection unnecessary, and this is a loss to both the man and the woman.

When a woman takes on masculine responsibility there will be losses to her and her husband. As the man is deprived of a portion of his function he will feel less needed, less masculine and therefore less fulfilled. As the woman assumes masculine burdens she tends to take on male characteristics to fit the job and acquires a certain coarseness. This means a loss of femininity, a loss of gentleness. The male responsibility adds strain to her life, more tension and worry. This results in a loss of serenity, a quality so valuable if she is to succeed in the home. And if she spends her time and energy doing the man's work, she will neglect important functions in her own role. This will result in losses to the entire family.

Man, the Guide, or Leader

The father is the head, or president or spokesman of the family. This arrangement is of divine origin. There is ample proof that the man is the intended leader of the family. The first commandment which God gave unto the woman was, "Thy desire shall be unto thy husband and he shall rule over thee." The Apostle Paul instructed women to *"reverence"* their husbands and said, *"Submit yourselves unto your own husbands."* The Apostle Peter said, *"Ye wives, be in subjection to your own husbands."* The Apostle Paul compared man's leadership of his wife to Christ's leadership of the church. *"For the husband is the head of the wife, even as Christ is the head of the church. Therefore, as the church is subject unto Christ, so let the wives be to their own husbands in everything."* (GENESIS 3:16, EPH. 5:3, COL. 3:18, I PET. 3:1, GENESIS 3:19, EPH. 5:23-24.)

There is also a *logical* reason why a man should lead, one arising out of the need for order. Every organization is designed with a leader at its head, whether it be captain, governor or president. This is a matter of law and order. Therefore, the family, a group of intelligent beings, must be organized, else chaos will result. It does not matter how large or small the family, even though it be just man and wife, there still needs to be a leader.

Since the man is by nature and temperament a born leader, he is the logical one to lead. Men have inherent traits of leadership, tend to be decisive and have the courage of their convictions. Women, on the other hand, tend to vacillate, and lack the qualities of good leadership. But an even more sound reason for men to lead is that they have the role of earning the living. If the man is to brave the world and bring back the bread—his role demands that he have control over his own life—the power of decision.

There is a great effort in modern times to do away with the "patriarchy" and replace it with "equality," in which the husband and wife make decisions by "mutual agreement." *This idea is the most impractical, unworkable arrangement for family leadership that can exist.* Although some decisions can be reached by "mutual agreement," many others cannot. There are situations in which a man and wife will never agree. Someone must take the lead or a decision will not be reached. Also, "mutual agreements" take time—sometimes hours of deliberation. Often decisions in daily living must be made quickly. For these reasons it follows that there must be a leader in a family, and as I have already pointed out, the man is the most logical one to lead. But, actually, keeping the man at the head of the family is not mainly a question of logic. It is largely a matter of following God's instruction, and like all other commands of God, it is for a divine purpose, one which will benefit all mankind.

Duties of the Guide, or Leader

1. *To Determine Policies, Rules and Laws for the Family to Follow:* If a family is to be organized, certain rules for living must be established, such as rules of conduct, use of the family car, expenditure of money, where the family spends its vacation, church attendance, school attendance, social connections, and many other things. Usually a family helps to shape these rules. A prudent father will consult family members about these matters or hold a family council meeting to get their ideas. Often a husband will delegate considerable authority to his wife in establishing rules of the household, since she more

121

closely supervises this area. But the point to stress is this: If the man is to be the head of the family, the right to final say is his. *A family is not a democracy where everyone casts his vote. The family is a theocracy.* In the home the presiding authority is always vested in the father, and in all home affairs and family matters there is no other authority paramount. This arrangement is neither harsh nor unfair. It is entirely a matter of law and order and compliance with divine command.

There is a tendency for women to claim jurisdiction over their children since they have given them life and are in charge of daily care. The wife may feel the right to determine discipline, instruction, religious affiliation, and many other things. When the wife clashes with her husband over these matters, she may feel an inalienable right to the final say. But this is not so. Although the wife has the sacred responsibility of motherhood, she is not their leader. *The husband is the shepherd of his flock and in full command.*

2. *To Make Decisions:* The second duty of the guide is to make decisions in his role as the guide, protector and provider on any matters which relate to the family. In an ordinary family many decisions must be made daily. Some of these are minor, such as "whether Jane walks to school in the rain with an umbrella or whether Dad takes her to school in the car." But, even though such a decision is small, it must be made, and often quickly. When the husband and wife cannot meet an agreement, the only way for order to exist is for one of them to assume the authority to decide, and as we have already pointed out, this authority is always vested in the father.

Many times *major* decisions must be made. The man may be faced with decisions about his work such as whether to enlarge his business, make investments, change occupations, or even move to a new community. These plans may mean a cut back in family expenditures or other adjustments. A wise father will consult his family, and especially his wife, to try to win her cooperation. However, he may not always explain his reasons for his decision or seek out her opinion. He may feel the situation is too complex for her to understand. Or he may feel, when it comes to business matters, that she does not have the background or knowledge. Perhaps the man may not know the reason himself. He may be guided solely by inspiration. But whether he explains his reasons or not, whether he seeks her advice or not, the decision is still his. He must be free to function in his role and this includes the power of decision. But, here again, the family is not a democracy in which each member casts a vote, but a theocracy in which the father presides. In marriage, the man and the woman are not like a team of horses which pull equally together. Husband and wife are like a bow and cord, as Longfellow has described in his poem *Hiawatha:*

> As unto the bow the cord is,
> So unto man is woman;
> Tho' she bends him, she obeys him;
> Tho' she draws him, yet she follows;
> Useless each without the other.

Although the man is the undisputed head of the family, a woman does have an important part to play in her husband's leadership role. Hers is a *submissive role, a supporting role* and sometimes an *active role* in which she expresses herself clearly and even strongly. A woman is not like a little puppy which follows along on a leash wherever her husband chooses to go, without any thoughts of her own. Her support is essential to him, and her ideas can be valuable if given in the right way. Much rests upon the man's shoulders. He has a family to lead and many decisions to make, some of them highly important. He alone will be responsible for these decisions, regardless of the outcome. Having his wife's understanding, support and even her ideas can be all important to him.

Mumatz, lady of the Taj Mahal, played an important part in her husband's leadership, even in governing his country. She was the daughter of the Prime Minister, was highly intelligent, well educated and of a worthy character. The Shah consulted her in many of his decisions, even in technical matters of government. There was no doubt about her subtle influence in his life, but she did it with such art that her husband felt not the slightest threat to his position as the supreme ruler of India. And the world at large had no knowledge of her contribution. A woman can be of great value to her husband in his leadership role if she does it in the right way. But, first, she must accept him as her leader, support him and obey him. Only then will he be open to her ideas.

1. *Ruling the Roost:* In some instances a woman will actually take hold of the reins of the family and run things. She is the boss. She makes the important plans and decisions and her husband goes along with her. She may consult her husband about family matters, but somehow she has slipped into the leadership position. She may have done this by default on her husband's part, or by demanding the position.

2. *Advising:* A common mistake a woman can make is in giving her husband too much advice. She offers too many suggestions. She tells him what to do, when to do it and sometimes how to do it. She appears to hover over him, watching, scrutinizing, and is overly concerned. All of this shows a lack of trust. It also indicates that she feels more qualified to lead than he, that he is incapable without her. The husband may get the impression that his wife feels self-sufficient, that she does not really need him and could get along just as well or better without him.

3. *Pressuring:* There are many strong willed women who, although they do not want to lead, still want to have things their way. They achieve this by pressuring, needling, hinting, using moral pressure, and exerting other influences to get their way. The problem is that sometimes a man becomes weary of her pressure and will give in against his better judgment just to keep peace. Although pressuring may be a victory for a woman, it is bad policy in marriage. Also, children tend to copy this habit from their mothers.

4. *Disobedience:* Some strong willed women refuse to follow their husband's counsel when they do not agree with it. They have a "mind of their own," and do as they please. Not only is this a complete failure to honor the man's leadership, but other serious consequences result, as in the following problems:

When the Wife Refuses to Obey

Serious consequences occur when the wife refuses to obey her husband. In the first place, she sets a pattern of rebellion in the family. Children tend to follow this pattern of rebellion for they have learned it from their mother. They begin to learn that they really do not have to obey rules if they don't want to, that there is some way they can get by without doing it. When such children are turned out into the world, they have difficulty obeying the law or higher authority such as leadership on campus or in their work. The problems of rebellious youth can in most cases be traced to homes where the mother has been disobedient to the father or showed lack of respect for his authority.

English satirist C. Northcote Parkinson has passed judgment on the campus revolution in America and blames the whole thing on women. He told a Los Angeles audience that the trouble in American colleges is based on disrespect for authority learned in the home. "The general movement, I think, begins with the female revolution," he said. "Women demanded the vote and equality and ceased to submit to the control of their husbands. In the process they began to lose control of their own children." Mr. Parkinson said that in his own Victorian childhood, "Pop's word was law, and Mother's most deadly threat was 'I shall have to inform your father.' Nowadays, the mother can't appeal to the children in that way because they have denied the paternal authority themselves."

Other serious problems occur when the wife "puts her foot down" and refuses to follow her husband. For example, years ago I knew a man who wanted to move his family to a metropolitan area where he could find better business opportunities. They were presently living in a quiet, small, beautiful town. The wife felt her children would be put to a great disadvantage and so refused to move. The man was very disappointed since he felt the move would be an advantage to his occupation. He did not become successful in the community in which he remained and felt that had he moved, his life would have turned out better. He felt thwarted. Because of this, he developed a resentful attitude towards his wife and started arguments over trivial matters. She thought the move would harm her children, but she did them a greater injustice by putting a wedge in her marriage.

Occasionally a man will give credit to his wife for putting her foot down and refusing to follow his decision, thus saving him from a drastic mistake. Don't let this confuse you. Just let her stand in his way when the outcome would have been a glorious success and see if he thanks her for it. The wife takes a grave risk when she refuses to follow her husband's decisions. No one can guess the outcome. And remember this rule: *It is better to let a man have his way and fail than to stand in his way and have him feel thwarted.* Now, there are problems women have in following a man which I would like to review at this time:

Problems in the Patriarchy

1. *When the Man is Wicked:* There are some instances when a father would lead his family into corruption, would encourage them to cheat, lie, steal, be immoral, or follow other evil practices. In this case the wife would have a moral obligation to take the children out of his household, away from the evil influences. If she is without children, she would have the same obligation to remove herself from the destructive acts.

However, there is a chance for misunderstanding on this subject. If the man has good intentions, but due to weakness has slipped so that he does not maintain the same high standards as his wife, or if he is negligent in his religious devotions or in other ways a weaker individual than she, then the wife should be patient with him and keep her marriage intact. It would be up to the wife to determine whether the man is actually wicked or just weak.

2. *When the Man is Cruel:* The same can be said for conditions when the man is cruel to his children. If he would abuse them so they are in danger of being injured physically or mentally, the wife has a moral obligation to stand in his way and protect them with her life if necessary. If his cruelty persists, she should take them out of the household until the man can be made normal, if this is possible. She would, of course, owe herself the same safety.

But here, again, the subject can be misunderstood. If a man is merely firm in his discipline of his children, the wife may interpret it as cruel. Women tend to be much more gentle in the discipline of their children than the men, and this is frequently a source of much conflict in marriage. But unless you are convinced the man will actually injure the child, it is better to give him free reign. Children grow up to respect a father who is firm, whereas they lack respect for one who is soft. The wife can do more for the child by supporting her husband's discipline and presenting a united front with him than standing in his way and confusing the child.

3. *The Wife's Fear That Her Husband Will Make*

126

Mistakes: One of the real difficulties that women face in trying to follow a man is her fear that he will use *poor judgment* which will lead to mistakes and failures. This may mean a loss of money, problems, regret, disappointment and unhappiness. When moved by this fear, she is tempted to oppose his plans and decisions with the thought of saving him from errors. A Christian writer, Orson Pratt, writes on this subject in the following words:

"The wife should never follow her judgment in preference to that of her husband, for if her husband desires to do right, but errs in judgment, the Lord will bless her in endeavoring to carry out his counsels, for God has placed him at the head and though he may err in judgment, yet God will not justify the wife in disregarding his instructions and counsels, for greater is the sin of rebellion than the errors which arise from want of judgment; therefore she would be condemned for suffering her will to arise against his ... be obedient and God will cause all things to work for good, and He will correct the errors of the husband in due time ... a wife will lose the spirit of God in refusing to obey the counsel of her husband."

4. *When the Man Flounders:* Sometimes the problem in the patriarchy is that the man vacillates and cannot bring himself to a firm decision. If the man is overly cautious by nature, then the wife should accept this tendency and learn to live with it. Very often, however, the man is moved by fear—fears that the woman needs to understand. One common fear is that his decision will put his family to disadvantage. For example, the man may desire to return to school to further his education, but fears that this may threaten the security of his family. If this is the case, the wife can encourage his decision by assuring him that she is willing to make the necessary sacrifice. Another common fear is that a decision will lead to the loss of money or prestige. The man may greatly desire to proceed with plans but lacks the courage to do so. If the wife can detect that his fears are groundless, she can build up his confidence and greatly aid him in making the decision.

5. *When the Man Will Not Lead:* Sometimes a woman would like very much for the man to take the lead. She wants a strong arm to lean on, but the man backs away from his position. In this case the wife can become frustrated and sometimes takes over the leadership of the family out of necessity. What can she do to help him take

127

his place at the head? First, she should read him the Scriptures which appoint him as the leader. She should reason that someone must lead and that he is more qualified than she. She should let him know that she does not want to lead and *needs him* to take this position. Then she should offer loyal support. After this, she can help by devoting herself to her domestic role and making a success there. By so doing, she more clearly defines the division of responsibility between the man and the woman. Then, she should learn to be a good follower using the following suggestions:

How to Be the Perfect Follower

1. *Let Go:* The first thing to do is to let go of the reins in the family. Step out of the leadership position. Let him lead and you follow. Stop giving him suggestions, advice, or telling him what to do and how to do it. If you "let go," you will be surprised to learn how well he can get along without you. This will build your confidence in him and his confidence in himself.

2. *Have a Girlish Trust in Him:* Being a good follower is largely a matter of trust. This is not the same trust as you would have in God, for God does not make mistakes. Men do. You will have to allow for his mistakes and trust in his motives and that his overall judgment is sound. In this way you help the man to grow, for nothing will make a man feel so responsible as when someone places a childlike trust in him.

Sometimes a man's decisions defy logic. His plans may not make sense at all to you, and his judgment may not appear the least bit sound. Perhaps it isn't, but there is a good possibility that it is. The man may be led by inspiration. We must realize that the ways of God do not always follow logic. Nor do inspired decisions always materialize favorably or lead to success. Sometimes God leads us directly into failures and problems for a wise, but pehaps unknown, purpose. We must all, at some time, "be tried in the refiner's fire," and God has mysterious ways of bringing this about. But, if we will follow devotedly, we can usually look back and see the hand of Almighty God in our lives and be grateful for how things turned out.

There are frightening times when a woman would like to trust her husband, would like to feel that her husband is being guided by inspiration, but she cannot. She can detect that vanity, pride and selfishness are at the bottom of his decisions and he is headed for a certain disaster. If the man will not listen to her, what can she do to avert this tragedy? If you cannot trust your husband, you can always trust God and turn to Him for help. He has placed your husband at the head and commanded you to obey him. You have a right to ask for His help. If you will obey the counsel of your husband and pray sincerely for right to prevail, things will turn out right in a surprising way.

3. *Be Adjustable:* A good follower is adjustable to her life's circumstances, following her husband where he wants to go and adapting to the conditions he provides for her. He is the leader and must be free to map out his life according to the responsibility he feels as both the leader and the provider. Follow these rules and you will find it easier to be adjustable:

A. *Don't have a lot of preconceived ideas about what you want out of life,* such as where you want to live, kind of house, life style, economic level, or plans for the children. These ideas may clash with your husband's plans, which he feels he must carry out to succeed in his masculine role. I remember in my own youth that I had a lot of preconceived ideas. I wanted to live in a two-story white house on an acre of ground, with tall rustling trees in the back and a cellar filled with apple barrels, and on the outskirts of a city of about 20,000 population. But I found through the years that this dream got in my way and made me less adaptable than I should have been.

B. *Make All of Your Dreams Portable:* A woman should have dreams, but they should be portable, so that she can be happy anywhere, in any circumstance—on a mountain top or on a burning desert, in poverty's vale or abounding in wealth.

4. *Be Obedient:* Obedience is probably the most important rule in being a good follower. If you agree with a man, obedience is easy, but if you disagree, it can be extremely difficult. It is the *quality* of obedience that counts. If the wife follows begrudgingly, dragging her feet every step of the way, complaining that she has a yoke around her neck or is bound by the shackles of male supremacy, she is not worthy of being called a good follower. Her obedience, however, is better than rebellion and worthy of some appreciation. But, if she will follow willingly, with a spirit of sweet submission, God will bless her and her household, and there will come into her home

129

a spirit of harmony that can never exist in the homes of the disobedient. And her husband will appreciate her and be softened by her yielding spirit.

5. *Support His Plans and Decisions:* A wife cannot sit back like a little dove, free of all responsibility and say to herself, "I will leave it all up to him," or tell him "Do what you want to do, it is not my concern." Often the man needs her wholehearted backing. He may not want to stand alone in his decision and take all of the responsibility for its outcome. He needs his wife's wholehearted support in important issues. This brings the wife into the leadership role to some extent for she will have to take a look at his plans or decisions before she can offer sincere support, but this is a necessary part she needs to play.

6. *When the Wife Does Not Agree:* It will be more difficult to support him when you do not agree, but it can be done, and it can be done *honestly*. You need not support his ideas. In fact, you can openly disagree with him if it will make you feel better. What is important is to support his office, his authority or his right to decide. You can say something like this: "I do not agree with your decision, but if you feel right about it, then follow your own convictions and I will support you in it."

7. *Present a United Front to the Children:* A woman can create serious problems when she openly opposes her husband when he is dealing with his children. If she has any opposition to express, she should talk with him privately. When with the children, it is always an advantage for mother and father to present a united front. Often a mother will take sides with the children, hoping to win their favor. But in so doing, she denies them favors from their father. A father will be most reluctant to yield to his children when their mother is "pleading their case." I had an experience which brought this clearly to mind. A girl wanted to attend a particular college, but her father said no. Her mother was "on her side," but they could not change his mind. I told the girl to go home and tell her mother to get on her father's side and stay there. Then I told her to tell her father that she respected his position and would do whatever he wished, but that she would like very much to go to a certain school. The girl followed my instructions, and as soon as the father felt his wife's support and his daughter's support, he immediately consented.

8. *Assert Yourself:* The points I have listed thus far

130

in being a perfect follower are all submissive qualities—let go, trust, be adjustable, obedient and supportive, even when you do not agree. There are, however, times when the wife should *speak out*. When she has a keen feeling about an important issue, she should express herself. This can be done clearly and, if necessary, strongly, but it must be done in a feminine manner, as I will now explain:

The Feminine Counselor

A man needs a woman at his side, not only to support him but sometimes even to advise him. Shah Jahan turned to Mumtaz again and again for advice. And David Copperfield felt a great lack in his life because he had no one to turn to. "I did feel sometimes," he said, "that I could have wished my wife had been my counselor; had been endowed with a power to fill up the void which somewhere seemed to be about me."

Women have special gifts to offer a man as a counselor—gifts of *insight* and *intuition* which are unique with their sex. They can be *fountains of wisdom*. Women also have a *perspective* of the man's life that no one else has. A woman is close to her husband, yet somewhat removed. She is near the center of his life's activities, yet stands back a step or two. She has a broader perspective than he does. She cares about him more than anyone else, is willing to make some sacrifices. Although she may be limited in knowledge, her advice may be more reliable than that of others because of her perspective.

There are some general requirements, however, for being a good counselor: First, it is important to drop any habit of giving *daily advice or suggestions*. Save your opinions for special occasions when they are extremely important. In this way your words will have more significance, more emphasis. If he hears your ideas only rarely, or when he asks, he will be more apt to listen and appreciate them.

Next, you will have to eliminate *negative thinking*. This is the tendency to have ungrounded doubts or fears or be overly cautious or anxious. If you have this habit, it is best to not give advice at all until you eliminate this tendency. Your advice could actually do him great harm or stand in his way. You can overcome this habit by reading some good books on the subject such as *The Power of Positive Thinking*, by Dr. Peale, or *Psycho-*

Cybernetics, by Dr. Maltz. There are many others. Overcome this habit or you will never be of any value as an adviser. Only positive thinking women make good counselors.

Then, a good counselor must have *something worthy to give.* She must have intelligence, wisdom, and be guided in her advice by a good character or spiritual qualities. She must also have somewhat of a knowledge about the world. This is not to surpass the man in knowledge, but to *supplement* him. This was the quality Dora lacked. She had nothing to give a man in the way of advice, for she lacked too much in herself. But the qualities of being a feminine counselor can be cultivated. We can gain knowledge, wisdom and good character and train ourselves to be good counselors. When giving advice, there are certain guideline rules to follow, as outlined here:

How to Give Feminine Advice

1. *Ask Leading Questions:* A subtle way of giving advice is to ask leading questions, such as "Have you ever thought of doing it this way?" or "Have you considered the possibility of . . . ?" The key word is *you.* In this way you bring him into the picture so the ideas will seem like his own. The man will either reply, "Yes, I have thought of the idea," in which case, if he puts it to practice, he will invariably claim the idea as his own. Or, he will say, "No, but I will consider it." In either case you have dropped an idea that he will likely mull over in his mind and, if he adopts it, will feel that he had a lot to do with it.

2. *Insight:* When expressing your viewpoint use words that indicate insight such as "I feel." Avoid the words "I think," or "I know."

3. *Don't Appear to Know More than He Does:* Don't be the all-wise, all-knowing wife who has all the answers and surpasses her husband in intelligence. If he has stumbled blindly along life's path and then finally turns to you for advice, don't give him the impression that "you knew all along what he should do" and wondered why he did not know better. Don't map out a course of action for him to follow, analyze his problems too closely, ask too many "whys" or give too many suggestions, as these things give the impression that you think you know more than he does.

4. *Don't be Motherly:* Don't take the attitude, "Here

132

is this poor little boy in the world who isn't getting along so well, and I must come to his rescue and help him."

5. *Don't Talk Man to Man:* Don't "hash things over" as men do and thereby place yourself on an equal plane with him. Don't say such things as "Let's come to some conclusions," or "Why don't we go over it again," or "I think I have spotted the trouble area." Remember, in giving a man advice, keep him in the dominant position so that he will feel needed and adequate as the leader.

6. *Don't Act Braver than He Is:* If you are giving advice to a man on a matter in which he is filled with fear, don't make the mistake of acting braver than he is. Suppose, for example, that he wants to create a new business, or change jobs, or ask for a raise, or try out a new idea. In advising him, don't courageously say, "Why are you hesitating?" or "You have nothing to be afraid of." Instead say, "Oh, dear, I know just how you must feel. There are so many problems that enter in. You really have reason to hesitate. How do you endure such tough responsibility?" Such meekness on your part will probably awaken his manly courage and cause him to say, "It isn't so tough. I think I can handle the situation." Whenever a man detects fearfulness in a woman, it just naturally awakens masculine courage.

7. *Don't Have Unyielding Opinions:* If you want your advice to appear feminine, do not have unyielding opinions. Do not speak with strong convictions in a way that will cause him to feel obligated to take your advice. To do so would be to threaten his right to decide for himself.

8. *Don't Insist He Do Things Your Way:* Use a "take it or leave it" approach. Let him take as much or as little of your advice as he would like. Use no pressure or forcefulness. To do so would, again, be to threaten his right to decide for himself. And always remember: *It is better to let a man have his way and make a mistake than to stand in his way and have him feel thwarted.*

Rewards

As we come to the end of the man's role as the guide, I would like to stress some important points: First, remember the guiding principle, that the man needs to function and excel in his masculine role as the leader. To help him achieve this, stay out of his masculine role, and help him feel needed and adequate as a leader. I would like to stress also that there are great rewards for putting the father at the head of the house.

First, a home where father presides is a house of order. There is less argument and contention, more of a spirit of harmony. Taking the lead will also help the man grow in masculinity. Out of necessity he acquires the traits of firmness, decisiveness, self-confidence and a feeling of responsibility. The wife also benefits. As she is relieved of the burdens of family leadership, she is relieved of worry and concern, is free to function more fully in her domestic role, to put her mind and heart to the womanly tasks and arts and succeed in her career in the home.

Children who grow up in a home where father's word is law grow up with a natural respect for authority at school, at church, or society as a whole. In a world where men lead we would have less crime, violence and unrest, less divorce and social problems, less homosexuality. There would be happier marriages, happier homes and therefore happier people. If the patriarchy could be achieved widely, it would indeed be a world of law and order. The rewards of the patriarchy are clearly indicated in the following true experiences.

I Was Always Advising Him

"I have been trying to run my husband for years. He has always worked for himself, and sometimes his business has been successful and sometimes it has failed. I was always there 'advising him' one way or another, until I became ill in bed one day and a friend loaned me Fascinating Womanhood to read. Next day I called my husband into my bedroom and said, 'Dear, I want to let you know that I have been wrong all this time. I am sorry. I will try to never nag you again. Your decisions are your own. I can't tell you how sorry I am for the past years.' He was sitting on the bed. He put his head in his hands and wept. 'You'll never know what your saying that means to me,' he said."

I Was the Domineering Type

"After 15 years and three beautiful children, our marriage was in serious trouble ... until my sister loaned me her copy of Fascinating Womanhood. My first impression was 'it may work for others but it will never solve our problems.' We had long forgotten the common little courtesies extended each other during courtship and early marriage . . . we had even talked of divorce. I was the domineering type. Not once in all those years had my husband introduced me or referred to me as his wife; it was always 'the little woman,' or 'the missus,' or, even worse, 'the boss.'

"Willing to try anything to save our marriage, as I started to live Fascinating Womanhood, surprising results began to happen. Imagine how thrilled I was when in the company of new acquaintances he proudly said, 'I want you to meet my wife.' It sounded like music to my ears. Now, no matter where we go, he can't say 'my wife' often enough. Ours is a happy home now. The children are more thoughtful and happy, and my husband even started bringing me candy and flowers and telling me that he truly loved me. Love reigns supreme. I bless the day I heard about Fascinating Womanhood and wish I could broadcast its many benefits."

The Battle Front

"I had been on the front lines of the battlefield of marriage for twelve years. I had fought daily for what I wanted out of marriage, and it had taken its toll. I had battle fatigue, shell shock, nervous tension and I was bitter and resentful, for no victory had been gained, not even a small one. I was constantly losing ground. I felt like I bore the total worry, cost, and all the responsibilities of this war and our children were the ones—innocent ones—who were suffering. After twelve years I felt I just couldn't continue this any longer, and it was then that I was invited to attend a Fascinating Womanhood class.

"Now I am giving up my war for peace; the tension and weariness are over; I'm happy and secure. I can again meet my domestic responsibilities with joy in my heart, because I have shed those that were not mine. Practicing Fascinating Womanhood has given me more victories in four months than I had ever seen in twelve years and I didn't fight for one of them. They were given to me without even asking. I feel loved and cherished, and it is beautiful. Even my appearance has changed; my face has a new light, my eye a new twinkle, and real joy radiates from my inner being. Friends compliment me on how pretty I look.

"Before, he was making big plans for building on—not to our home, but to the garage—a 'bachelor's' apartment where he could get away. Plans included a fireplace, sliding glass doors with a beautiful view, a Jacuzzi bath, pool table, bar, colored T.V., etc. After Fascinating Womanhood, he is now drawing up plans to remodel our house, instead—including a huge family room with a fireplace, a new bedroom for us (he has been sleeping on the couch for six years), and a service room for me with washer, dryer and a place to sew and iron."

How to Be the Perfect Follower

1. Let go of the reins.
2. Have a girlish trust in him.
3. Be adjustable.
   A. Don't have preconceived ideas.
   B. Make your dreams portable.
4. Be obedient.
5. Support his plans and decisions.
6. When you don't agree, support his "right to decide."
7. Present a United Front to the children.
8. Assert yourself.

How to Give Feminine Advice

1. Ask leading questions.
2. Use "insight" words, like "I feel."
3. Don't appear to know more than he does.
4. Don't be motherly.
5. Don't talk man to man.
6. Don't act braver than he is.
7. Don't have unyielding opinions.
8. Don't insist he do things your way.
   Remember: It is better to let a man have his way and fail than to stand in his way and have him feel thwarted.

Assignment

If your husband has not been the leader, read him the Scriptures at the beginning of this chapter. Then say, "I believe these things are true, do you?" Then, if he is interested, read him parts of Fascinating Womanhood, Chapter 8, and discuss with him his role as the guide, protector and provider, and especially his role as the leader. Tell him something like this: "I want to support you as a leader and be a good follower. I will support your plans and decisions even though I may not always agree. I want to let you do the masculine things so that I can become more feminine."

9

Man, the Protector

Characteristic No. 6: The Man's Need to Function in His Masculine Role (as the Protector), to Feel Needed in His Role and to Excel Women in His Masculine Responsibility

When we consider the natural man, we can see that he was created to be the protector of his wife and children. Men are larger, have more powerful muscles, and greater physical endurance than women. Women, on the other hand, are more delicate, fragile, and weaker than men. They are like a fine precision machine which was created for the more delicate tasks and which runs smoothly and efficiently when used for the purpose intended. Men are blessed with courage to face dangers and difficulties, whereas women are inclined to be afraid of dangers.

What Do Women Need Protection From?

In all periods of time women have needed protection, from *dangers, strenuous work,* and *difficulties of life.* In the early history of our country, the very conditions under which people were forced to live made manly protection necessary. There were dangers everywhere. Savage Indians, wild beasts and snakes created situations which called for masculine courage and ability. Women have also needed protection from the heavy work, work which was beyond their capacity—hard labor in the fields, hauling, lifting, and anything requiring masculine strength and endurance.

Protection Needed Today

1. *Dangers:* The great danger of today is that of sexual assault and in connection with it—the threat to life itself. Most of us are aware of the tragic number of cases in which women have been raped and even murdered. This

is a real danger to all women and one we need to face realistically.

There are also *unreal* dangers which many women are afraid of. Amusing as it is, women are still afraid of such things as lightning, thunder, strange noises, spiders, mice, and even dark shadows. It is not likely that these things would actually harm a woman. But, whether the danger is real or not, *if the woman thinks it is real,* she will feel a need for masculine protection. And the man, if he is to serve as her protector, will do what is necessary to quiet her fears.

2. *Strenuous Work:* Because of her weaker physical structure, a woman needs protection from strenuous work such as lifting heavy objects, moving furniture, mowing the lawn, painting, repairing mechanical equipment, carpentry and other heavy or rough work. This heavy work can be injurious to a woman physically and lessen her feminine qualities.

3. *Difficulties of Life:* Women have many difficulties they need to face alone—failures in homemaking, mistakes in household management, problems with the care of the children, and disappointments. A wife should face these quietly, without expecting her husband to come to the rescue. But there are other difficulties of a different type for which she needs masculine assistance. These are such things as financial entanglements, belligerent creditors, or any dealings with people who are harsh, offensive, imposing, or who make unreasonable demands. Here is the "maiden in distress," dependent upon masculine chivalry. Women tend to be emotional and less objective in dealing with this type of assault than are men. For this reason they need the man to step in and cope with the situation.

Mistakes Women Make

Women of today do not always rely upon men for protection. We see them walking down dark streets alone, taking long distance automobile trips alone, and even hitchhiking. Women in our generation have become independent, capable, efficient, and able to "kill their own snakes." We see them doing the heavy rough work, lifting heavy objects, repairing automobiles, changing tires, driving heavy equipment, fixing the roof, doing the carpentry, and many other masculine tasks. In the working world, women are asking for the men's jobs. They are hauling lumber, driving trucks, and climbing scaffolds. We see women policemen, steel workers, pilots, and even engineers. Day in, day out, they are proving by their strength and capability that they do not need masculine care and protection, that they are well able to take care of themselves.

Women also battle the world of difficulties. I knew a woman who helped her husband in his food market. When a competitor built a larger market across the street, his business was reduced to near bankruptcy. His wife was the heroine of the occasion as she faced the angry creditors and fought the financial battles. But where was the husband? In the background, of course. Obviously she did not need him. She was able to cope with the situation herself.

A similar situation was of a couple who purchased a home which was to be vacated on a specific date. When the time for occupancy arrived, the former owners refused to move. After the wife battled with them a few weeks, the occupants became angry and said, "We are going to remain here until our new home is finished, and there is nothing you can do except take us to court." The wife, in this case, was the buffer for the difficulty. Her husband had retired into the background since his wife appeared qualified for the battle.

It is difficult to describe how seriously women rob men of their masculinity by becoming independent. A competent woman stands as a threat to the male ego—to his position and capabilities as a man. When he comes in contact with a capable, efficient woman, well able to get along without him or any other man, he does not feel masculine any longer. It is an unpleasant feeling that he does not care to repeat.

The woman who becomes capable and independent suffers losses herself. As she takes on self-sufficient qualities, she tends to lose some of her feminine charm. A *feminine* woman is *dependent* and in need of protection from men. As she lessens her need for him, she lessens her femininity. As we view this generation of capable women, who are able to make it on their own in the world, it is not surprising to see the loss of respect men have for them, and that men no longer offer them the chivalry they did a generation ago.

140

Men Enjoy Protecting Women

The important thing to remember is this: Men *enjoy* protecting women. Do not think, therefore, that it is an imposition on a man to protect a dependent, feminine woman. One of the most pleasant sensations a real man can experience is his consciousness of the power to give his manly care and protection. Rob him of this sensation, of superior strength and ability and you rob him of his manliness.

The inborn desire to protect women was evident in John Alden's feelings for Priscilla. "Here for her sake will I stay and like an invisible presence hover around her forever, protecting, supporting her weakness." And Victor Hugo made known his desire to protect his love when he said, "My duty is to keep close to her steps, to surround her existence with mine, to serve her as a barrier against all dangers; to offer my head as a stepping stone, to place myself unceasingly between her and all sorrows ... if she but consent to lean upon me at times amidst the difficulties of life."

Is this kind of chivalry dead? Is the tender care and protection offered by John Alden and Victor Hugo in existence any longer? Do we see men hovering around their women, protecting their weakness, defending them or serving them as a barrier against all dangers? It sounds like something from a romantic novel, and yet it existed at one time. If chivalry is dead, women have killed it. If so, they can revive it again. Let's review some things we can do about it:

How to Awaken Chivalry

If you are to awaken the man's desire to protect you, the first thing to do is to stop doing the heavy work. Stop mowing the lawn, fixing the roof, painting the fence or repairing the furnace. Stop doing anything which requires masculine strength, skill or ability. Then, let him do things for you. Let him open doors for you, lift in the groceries, offer his hand at a busy street crossing. Give him time to offer. Hesitate at the street corner. Indicate in some way that you need him. If he does not offer to help you move the sofa or lift in the groceries, then ask him to.

Then, you will have to eliminate any tendency to be

independent, efficient, or *capable* in masculine skills or abilities. You will also have to stop fighting the battles of life without him, or going on long distance car trips alone. Plane trips seem to be safe in our modern world, if transportation at your destination is also safe. Automobile trips are in too much danger of mechanical breakdown, which would leave a woman in a helpless situation, or even a dangerous one.

And be sure to remember Characteristic No. 6—the man's need to function in his role and to excel women in this role. So, you will have to *need him* as your protector, to help him to *feel needed,* and to not excel him in anything which requires masculine strength or ability. The most important quality to arouse chivalry is *femininity.* It is femininity to which masculinity responds as evident in the following experience as written to me:

Feminine Wiles and Ways

"I was raised on a farm and worked like a boy, gardening, doing chores etc. I never had any frilly feminine things as a girl, and never thought such things necessary. Perfume, nail polish, eye makeup, frilly lingerie were for fancy town women who never did anything useful, or helped their men.

"I married my husband with the idea of making him into something acceptable. I thought he should appreciate my efforts. He had been dominated a great deal by his father and so took a lot of my bossiness without comment. Between his Dad and me he's never really had a chance to be himself. I felt responsible for what he did and he let me.

"I worried about money and church. He blithely spent whatever he liked, writing out checks, going into debt. His family was not religious, mine was. I tried to get him to go to church, and he did, but embarrassed me by acting bored, etc. He continued a few bad habits he'd promised to break before we were married.

"In spite of this we had a pretty good marriage. We were in love and thought our problems were normal ones. But our quarrels grew more frequent and violent. Money was the main bone of contention, along with his refusal to give me things I thought rightfully due me.

"Worry over money was making me old before my

time. He refused to try to get a really good job after getting fired from an excellent one. I tried to budget on what little was left after his weekly 'pocket expense and check writing.' I bravely chased and bribed creditors. I even left my three little kids and went to work.

"But while I worked he spent enough on dog food, ice cream, cola, treats for buddies, car repairs, gas, etc. that our rent checks bounced and we ended nearly $300 in the hole. The way things were going, separation was inevitable. I had plans to leave him as soon as the kids were in school.

"About this time he became active in scouts, at my insistence. Soon we had scouts 'coming out our ears.' He spent so much time with them we hardly saw him. He broke promises of carnivals with me and the kids to go hiking with the scouts.

"At the time the Fascinating Womanhood class started I was taking a chorister class once a week. I decided not to take Fascinating Womanhood because I thought it would take me away from home too much at night.

"The night I took my first chorister class my husband was planning to stay home and paint the floor on my back porch for me. When I got home I found he'd called three of the scouts to do it so they could get their 'floor painting' merit badge. Not only was the floor painted, but the walls were spattered. It looked awful and I was furious! I told him that since he was so glad to get me out of the house to be with the scouts I was going to take the Fascinating Womanhood class the very next night. And that's how I happened to take Fascinating Womanhood. I know we would have separated by now without it.

"My husband is a changed man now. I've never been so blissfully happy. Freedom, acceptance, praise, feminine ways and wiles and love—these are my secrets. It's really fun to be a feminine woman. I'm hardly unfulfilled.

"My husband has an extremely good job now and he loves it and is making as much in one week as he used to in two. His love and consideration for me has doubled. It is apparent in all he does. He acts romantic as a school kid. He brings me presents, helps me with the dishes (occasionally) and our love life is wonderful. I couldn't ask for more."

Assignment

Tell him "I am glad I have a strong man to protect me. I think it would be difficult to go through this life without you." If you need him to lift something for you, say something like this: "Will you please lend me some of your masculine strength?"

10

Man, the Provider

Characteristic No. 6: The Man's Need to Function in His Masculine Role (as the Provider), to Feel Needed in His Role and to Excel Women in His Masculine Responsibility

Since the beginning of time, the man has been recognized as the provider. The first commandment given to him was, "In the sweat of thy face shalt thou eat bread, till thou return unto the ground." This command was given, not to the woman, but to the man. The woman was instructed to "bring forth children." From this time since, the man's and woman's duties have been thus divided. This arrangement has been carried forth by tradition, custom, and even courts of the law. Men are legally still bound to pay alimony in the event of divorce. However, this principle is important to live, not because it is custom or law, but because it is God's command.

There is another reason the man should provide the living. It has to do with masculine fulfillment. Inborn is a masculine pride in making the living, in taking this burden upon his shoulders and being solely responsible for it. Being successful in this area of his life brings him fulfillment just as it does for a woman to "keep the home fires burning" and make a comfortable home for her loved ones. It is thrilling to picture the man going out into the world sweating, toiling, struggling against the elements and oppositions of life to bring home the necessities and comforts to those he loves. This is a major part of his masculine fulfillment. Rob him of this struggle and you rob him of pride in his manliness.

Not only does a man have a pride in *providing* the living, but he needs to *feel needed* in this responsibility, that his wife depends upon him for financial support and could not get by without him.

He also has an inborn need to *excel women* as a provider. This means that in the working world, a man's pride would be threatened if a woman were to do a better job than he, or be advanced to a higher position or bring home a bigger paycheck, or even be equal with him. He would feel threatened not only by his own wife, but by any woman. Keep in mind Characteristic No. 6, the man's need to function in his masculine role as the provider and to excel women in doing so.

What Should a Man Provide

An excellent description of what a man should provide is found in my husband's book *Man of Steel and Velvet*, which pictures the ideal man. "Simply stated, the man should provide the *necessities*. This means food, clothing, and a shelter—plus a few comforts and conveniences. . . . It is important that the man provide a shelter separate and apart from anyone else. This is important for the sake of privacy and giving the wife the opportunity of making her home a home in her own way. Perhaps this is why a special instruction was given by God, immediately after he created the man: 'Therefore shall a man leave his father and mother and cleave unto his wife.' (GEN. 2:24)

"Although a man has a sacred and binding obligation to provide the necessities, he is under no such obligation to provide the *luxuries*. Women and children are not entitled to ease and luxury, to style and elegance. The man's duty is not to provide a costly home, expensive furniture and decor. Concerning the education of his children, he does have some obligation to provide them with a basic education, but such a binding obligation does not extend to a higher education, music lessons, the arts and cultures. He may wish to provide these—and it may bring him much pleasure in doing so, but it is not his responsibility.

"In providing a high standard of living, some men make near economic slaves of themselves, with great disadvantage to themselves and to their families. Too often a man is so consumed with meeting ever-increasing demands placed upon him—not only by his family, but by himself—that he does not preserve himself for things of greater value. He has little time to give to his wife and children—time to teach them the great values of life, how to live, standards to follow—and time to build strong family ties. A man also is entitled to some time for himself, for recreation, study, meditation, etc. And he has a need to be of service outside his own circle. . . . It is not

146

right for a man to spend his entire time and energy to provide luxuries for his own family circle." Now, with these thoughts in mind—providing the necessities, plus his God-given responsibility and pride in doing so—let's take a look at society to see how this is applied:

The Working Wife

We have in America approximately 44 million *married* women with families. Out of these homemakers, 24 million work outside the home and 20 million do not. This means that over half of the homemakers of America are working. Women are employed as secretaries, clerks, teachers, technicians, and even doctors and lawyers—in almost every field that men are. Many of them are highly educated and skilled and excel men in ability. Some are in top positions, have become office managers or presidents of their companies with men working under them. They may draw a top salary, even to exceed their husbands.

Now, why do these homemakers work? In certain rare instances it is because their husband has failed to provide the necessities or other financial emergency. But in most cases the homemakers are working for one of three reasons—*for luxuries, because they are bored at home, or to find more fulfillment in the challenging and exciting world of men.* Now, there are times a woman is justified in working and times when she is not, as we will now review:

When Women Are Justified in Working

Single women, widows and divorcees are certainly justified in working. Women whose husbands are ill or disabled are justified. But what about the homemaker whose husband is working; when is she justified in working?

1. *Compelling Emergencies:* The homemaker would be justified in working when the family is faced with heavy expenses or financial distress, when there is no alternative but for her to seek employment. But, these times are rare. Most financial problems can be solved by trimming off luxuries and comforts to meet the husband's income. The times a homemaker truly must work are unique situations which seldom occur. And, in these rare instances, the family understandingly accepts the wife's employment as a

necessity, considers her unselfishness a noble sacrifice, and there is little harm because of it.

2. *Furthering the Husband's Education or Training:* When the husband is attending college or training for a career is another time a wife is justified in working. Often a man has no other alternative to secure an education than to depend on his wife for financial support. And since he is working to prepare himself to be a more adequate provider and the situation is only temporary, there is just reason for the wife to help him accomplish his goal. However, when a wife works to help her husband through school, there is a temptation for her to continue after he graduates. He will need to get established, and they need many things after going without for so long. They both see no harm in her working a little longer. But, they soon become accustomed to luxuries and gradually raise their standard of living, so that there is still a need for the wife's income. Often this is just how a wife gets started on a lifetime of working outside of the home.

3. *The Older Woman:* When a woman has raised her family and has a great deal of time on her hands, she may feel a need to work just to occupy her time. Her sense of values may tell her that useful employment would be better than idling away her time with hobbies or things which are of no real importance. She may seek employment where she is greatly needed. If she is a gifted, talented woman, she may be extremely useful and in real demand.

Whether the older woman is justified in working or not, depends upon her motive. If she is working to be more useful, to render service, or to give important talents to the world in an area where they are greatly needed, she may be justified. But if she is working to bring in more money, she stands as a threat to her husband's pride as a provider. There is another thing to consider. If she has children, even though they are married, they may still need her. A mother is a mother all of her life. If her work divides her interest from these important things, it may not be justified.

When the Wife Is Not Justified in Working

1. *Working for Luxuries:* In the majority of cases women work for additional luxuries and conveniences, whether they like to admit it or not. They want the latest

148

in household equipment, new furniture, draperies, carpet, or a better house or better clothes. It may be that they have a drive to meet the standards of their friends and are overly material-minded. Or, it may be the husband who has the drive for luxuries and encourages his wife to work. He may be the one who is material-minded, wants a boat, swimming pool or cabin in the mountains. Or they may want greater advantages for their children, music lessons, better clothes and opportunities. But, these luxuries are purchased at a great price in the harm that comes to the family when the wife works.

2. *When She is Bored at Home:* This is a common reason for women working. The wife is bored with the menial tasks of housekeeping or tending children. If the husband detects her boredom, he may even suggest she work, just to keep her happy. And when she works, she will undoubtedly feel a relief from this boredom and learn to enjoy working. Is she, then, justified in working? No, working is not the answer to her problems. She needs to be taught *how* to be happy in her domestic role. She may never have understood that it takes a wholehearted effort and devotion to find enjoyment in anything we do. Learning to be happy at home is a matter of following principles. Effort in this direction will bring great benefits to her and her family, whereas working will bring only temporary relief.

3. *To Find More Fulfillment:* Some women find little satisfaction in the domestic role as the wife, mother and homemaker. They feel trapped in the isolated household and that their homemaking role is one which frustrates their own development. They think that the men have the more interesting, challenging and important jobs and feel that if they are to find fulfillment, it will have to be in the world of men. These women suffer a serious mistake in their values and basic philosophy of life. They have greatly underestimated the importance of the woman's role in the home, her contribution to the well being of society, and the satisfaction and personal development which results. And they have exaggerated the importance of men's work. Their distorted, mistaken philosophy and the harm which comes to their families and especially to themselves, make it safe to say that seeking fulfillment is not a justification for working, but a damaging one which will harm society.

4. *To Ease the Load for the Man:* When women see

149

their husbands work long hours, often under pressure and strain, and when they see them worry about problems, money, paying the bills, meeting expenses and the demands of a growing family, they may feel that they must ease the load by seeking employment. They may not want to work, may even consider it a sacrifice, but feel it is the Christian thing to do. Our men *are* under strain, and women can help; but working outside the home is not the solution.

First, we must remember that men have a great capacity for their role as the provider. The man was blessed with strength and endurance for difficult tasks. He also has the emotional make-up for his work, for the stresses and strains of the marketplace, the uncertainties of the crops in the fields, and the financial challenges of the office. He can endure worry and has the capacity to overcome his obstacles, solve his problems and thus succeed at his work.

But in spite of the man's inborn capacity to meet the demands of his work, some are faltering. Many men suffer heart attacks and other breakdowns in health. What, then, is putting a strain on our men and causing them to be over-burdened in their work? A number of things are responsible. He may not have taken proper care of his body, may have neglected it, or filled it with bad food, drugs, alcohol, tobacco, etc. Or, he may suffer from frustration in his marriage or tension in the home. Or his family may be overtaxing him by demanding too many luxuries.

A woman can help a man in all of these ways. She can protect his health by studying the principles of nutrition and providing him with a proper diet. She can remove the frustrations of marriage and tension in the home by living the principles of Fascinating Womanhood. And she can greatly ease his financial burdens by cutting down on luxuries and employing the principles of thrift. A woman helps a man financially, not by joining the working forces herself, to work side by side with him, sweating, toiling, and facing all of the perplexing problems that men face in their work; but by *being feminine, radiant, relaxed, and providing a peaceful home atmosphere where he can be renewed.* This gives him incentive in his work, a reason for striving and struggling against difficulty.

Harm in Women Working

1. *Harm to the Man:* When we consider the man's feeling of responsibility to provide the living, and his pride in doing so adequately, we can see that when his wife works it would be a threat to this feeling of masculine fulfillment. As she becomes capable, efficient and independent in earning money, able to make it on her own in life, he would feel less needed and, therefore, less of a man. He would also feel less tender towards her, since her dependence upon him helps to awaken his feelings of tenderness.

2. *Harm to the Woman:* When a woman works by choice, she tends to lose some of her womanliness. This would depend, of course, on the type of work. Some jobs are quite feminine—secretarial, clerical, nursing, school teaching and many others. In this case she would have much less tendency to lose her feminine qualities. But, any woman who works and learns to support herself, who is able to make it in the world without masculine assistance, develops independence, which means a loss of quality of feminine dependency.

Some jobs are somewhat masculine—in science, industry, politics, engineering, technical fields. Some of these, however, are very masculine—steel mill workers, airplane pilots, truck driver, policewomen, and many others. A woman must develop masculine skills if she is to succeed in these jobs. This would also be true in managerial jobs where the woman must develop leadership qualities, efficiency and drive to meet the demands of her work. When this occurs, femininity diminishes. Women in top positions will invariably deny this is true, since women are usually the last to notice any loss of their femininity; but the general observation makes this statement undeniably true.

There doesn't seem to be any way that a woman can step into the man's world and be a shining light there, without losing some of her womanliness. When she attempts to play a part not intended for her, she sacrifices her own special beauty and grace. The moon, when it moves from its sphere of night into day, loses its lustre, its charm, its very poetry. And so it is with a woman, when she attempts to play a part not intended for her, gone is the lustre, the charm, the poetry that says, "She is a phantom of delight." Again, I would like to quote from my husband's book *Man of Steel and Velvet:*

"Another harm is this: When a woman divides herself between two worlds, it is difficult for her to succeed in either. In her world alone she has challenge enough if she is to reach success, to be the understanding wife, the devoted mother and successful homemaker and gain the satisfaction from a job well done. This takes great effort. But as she divides her time and interests between two worlds, she is not likely to succeed in either.

"When a woman works because it is her husband's idea, an even greater harm can come to her. His suggestion that she work casts doubts in her mind as to his adequacy as a man. If he must lean on her for the necessities, she will question his ability to solve his problems and face responsibility that is his. This can cause her to feel insecure.

"Still another harm is her relationship with her employer, especially if he is a man. The wife is accustomed to looking up to her husband as the director of her activities. When she finds herself taking orders from another man, it is an unnatural situation for her. She owes him a certain obedience as her employer, and in countless hours of close contact she may find herself physically attracted to him. Seeing him at his best and perhaps as a more dynamic and effective leader than her husband, she makes comparisons unfavorable to her husband whose faults and failings she knows all too well."

3. *Harm to the Children:* "When a mother works due to a compelling emergency, children seem to adjust to the situation quite remarkably. They are able to comprehend circumstances and seldom hold them against their parents. They may suffer neglect, which may be harmful, but will not suffer lack of love or concern. If however, the mother works by choice, great harm can come to the child. When he realizes that she prefers to work instead of take care of him, that she places her interests, or luxuries, as more important, he will be apt to interpret this as lack of love and concern for his welfare.

"The children of working mothers usually suffer considerable neglect. Not in all cases, but in most. The woman who works must dedicate herself to her job, in order to succeed and to earn her pay. During the working hours her job has priority. At times it may be demanding. Her children are less demanding, so they are naturally the ones who suffer neglect."

Working mothers often make this statement: "It is not the quantity but the quality of time you spend with your children that counts." When they come home, they try to make up for their absence by spending devoted time with their children. Most of this is just talk. A working mother is too busy in the evening to do anything extraordinary with her children that other mothers do not do. But, even if she does give her child extra attention of a high quality, there is something else to consider:

The mother's presence in the home during the day means everything to the child's feeling of well being and security, even though she may be busy with homemaking tasks. It isn't always possible or even necessary for a busy mother to take time away from her work to actually play with her children. And too much attention can harm the child and make him demanding. But her presence in the home is a security to him and helps him to develop normally. When a child comes home from school he may not pay much attention to his mother or be overly aware that she is home, but her presence is felt and the child is benefited. If the mother is away from home for long hours, the child may not complain, but this does not mean he does not feel the lack. We must understand that children do not know how to interpret their feelings, let alone reveal them to adults. But they will nevertheless experience the lack of their mother's presence. Now, I would like to again quote from my husband's book *Man of Steel and Velvet* in explaining this next point:

4. *Harm to Society:* "The trend for the mother to be out of the home is a pattern of living which has extended for thirty years in America, since the emergency of World War II took millions of women into the factories. It has been during this time that we have developed some of our most threatening social problems—marriage problems, divorce, violence in the streets and on the campus, drug abuse, rebellion against social customs and moral standards. Many of these problems can be traced to homes of working mothers. The children fail to develop properly, or develop into mental cases or fail to find purpose or happiness from life. They turn from the ways of the parents and seek new ways.

"Dr. David V. Haws, acting chairman of psychiatry,

General Hospital in Phoenix has said, 'Mother must be returned to the home. The standard of living is a fictitious thing. It is a woman's primordial function to stay home and raise children. She should not join the hunt with men. A man, too, feels less of a man when his wife works. If you don't leave a family of decent kids behind, you have left nothing. Basic to the solution of adolescent problems of any generation is an intact home.' "

Mistakes the "Stay at Home" Wife Makes

The wife who does not work eliminates the above harm which can come to herself and to her children. She can, however, still make mistakes which will injure her husband's pride as a provider. For example, she may say "We can't afford it," or "I wish we had a little more security." She may offer suggestions about how he may increase his income, or she may admire another man who has been financially successful. All of these things make a man feel like an inferior provider, rather than an adequate one.

Another way the non-working wife makes her husband feel like an inferior provider is by reminding him how she scrimps and saves to make his salary do. The following dialogue illustrates:

Tom and Mary

Tom: As he looks over his bills, "It takes a lot of money to support a family now-days." (Hoping for praise.)

Mary: "Well, it's not my fault! I scrimp and save, sew all the children's clothes myself, make our bread, and never buy a thing for myself. Other women go to the beauty salon to have their hair done and buy a lot of expensive clothes, but I go without these things." (Hoping to win appreciation.)

Tom: "Do you really go without?" (Hoping she will reassure him that she doesn't.)

Mary: "I'm only trying to help. I would rather go without the things I need than to see you worry." (Hoping again for appreciation.)

Tom: (Something inside of him happens—a mixture of resentment towards his wife for making him feel like a

154

failure and a miserable feeling of being one.) He says with irritation, "Guess I'm not much of a provider in your eyes, am I?"

(Mary looks up in bewilderment at his irritation and lack of appreciation for her self-sacrifice.) This is a perfect illustration of the lack of understanding between the sexes. The only reason Tom complained about the high costs of living was to win Mary's appreciation. But she took it as criticism. And her defense as the scrimping wife was only to let him know she was trying to help. But this was too much of a blow to his pride. The following dialogue is an illustration of what she should have said.

The Right Way

Tom: "It takes a lot of money to support a family now-days."

Mary: "Doesn't it, though. How have you managed so well? Isn't it a tremendous responsibility to be a man and have to provide for a family?

Tom: (His self-esteem has doubled.) "Well, now, I don't mind the load at all. Of course, it does have its trying problems. But I feel capable of the job! Yes, quite capable!"

Mary: "It is wonderful to feel secure and to know that I have a man that will always provide for me!"

In the first illustration Mary made her husband feel like a failure, but in the second—like a hero!

Suppose the man is really not a good provider. Suppose that he is lazy and irresponsible and as a consequence does not make an adequate living, so that the family really does go without essentials. It is not expected that his wife be dishonest and give credit where credit is not due. But neither should she depreciate him. Do not think that you can inspire a man to be a better man by making him feel like a failure. If he is negligent about his responsibility to provide, his wife will have to accept this weakness in him and look to his better side. However, I must point out that the man does have a binding obligation to provide the necessities—food, clothing, and a house of her own. These she can rightfully expect. But it is best to let him decide how much beyond this he is willing to provide.

Assignment

If your husband is an adequate provider, tell him something like this: "I appreciate how hard you work to provide the living. I don't see how you can take the year-in, year-out responsibility. I'm glad I am not a man. It would be tough for me to worry about making the living." In this way you help him feel adequate as a provider and that he is doing a better job than you could do.

How to Help Him Feel Fulfilled as The Guide, Protector and Provider

(Application of Characteristic No. 6)

1. Allow him to be the guide, protector and provider.
2. Need his masculine care and protection. Be dependent. Let him know you need him.
3. Do not excel him in anything which requires masculine strength, skill or ability.
4. Have a girlish trust in him, but allow for mistakes and inadequacies.
5. Express appreciation to him for his capabilities as the guide, protector and provider.

Summary of Understanding Men

As we come to the end of the section on Understanding Men, it appears that we must do a lot of *giving*. We are expected to *yield* to his authority, to *allow* for human weakness and errors in judgment, and to *give* admiration, sympathy, and make him *Number One*. If it seems to you that you are asked to do a lot of giving without taking much thought of reward, remember, *when you cast your bread upon the waters, it comes back buttered.*

As you apply these principles, it will awaken your husband's love and tenderness. As one wife put it, "Our marriage blossomed like a plant that had been placed in the sun after a long, dark winter." Love is awakened as a man begins to feel accepted, free, respected as a man, and understood. But, remember, you are not to expect material rewards, such as new clothes, a new dishwasher or color T.V., or even flowers and frilly night wear. These things may come as fringe benefits, as they often do, but the promise of Fascinating Womanhood is not material rewards, but a stronger relationship and a tender, romantic love. And now, I would like to describe a surprising problem which may occur as you begin to practice the principles of Fascinating Womanhood.

Pandora's Box

When a marriage has had real problems, and then the wife makes a devoted effort to improve it by applying the principles of Fascinating Womanhood, it can cause a peculiar reaction in her husband which I call Pandora's Box. In this case, when Fascinating Womanhood is applied, instead of the man being loving and tender, he may become violent and pour out resentments and hostile feelings towards his wife.

It is important for the wife to understand the change which is taking place within the man, which causes this violent outburst. I can explain it in this way: If a man's marriage has been "shaky," he may have suppressed resentful feelings towards his wife in order to hold his marriage together. When she has made mistakes which have hurt him or disappointed him, instead of expressing these troubled feelings, he may have felt it necessary to suppress them in order to avoid further marriage problems or even a marriage failure. This is not to say that he acted wisely, but only to say that he did so out of what he felt was a necessity. A high principled man who loves his children dearly will make great effort to hold his marriage securely together. When his wife begins to apply the teachings of Fascinating Womanhood over a period of time, he gradually begins to feel secure in his marriage. He no longer feels he must hold his troubled feelings within and begins to lose his fear that "speaking out" will cause marriage problems. Then, one day, at last, he dares to open Pandora's Box and release all of the resentful feelings he has kept hidden there.

The wife should understand this reaction and allow him to empty Pandora's Box. She should, in fact, encourage him to speak freely and completely. And she should not make the mistake of defending herself, justifying, or fighting back. She will have to sit there quietly, taking it all and even agreeing with him by saying, "I know, I know, you are right." But, when the last resentful feeling has been expressed and Pandora's Box is empty, he will have a feeling of relief, and a love and tenderness for her not

157

known before. And if he has had a reserve, it will probably come tumbling down along with the Pandora's Box reaction, as in the following experience as written to me.

Wham! A Pandora's Box Reaction

"After learning and applying Fascinating Womanhood, my husband seemed happier, but that lasted only about 3 to 4 months, when tension began to build a little (not bad). Then one evening, wham! A Pandora's Box reaction. It seems as if all the pent up feelings he had came out, and at the same time the walls of reserve came tumbling down. Pretty dramatic—and pretty wonderful! Now he tells me he has never been so happy in all his life, and I feel the same way. Even friends comment on it and ask if I am really as happy as I look.

"I really feel the spirit of Fascinating Womanhood and the deep happiness it can bring when one lives it. Tonight my husband spent three hours just talking to me, telling me more about himself, his past and dreams than I have learned in ten years of marriage. He also said that he came closer than I had realized to leaving me during that time and would have if it hadn't been for the children."

He Opened the Lid of Pandora's Box

"I had been extremely happy all day, but when my husband came home he cast a shadow of gloom and was grumpy. I was determined to not let his gloom rub off on me. I made him comfortable and invited him to talk over the day. He just wanted to relax, so I continued to prepare dinner.

"When I went to call him to dinner, his head was bowed and wet tears on his cheeks. Tenderly, I softly said, 'Dear, share it with me.' All of a sudden he burst into deep sobs, and he opened the lid of Pandora's Box. He had lost all faith in womanhood through the tragic experience of a previous marriage. Out stormed all of his resentments, hatred towards women and fears of the future. He had opened his shell. Since that evening, our love has had the freedom to grow, even to the height of him telling me with a big hug that I am everything a man could want in a wife."

"My husband and I have been married 6 years—we have 2 children. When I became pregnant with my last child, my husband became very cold and indifferent. He said he didn't love me and said I was like a mother to him. He began having an affair with another woman. After the baby was born, I filed for divorce, and we got a settlement and separated. But my husband didn't want a divorce. We went to a marriage counselor for help, and he told us what was wrong but didn't tell us how to make things right. After being separated for three months, we went back together on a six-months trial. We were both miserable separated. We were from very religious homes and attended and were very active in our own church when this happened.

"During this trial period our marriage was doing fairly well, but was shaky and wasn't what I wanted. I didn't feel the tenderness I wanted and needed so desperately. I didn't feel loved like I wanted to be. I felt like our marriage was very insecure, but I didn't know what to do about it. I felt helpless and worried constantly that my husband would find another woman to have an affair with.

"At this time I heard about Fascinating Womanhood. I read the book and attended the classes. The first time I practiced it, I saw my husband's face light up and felt a tenderness, though small, towards me. We had had very little communication, but when I started *admiring him* and giving him the *sympathetic understanding* that you describe, he became a changed man. His shell has disappeared, and he tells me all his problems and treats me with a lovely tender feeling. It is a marvelous experience—one I have always dreamed of but never had. The more I admire him, the more love I feel from him.

"I now have a wonderful peace within. I have no fear of him leaving me for another woman because I am giving him the admiration and love he needs and wants, and in turn I receive the love I so desperately need."

He Wonders What Kind of Pill I Am Taking

"I feel a person either wants to make a marriage work or she doesn't. After ten years I still want mine to work, so

I have tried hard to live Fascinating Womanhood. I read the book last summer and started trying. My husband is still wondering what kind of pill I am taking. 'Whatever it is,' he said, 'I hope they don't run out.' I know and believe that Fascinating Womanhood works. My husband hasn't spoken a cross word to me for months. He comes home earlier than he has in years. In the last six months, his earnings have increased each month. He can't seem to do enough for me. I could go on and on. I have never been happier or had a happier family. I know that your *bread comes back,* not only *buttered,* but *with a little jam on it.*"

Six Characteristics of Men

1. His need to be accepted at face value.
2. His need for admiration.
3. His sensitive masculine pride.
4. His need for sympathetic understanding.
5. His need to be No. 1.
6. His need to serve as the guide, protector and provider to feel needed in this role, and to excel women in doing so.

11

Family Finances

The man, in his duties as the leader and the provider, and the woman, in her duties as the wife and homemaker, share the responsibility of family finances. The proper division of concern is this:

Husband's Responsibility	Wife's Responsibility
1. Provide Money	1. Support husband's financial plans
2. Manage money	2. Provide a peaceful home atmosphere.
3. Necessary worry	3. Make a dollar stretch

If we accept the holy Scriptures, we have no doubt that the man has the responsibility to provide the living. And as the leader, he also has the responsibility to manage the money and worry about it. The wife, then, is not responsible for earning the living, managing the paycheck or worrying about it. She should be given a household budget, but is not responsible for the overall management of the income.

But the wife does have an important part to play in the success of family finances. If the man is to succeed in providing an adequate living, he will have to make plans from time to time to meet this challenge. Her support, her willingness to sacrifice when needed, and to adapt herself to circumstances is a vital part of the man's success. Also important is the part she has to play in providing a peaceful home atmosphere, one where he can think, where he can be renewed in body and spirit so that he can go back into the world prepared to make another effort. A man is definitely influenced in his work by his home environment. When his life at home is on an even keel, he is much more apt to succeed in his work.

The wife has an additional part to play in managing the household budget, or in making a dollar stretch. We can measure our standard of living, not so much by the amount of income the husband brings in, as by how well the money is managed. The wife does her part to create a good standard of living by being thrifty. If the husband's income is low, the wife can be the key figure in the financial success of the family, being in a position to either make or break her husband. There are families with high incomes who live in much less comfort than families with far less, and this is due to the difference in money management. The wife, then, plays an important part in achieving a good standard of living for the family by learning to make a dollar stretch.

Family Finances Today

The problem in our society is that some men and women have their financial roles confused. Many men think that their only duty is to provide the living. The man brings home his paycheck, hands it over to his wife and expects her to worry about making it cover expenses. And she does worry; oh, *how* she worries about the bills and expenses and where the next dollar is coming from. And if, through her initiative, she is able to save part of this income, what happens? The husband, because he is the leader and in full command, may reach into the savings and spend the money for investments or luxuries. Let me make this point clear: If the husband manages the money and worries about it, then he has a right to use the excess according to his best judgment, but not otherwise. The role of money management and control of the purse strings belong inseparably together. If the wife is to manage the money and worry about it, she should have the power of decision in spending it. In our society we also find women everywhere working, helping to share the financial burden of earning the income. So women have stepped over into the man's financial responsibility and in some cases have pretty much taken it over.

And what has happened on the home scene? Because women are so busy working, worrying about finances and helping the man with his financial responsibility, they have neglected their own. There are homes that are in such a state of confusion that when the man comes home, he does not have the peace he needs to revive himself. No wonder he has difficulty solving his money problems or making greater headway as a provider. And because women spend so much time away from home working, they develop extravagant habits of spending to save time. Food, clothes and household goods are bought to save time rather than money. Fast disappearing is the feminine art of thrift, which is such a feeling of security to a family. What is the solution to these common problems we see in our society? For the man and wife to recognize their financial roles and make a success of these responsibilities.

The Wife's Budget

A simple solution to common money problems between husband and wife is the wife's household budget, which covers food, clothing, household goods, personal items, miscellaneous or any items in regular demand. It would not include occasional items such as household furniture, house repairs, or remodeling, etc. The budget money can be advanced weekly or monthly. It should be a fair allotment, based upon the husband's income, but hopefully generous enough to have some left over. This she should be allowed to keep, to save or spend as she pleases with no questions asked. This will provide strong incentive for her to be thrifty.

The husband would manage the remainder of the money and pay the monthly bills such as gas, electricity, telephone, water, house payments, insurance, yard care, car expense, income taxes and other expenses. And if he manages his money well and accumulates an execss, he should have jurisdiction over it *with no questions asked*. This would be an incentive for him to be diligent in his work and try to increase his income. When the man contemplates investments or spending considerable amounts of money from his savings, it would be wise for him to consult his wife, but it is bad policy to make this a binding obligation. Disputes over money matters are a source of painful problems in marriage, and whatever is gained by the wife in more control of the money, is lost in a dampened relationship. Try to understand that a man works hard for his money, and it is well to allow him freedom over his excess as long as you are not deprived of what you need.

When the Wife Manages the Money

Serious problems occur when the wife manages the money. I can best explain this by giving a living example.

A couple of my acquaintance had their financial roles confused. The husband, of modest income, brought his paycheck home each week and handed it to his wife. She managed it well until several more children came along. It became increasingly difficult to cover expenses, and she began to almost break with worry. In the meantime, her husband was quite carefree about money matters. She tried to explain the problems they faced, but he was not used to thinking about them.

An opportunity arose in which the man was offered a higher paying position if he would move to another state. When the husband and wife considered the proposition, the wife wanted to move for she could see a solution to their financial problems. But the husband wanted to stay in the comfortable environment he was in. Because he was not managing the money he did not feel the financial pinch. However, because he was head of the family he was in a position to refuse the offer. The wife was heartsick over this decision, but felt there was nothing she could do about it. The only fair solution is this: If the wife is to handle the entire paycheck, she should also have the leader's right to decisions which relate to finances. When the man does not assume his position as money manager, he should forfeit his power of decision.

Also, serious harm can come to the *woman* if she assumes full financial responsibility to manage the money. Women are not designed by temperament to worry extensively over money. They become depressed, mentally ill, physically ill, lose their health, become disagreeable, lose their sparkle and feminine charm. It can also cause them to fail in homemaking responsibility. Perhaps the reason women worry intensely over money is because they are not the breadwinner and so are rather helpless to do anything to solve acute money problems. Of course, they can go to work, as many of them do. Men worry about money, too, but they have more of a temperament for it and can do more to solve problems. If they do not have enough money, they can, by their initiative, cleverness, or hard work, earn a greater income. Men would rather work than worry, and so when faced with this problem, they usually work a little harder.

There are women who take over the role of financial management by choice or even by demand. This is usually because they do not trust their husband to do a good enough job, so would rather do it themselves. But even if the wife assumes this role by choice, there are still some losses to her. Being an efficient money manager can burden her with responsibility which can interfere with the domestic role. And if she becomes capable as a financier, it can mean a loss of womanliness. It also robs the man of his rightful role.

When a Man Makes a Mess of Management

Now, how does a woman face this problem: She willingly hands the money management over to her husband. He willingly accepts. Then she peacefully turns her back on this part of life and trusts that all will turn out well. But what happens? He gets behind in the house payments, doesn't pay all of the bills, overdraws the bank account and a few other things. The wife is a nervous wreck. She doesn't want the job back, but what can she do? The only thing to do is the following:

When a woman gives a man the financial burden of money management, she should "let go" and turn her back on it completely. It must be a wholehearted and complete thing. She cannot be on the anxious seat, checking on the books to see if he added right or constantly wondering how he is doing. If he makes a mess of things for awhile, let him suffer the consequences, no matter what they are. This is the only way he will learn. Remember that if you have been handling the money, he has been denied experience in this role and will have to learn by doing.

Also, if the wife lets go completely, the psychology is right. The man will feel his *full responsibility,* will begin to know that if anyone is to worry about the money, it will have to be him. Also, as you turn your back on the money matters, he will be able to see your relief, that you are happier. Let him know you are. And as he sees you bloom a little, he will try harder to make a go of it so he can keep you happy. Some interesting things happen when a woman hands finances over to her husband, as in the following true experiences:

He Exploded

"The turning point in my marriage came dramatically when I learned through Fascinating Womanhood of the separate responsibilities of husband and wife. During the six years we have been married, my husband has handed all but a small amount of his salary over to me to spend and pay bills as I wanted. After the third Fascinating Womanhood class, I drove home with my mind made up that I didn't want control of the money. I approached my husband by saying that I could no longer carry the burden of handling the finances, that he could do it much better and that all the worry was getting me down, and that I was not doing a very good job.

"Well, he just exploded, saying, 'So, you do not want to worry! Tough, you are going to, because I do not want it. If you have not done a good job, it is your fault and you are going to learn to do a good job, and you are going to continue.' He walked around saying he had never had a say in the money or what I did. I assured him I would change and I would consult him before I did anything. He just laughed as though he did not believe me. I was crying, but his attitude did not change. He was so angry he threw all of the books and bills on his footstool.

"I then got my Fascinating Womanhood book and asked him to please read the pages I opened for him, the ones my Fascinating Womanhood teacher said to have our husbands read. After reading the first pages of Man's Role in Life, where he is to be the guide, protector and provider, his voice softened and he asked me about the book. I had not told him about my classes or the book before. I then had him read about family finances and the man's and woman's responsibilities there. He was quiet for a little while, then a very small smile came across his face and he said to please bring all the bills, bankbooks and checkbooks. He worked from 10:30 until midnight.

"The next week he gave me $15.00, saying he had that much extra and to buy some things I had been wanting. My husband has complete control of the money now, and I am very happy. I used to spend several hours a week placing the money here and there. My husband spends only a few minutes every two weeks and has everything under control. I now ask my husband for what I need. I know he will give it to me if my desires are not selfish and if he can afford it."

My Mathematical Jungle

"After we lost two homes, one new car and went through bankruptcy, I was almost a nervous wreck, trying to make the money go around. My checkbook was a mathematical jungle and statements never balanced. My husband was after me because we were always overdrawn at the bank. He wrote checks for what he wanted, and then I had to worry about bills. Then came Fascinating Womanhood. I soon found out that I shouldn't worry about these things, so I really made an effort to stop worrying. Now, I don't open the bills when they arrive.

"We recently had some friends come to visit us on their vacation. We hadn't seen them for about three years. She had only been in the house a short time when she said, 'What has happened to you?' I said, 'Nothing, just that I have gained weight.' 'No, not that,' she said, 'you aren't nervous any more. You used to shake all the time.' So I told her about Fascinating Womanhood and what it had done for me. She said she often wishes she didn't have to take care of the finances, so that night she told her husband about Fascinating Womanhood and the way to handle finances and asked him to take over the responsibility. Much to her surprise and delight, he said as soon as they got home he would try. It is so good to be free of the worry of the bills, and we are doing better financially than we have ever done before. Thank God for Fascinating Womanhood."

It Was a Risky Feeling

"In the past I have tried to handle the finances in the family, since my husband has been very irresponsible about money. You just can't imagine how foolish he has been—spending his money on motorcycles and other luxuries, always negligent about paying bills, and never able to hang on to any money. After studying Fascinating Womanhood, I became convinced that I should hand over the finances to him, regardless. It was a risky feeling, but he was willing to do it. To my surprise—even amazement—he has become a changed man; is responsible and thrifty with his money and has developed leadership qualities. He now manages our money better than I used to."

Assignment

If you have had the burden of managing family finances and would like to be relieved of this worry, read him the principles in that section and discuss it with him. Then ask him if he agrees. If he does not, then say, "I don't think I can carry this responsibility any longer, for it is a burden to me. I don't feel it would be nearly as difficult for you, for you are a man. Will you please relieve me of it?" Assure him that you will work efficiently to do your part to "make a dollar stretch" and provide a peaceful home atmosphere. If he accepts, offer sincere appreciation. If he does not, then don't make an issue of it at this time. Wait until you have applied all of the principles of Fascinating Womanhood.

12

Deep Inner Happiness

Deep inner happiness is a happiness of spirit, a *serenity, tranquility,* and *peace of mind.* Agnes had this quality of spirit—"a *placid* and *sweet* expression and a *tranquility* about her, a *quiet, good, calm spirit.*" Inner happiness can carry one through the turmoils of life with a calm stability. A woman who has inner happiness is not necessarily free of problems, but she has power to face these problems or disappointments with a spiritual calm. This quality of spirit seems to be pretty important to a man. I know of at least two men who told me they would not consider a reconciliation with their wives if they did not learn to be happy within.

When a man detects that his wife is unhappy, if he is a kindly man he will be greatly concerned and sympathetic. And he certainly should try to help her and cheer her up. But, this is *not* something he admires in a woman. Men do not appreciate this deficiency in women. They expect women to give happiness. They know women will face many problems, but expect them to do so with a stability of spirit.

What is the cause of unhappiness? It arises from a failure on the part of the individual—a weakness in character, sin, failure to fulfill responsibility or self-centeredness. We are unhappy when we are doing something wrong, failing to do something right or in some way breaking the eternal laws of life. People become happy, then, by overcoming their weaknesses and putting themselves in harmony with eternal principles. We will discuss these routes to happiness in this chapter but first, let's define the difference between happiness and pleasure:

Happiness Versus Pleasure

The word pleasure comes from the word *please.* Pleasure is derived from those things which please the *senses,* such as the eyes, nose, ears, mouth and sensual feelings. There are both good and bad pleasures: Good pleasures are derived from such things as sunshine, rain, flowers, nourishing food, the laughter of little children, music, wholesome recreation, the arts, and many more of the finer things of life. We can receive good pleasure from attractive clothes, beautiful homes, gardens, furniture, and the conveniences of modern equipment such as vacuum cleaners and washing machines. These things are enriching to life, but we must realize that they bring *pleasure*, rather than *happiness*. This can be proven by the fact that people who have all of the pleasures of earth may yet fail to be happy.

Bad pleasures are derived from sin and bring us harm, rather than good. They are such things as immoral sex, bad literature, unwholesome entertainment, improper food, alcohol, smoking, gambling, riotous living, and many more vices. These things do nothing good for the body or spirit and should be avoided completely. Excessive material goods, extravagances, and too much emphasis upon and enjoyment of material things are also considered sources of bad pleasure and should be avoided.

Happiness is quite different from pleasure. While pleasure comes from those things which please the senses, happiness may arise from unpleasant experiences. The mother who desires the joys of a family will first know the pain of childbirth, then the tiresome labor to care for her children. The father will know the weariness, pain and toil to secure comforts for his loved ones. Any person who sets a high goal for himself and is dedicated to reaching that goal, will know the struggle and opposition involved. But he will also experience a new-found joy—not only the joy of his accomplishment, but the joy of a new-found strength, a strength gained in conflict and experience. Sometimes happiness comes as a result of knowing misery, sorrow, pain and suffering. Pleasure may be derived from sin, while happiness is a direct result of the struggle to overcome sin. No person who lives a mere innocent life, protected from unpleasant experiences, can know what happiness is.

Although happiness can arise from unpleasant experience, even misery and pain, the feeling of happiness itself is the opposite of misery. Happiness is a deep feeling in the spirit, a combination of peace, joy, serenity. But even this cannot adequately describe it. It has always been difficult to describe real happiness. The Apostle Paul, when he attempted to explain the eternal happiness in store for the faithful, said, "Eye hath not seen, nor ear heard, neither entered into the heart of man the things which God hath prepared for them that love him." (I Cor. 2:9) And so it is with earthly happiness. We cannot comprehend its magnificence, without personal experience. But when it is experienced, it is unmistakable. How can we acquire this deep inner happiness? What conscious effort must we make to achieve it?

How to Gain Deep Inner Happiness

We sometimes hear the statement, "People are about as happy as they make up their minds to be." Although there is some merit to this positive outlook, the statement is not entirely correct. A wicked person cannot be happy by merely determining to be. In fact, no one can gain inner happiness by suddenly deciding to be happy, as you would suddenly decide to smile. Inner happiness is a quality which must be *earned*. Henry Drummond has said, "No one can get joy by merely asking for it. It is one of the ripest fruits of the Christian life, and like all other fruits, must be grown." And Robert Ingersoll has said, "Happiness is the bud, the blossom and the fruit of good and noble actions. It is not the gift of God. It must be *earned.*"

Inner happiness is acquired by following eternal laws. There are spiritual laws governing happiness, just as there are laws governing the universe. When people are happy, it is because they are following the laws upon which happiness is based; and when they are unhappy, it is because they have broken these laws. Inner happiness can be reached by everyone who will obey its laws. Happiness for a woman can be gained by doing the following:

1. *Fulfilling Domestic Role:* The most basic area in a woman's life where she must succeed if she is to be happy is in the home, serving as the understanding wife, the devoted mother and homemaker. Success in the home follows eternal laws which will inevitably bring happiness. Many women do not realize that their "bluebird of happiness" lies within their own four walls. They reject this domestic role and seek happiness in the world of men. Of course, it takes a "wholehearted effort" to earn happiness from homemaking. You have to "go the second mile," doing more than required, to get any joy out of it. If you

merely do enough to "get by," you cannot expect any great rewards of happiness.

If a woman were to fail in the home, she would inevitably reap unhappiness. She would be breaking eternal laws and must suffer the consequences. A failure in the home, for a woman, is a failure in life. Even though she fail in only one area of her domestic role, for example, homemaking, she would still be somewhat of a failure as this is a vital area where she must succeed. She must succeed in all three responsibilities in the home if she is to gain the rewards of deep inner happiness.

2. *Development of the Character:* Happiness comes from righteous living and the development of a noble character. You can observe this yourself by noticing that people who are truly happy are also people who are honest, unselfish, kind, responsible, and have high moral standards. On the other hand, unhappy people are invariably selfish, lazy, irresponsible, and lacking in self-discipline. These are the common lacks in character that cause so much unhappiness, even among people who claim to have high standards. There are other people who are grossly sinful, immoral, dishonest and wicked. A sinful person is so removed from inner happiness that they would not even be familiar with the feeling. Sinfulness never leads to happiness, but to depression, nervousness and mental illness.

It is encouraging to find that modern psychiatry is turning to religion to cure the ills of the spirit. Dr. J. A. Hadfield, one of England's foremost psychiatrists, has said, 'I am convinced that the Christian religion is one of the most potent influences for producing that harmony, peace of mind and confidence of soul needed to bring health to a large portion of nervous patients." And the Bible promises, "He who hath clean hands and a pure heart; who hath not lifted up his soul unto vanity, nor sworn deceitfully, he shall receive the blessings of the Lord."

The struggle to overcome weakness or sin is not an easy one. There is always a tendency to slip back into old habits. But overcoming the weakness is the very thing which will bring inner happiness, not only because of overcoming the habit itself, but because of the strength gained in conflict, a strength of spirit which is a new-found joy. The weaknesses we need to overcome and the basic strengths we need to achieve in the development of a noble character will be taught in the next chapter.

3. *Service:* Dr. Norman Vincent Peale has said, "The way to be happy is to be *involved* in something—something worthwhile." Benevolent service outside the home can greatly enrich a woman's life. Our first responsibility is to our family, but each woman does have a certain obligation to give beyond her own sphere, for the betterment of society. Those who limit their devotion to their own small family unit, focusing on their own children and household affairs, will narrow their lives and thus limit their happiness. Dr. Max Levine, psychiatrist of New York, has said, "I speak not as a clergyman, but as a psychiatrist. There cannot be emotional health in the absence of high moral standards and a *sense of social responsibility.*" When we share the burdens of society and help make the world a better place, we gain a compensating inner happiness.

4. *Creative Work:* Did you know that working with your hands and mind, creating things of beauty and worth, builds inner happiness? And do not think that you lack this power within you. Boris Bali, Dean of Fine Arts, Temple University, has said, "I am convinced that every human being possesses a creative urge to make beautiful things, that this urge can be brought out and put to work with proper encouragement, and that suppression of it results in maladjustment." A routine therapy used in mental hospitals has been to give the patients things to do "with their hands."

We can be creative in the things we do at home, such as cooking, sewing, decorating and gardening. It is not creative, however, to merely copy someone else's idea from a pattern, recipe or picture. This is the creative product of someone else's mind. Creative opportunities are found in the fields of art, sculpture, music, creative writing, designing, and many more. Almost everything in the world can be creative. Whenever you have an original idea, or whenever you build something out of your imagination, something that is good or beautiful, you are creative. And when you create something of real worth or supreme beauty—like those rare treasures that are left to the world, you can experience a great satisfaction in your soul. When I think of the great joy in the modest creative efforts of man, I wonder how God must have felt when he created the world and, viewing the workmanship of his own hands, said, "It is good."

5. *Accept Ourselves:* If we are to be happy, it is

173

important that we accept ourselves and allow for our human errors and weaknesses. In the process of becoming angels, we are still human beings and are apt to make mistakes and failures. We do such things as burn food, spend money foolishly, break an expensive object, lose something, or we are late for an appointment. These errors can cause us to become quite upset with ourselves. Even little things disturb us and rob us of happiness. It is not fair for us to be "hard on ourselves." If we can learn to be forgiving of others, we must do the same for ourselves. Just as we learn to accept our husband, we must learn to accept ourselves as human beings and allow for mistakes and weaknesses.

The businessman allows in advance for business failures. We should allow for some mistakes in our routine. Tell yourself that each year, each week and even each day, you will make your share of mistakes or unwise decisions. When you plan a wardrobe, remember that you may not choose wisely with every item. We learn by experience, and this means we make our share of mistakes. Accepting ourselves, however, does *not* mean *contentment*, that we are satisfied with ourselves just as we are and will make no effort to improve. This would block our progress.

6. *Appreciation of Simple Pleasures:* If we are to be happy, it is important that we appreciate the simple joys of life such as rain, sunlight, and fresh crisp curtains. It is not so much these simple pleasures themselves that bring happiness as it is our ability to appreciate them.

The appreciative woman will enjoy drinking water from a tin cup, while another feels she must have china dishes. One woman will enjoy sitting on an apple box in her back yard, letting the warm sun shine down upon her shoulders, while another may feel she must have patio furniture to be happy. An appreciative woman will enjoy the sounds of the forest or the birds and the leaves rustling, while another must have grand opera. One will enjoy a simple wardrobe of cottons, while another, less appreciative, lives for the day she can buy her clothes on Fifth Avenue. One feels joy in pushing her baby carriage in the park, while another must have the bright lights and gay places. One will enjoy the simple cottage, while another must have a modern home with a view. Little children have this ability to enjoy simple pleasures. A ray of sunshine, a tub of water to splash in are common things they enjoy. The appreciative woman who learns to enjoy these common pleasures always has a source of joy near at hand.

7. *Seek Knowledge, Wisdom:* Knowledge unlocks the door to happiness, and wisdom is the most important tool for attaining it. Knowledge comes first, and then the application of knowledge, which is wisdom. The search for wisdom, then, should be the greatest, most inportant pursuit of our lives, and the attainment of it our most priceless possession. This thought is born out in the Holy Scriptures, Proverbs 3:11-18:

"*Happy* is the man that findeth wisdom and the man that getteth understanding. For the merchandise of it is better than the merchandise of silver, and the gain thereof than fine gold. She is more precious than rubies; and all the things thou canst desire are not to be compared to her. Length of days is in her right hand; and in her left hand riches and honor. Her ways are the ways of *pleasantness*, and all her paths are *peace*. She is the tree of life to them that lay hold on her; and *happy is everyone that retaineth her.*"

If knowledge can bring happiness, then lack of knowledge can bring *unhappiness*. This thought is expressed by Dr. Abraham Maslow, psychologist: "Knowledge, insight, truth, reality and facts are most powerful curative medicines. . . . If knowledge can cure, then lack of knowledge can sicken. . . . We must take seriously the fact that blindness can be sickness producing and that knowing can be curative. The old saying 'what you don't know won't hurt you' turns out to be false. Just the contrary is true. It is just what you don't know that *will* hurt you. What you don't know has power over you; knowing brings it under your control." A good example of this would be in marriage and family relations. Those who experience unhappiness and lack of peace in the household, suffer a lack of knowledge or wisdom. And when they gain this wisdom, they will find peace and happiness.

Is Love of Husband Necessary?

As we come to the end of these seven things we must do to gain inner happiness, you may wonder "Is it necessary for me to have the love of my husband to be happy?" If you are a woman who feels unloved, you may be inclined to think, "If my husband really loved me, then I would be happy." Although the husband's love is essential

175

to our total happiness in the highest sense, it is not essential in acquiring the inner-happiness I have described. In fact, you must first find inner happiness before your husband can really love you, as this is one of the qualities that men desire in women. Men all over the country are turning from their wives to someone else, partially because their wives are unhappy. This is a quality that men seem to insist upon before they will offer their true love.

But, if you do attain inner-happiness without your husband's love, it cannot be considered a complete happiness. A good example of this would be, again, Agnes Wickfield. Although she did have the quality of inner-happiness—a tranquility and a good calm spirit, she did not really experience complete happiness during most of the story. David Copperfield noticed frequently an unhappy expression in Agnes' beautiful face, but he did not realize that it was due to unrequited love. It was an indication of a missing ingredient to happiness, but it did not detract from the tranquility of her spirit.

How Do Others and Circumstances Affect Happiness?

You may wonder how much others or circumstances contribute to your happiness. The truth is that other people—your husband, children, relatives, and friends— can contribute greatly to your happiness, as do favorable circumstances. However, the point I wish to stress is this: They are not *necessary*. If you do not have the advantage of these things, if other people have let you down or if the circumstances of your life are not at all favorable—you can still be happy within by living right principles. And if you are able to succeed, without the advantage of other people and circumstances—it will prove that you are a finer, more courageous and stronger individual.

How to Find Inner Happiness

1. Fulfill domestic role.
2. Develop character, overcome weakness.
3. Give service to others.
4. Creative work.
5. Accept ourselves.
6. Enjoy simple pleasures.
7. Gain knowledge, wisdom.

Assignment

Make an evaluation of your life and try to decide if you have achieved inner happiness, fully. If not, which area of your life do you think is lacking? What can you do to gain a greater happiness in that area?

Inner happiness is a quality of spirit which must be earned by a victory over our weaknesses and an upward reach for the perfection of our character. It is like swimming upstream. It is found in the great efforts and achievements of life and in faithful devotion to duty.

13

A Worthy Character

A man wants a woman of fine character, one he can place on a pedestal and hold in highest regard. Not only does he expect her to be good, but he expects her to be better than he is. He hopes that she will be kinder, more patient, forgiving and unselfish than he, and hold more valiantly to principle. He considers himself to be less refined in spirit. If he becomes thoughtless, harsh or critical, he may be willing to overlook these weaknesses in himself, but is disappointed to see a woman, who has always been regarded as the more angelic creature of the human race, fall onto his level.

At times a man will shake a woman's pedestal by suggesting she do something wrong. He does this deliberately to see if she is as worthy as she appears. What a disappointment if she lowers her standards and what a joy if she remains unshaken. Remaining on the pedestal when she is tested is further proof that she belongs there.

Before a man will place a woman on a pedestal, she must develop a character worthy of that position. Your first impression may be, "This subject is not too essential for me to know. I have been trained all my life in the development of the virtues. I am honest, kind and benevolent. You see, I have a fine character." Such a thought indicates one's failure to understand what good character includes. The virtues mentioned are essential, of course, but good character includes much, much more. Dora was kind, honest and benevolent, but she did not earn the eminence of the pedestal. We will now devote ourselves to a study of good character and what it includes. There are many virtues of character, but the following are some of the most essential:

1. Self-Mastery

"He who rules within himself, and rules his passions, desires and fears, is more than a king."

MILTON

Self-mastery is the foundation of a worthy character. We cannot even apply the knowledge of this book if we do not have the *will* to apply it. Self-mastery means control over one's thoughts, feelings, desires, passions, fears and actions. It means deciding what is right or wise and then having the will to do it. It means sticking on diets, controlling our words, schooling our feelings, keeping confidences or secrets that have been entrusted to us. It means being on time, fulfilling responsibility assigned to us, holding to the standards that we set for ourselves and reaching our goals.

So important is self-mastery to spiritual achievement that the greatest person of all time felt a need for it. Jesus Christ did not even begin His ministry until He first went into the wilderness and fasted for forty days and forty nights. During this time He gained spiritual strength and was able to endure severe temptations. He gained mastery over Himself which was necessary for the completion of His mission in life.

There are numerous ways of gaining self-mastery. One of the most useful is the example set by the Savior, that of *fasting*. By depriving ourselves of food for a period of time, we gain a self-control that strengthens us for the challenges of life. Usually a 24-hour fast is sufficient and all that many people can endure, to begin with. It is also important to seek the Lord's strength through *prayer*. If we are to reach upward, sufficient to conquer our passions, weaknesses and fears, or to reach high objectives, we will need the help of God. Fasting and prayer can be practiced regularly to gain self-mastery as a virtue of character, or at a specific time to gain mastery over a particular situation.

Another way of gaining self-mastery is by *training the will*. Some ways of doing this are: 1. *Every day do something unpleasant*, such as take a cold shower or give up coffee, smoking or candy. 2. *Do something difficult*, such as set a high goal for yourself, take an extra responsibility (if you have time), or develop a talent. 3. *Demand definite quotas of yourself*, such as arise every morning at 4:30, get a specific number of jobs done at a particular time each day, exercise regularly, or outline a definite program of responsibility, and follow through consistently.

Training the will develops self-mastery so that when temptations come, we are fortified against them. Most of us have sincerely desired at times to be better than we are,

179

to overcome weakness, bad habits, or reach higher goals, only to find that we let one thing and then another interfere. This is due to a lack of self-mastery in most cases. As we practice measures of self-control through fasting, prayer and training the will, we gain a self-mastery which will greatly aid us in sticking to our objectives and eventually becoming more nearly perfect individuals.

2. Unselfishness

First, let's take a look at the word *selfishness:* The dictionary defines it as "caring unduly or supremely for oneself; regarding one's own comforts, advantages, etc., in disregard or at the expense of others." There is a natural tendency in us all to be selfish, beginning in infancy. We observe this trait in tiny children who take things away from each other without a tinge of conscience, or gather up every toy in sight and claim them for their own without regard for another child who may be crying at the top of his voice. Children tend to grow out of this selfishness quite readily, partly because of the teachings of their parents, but more because of their experience in the world. They soon realize that they must lose their selfishness if they are to get along with other people.

The trouble is that most people lose only the amount of selfishness necessary to get by in the world. They learn to share, yield and give, because they know they must and will be criticized if they do not; but the main focus is still on themselves and their own comforts and advantages. Women, especially, are inclined to be selfish, thinking in terms of "my children, my house, my husband, my wardrobe, and my problems." Such a narrow concern leads to a selfish life.

Unselfishness is a willingness to give up one's own comfort or advantage for the benefit of someone else. There must be an element of *sacrifice* in a truly unselfish act. This means giving up some pleasure, comfort, time, money, material thing of value to you, or going to some trouble, risk, inconvenience, or out of your way for the benefit of someone else. There are acts which are imagined unselfish which in reality are not, such as giving away something you do not want or need, doing something which is little trouble or expense, giving a small donation to the church or poor, etc. These may be acts of kindness, but they are not truly unselfish acts since they do not require sacrifice. On the contrary, if you give something of your own which you like or need but which you recognize that someone esle needs even more than you do, or if you go to some trouble or inconvenience to help someone in need, these are truly unselfish acts.

As we become unselfish, not only does it enlarge our character, but it leads to a general spiritual growth. In fact, our spiritual growth is parallel to our growth in unselfishness. If we are growing to be more and more unselfish, then we are growing in spirit; but if we retain our selfish tendencies, then we fail to grow in spirit.

3. Humility

Humility is a freedom from pride or arrogance. One who is humble may have many virtues, talents and advantages, but realizes his own weaknesses, mistakes and limitations. A woman who is humble does not lift herself up in pride over her friends or associates, thinking she is better, smarter, or more fortunate than they. Although she may have some talent or advantage over them, she realizes her lack in other areas. She knows that others have qualities that she does not have. She also knows that although she may have abilities for which she can honestly be proud, she is far removed from the woman she ought to be, that there is still much more to overcome and to attain.

Humility is not, however, a groveling or self-effacing attitude in which one deliberately depreciates himself beyond justification, to quote from my husband's book, *Man of Steel and Velvet*. "It is not thinking of ourselves as less than we are, or more than we are, but just as we are. It is a correct estimation of ourselves as God sees us. Humility is not pretended modesty in which we control bragging for the purpose of impressing others. There must be a quality within which causes one to truly feel his own limitations and weaknesses.

"The Savior set a perfect example of humility. Although He was the chosen Son of God, having no sin, and was able to overcome all things, yet He lived among the common people and dined with sinners. Although His disciples worshipped Him, He did not rise above them in an attitude of superiority. He demonstrated His humility when He bowed before them and washed their feet. By this act He impressed upon them in a dramatic way the requirements that men remain humble. How can anyone elevate himself above others when he remembers this action of the Savior?"

Humility can best be understood by reviewing its opposite—arrogance or pride. Arrogance is an ungrounded feeling of superiority over others and an inability to see one's own weaknesses or limitations. This fault can be commonly viewed in the following areas of life:

1. *Worldly Goods:* It is difficult for those who have money and material possessions to keep from being proud. There is a natural tendency for women who are dressed in expensive and stylish clothes and who drive the latest model automobile and live in luxurious surroundings to feel superior to women who have less. In some cases they take pleasure in parading their fine possessions before those who have little material wealth, for the purpose of making the other person feel inferior and thereby gaining a feeling of self-importance. This pride causes men and women to glory in the corruptible things of the earth and is a sign of moral and spiritual weakness.

2. *Knowledge:* Another source of unwholesome pride is knowledge, which can come from higher education, native ability, gifts, talents, and what some consider higher intelligence. A recognition of these special gifts or accomplishments is not wrong, but a feeling of superiority can be, and demonstrates a lack of humility. People who are highly intelligent and have great stores of knowledge are seldom proud and haughty about their abilities, but usually have a noticeable amount of humility. They realize that in spite of their talents, there is yet a vast sea of knowledge which is undiscovered and which they may feel limited to explore. They recognize the greatness of those who have gone before them and those in the future who may yet discover knowledge that would dwarf the present-day accomplishments. They live in between a realization of their own contributions and an awareness of their limitations. They also realize that others in their own way know far more about certain subjects than they. Their knowledge, great as it may be, is limited to specific fields.

3. *Humility in righteousness:* There is a tendency to be lifted up in pride because of the goodness of our lives. We may be making an honest effort to live a pure and wholesome life, to hold to high standards and overcome weaknesses. When we compare ourselves to others who do not appear to be making an effort according to our terms, we are naturally tempted to feel superior to them. To feel

182

humble in this situation is extremely difficult, but is a real mark of character. The thing to do is to tell ourselves that "we are no judge of a person's true worth." This person may now appear to be weak and irresponsible, but he may yet live a life more worthwhile than our own. He may have hidden qualities that have not yet come to life or been brought to the test. Also, we must consider the person's background. He, or she, may not have had the advantages of proper training. They may not have been inspired by good parents and other family members, to a better way of life. If given a proper chance or equal opportunities to your own, they may show their better side.

God has strongly condemned pride. We read in Proverbs 6:16-19: "These six things doth the Lord hate; yea seven are an abomination to him; A proud look, a lying tongue, and hands that shed innocent blood, an heart that deviseth wicked imaginations, feet that be swift in running to mischief, a false witness that speaketh lies, and he that soweth discord among brethren." It is significant that pride is described as an abomination to God and listed in company with lying, wicked imaginations and even murder.

Did you know that lack of humility can lead to a critical attitude? It follows, then, that humility can cure criticism. First, why do we criticize? There seems to be a tendency to enjoy faultfinding since it may serve as an ego builder for the one criticizing. This is particularly true if the fault in question is not one he has himself. There is also a tendency to demean a person of real *importance* in effort to elevate oneself. Or, one may criticize in an effort to actually help another person, to encourage better habits of living and greater happiness. If one's motive is actually to point out a better way, we must realize that this is the poorest way of helping someone. Instead of responding to the criticism, the natural tendency is to withdraw or to even become rebellious.

When we are tempted to be critical of someone, we can keep ourselves humble by remembering our own faults and imperfections. We may be superior to the person in some ways, but not all. As a total person, we are unlikely to be better than they. At least we are in no position to judge another person's worth. True humility brings with it the qualities of patience, forgiveness, acceptance and appreciation. With these qualities it will be impossible to feel critical.

183

True humility is one of the most essential elements of a worthy character. All of the really great people in this life have been humble, regardless of their position or outstanding qualities. They have been able to see themselves in a true light, have been able to recognize their greatness, and yet have acknowledged their weaknesses and limitations. No one is so great or good that he has no need of humility.

4. Honesty

It is difficult to say which of the virtues are the most important, but honesty is certainly one of them. One cannot lead a moral and wholesome life if one is not honest. Most of us have been trained in the basics of honesty in that we would not think of stealing, cheating, or telling bold-faced lies. These standards, however, do not necessarily make us an honest person, for we may be dishonest in the more subtle forms.

Some of the more obscure forms of dishonesty are such things as lying about a child's age to save fare in public transportation, a movie or the circus, returning items to a store under false pretenses, buying items wholesale by deceptive means, failure to leave identification for a damaged car, making excuses which are not entirely true, exaggerating the truth, failing to return money or goods which do not belong to us or which have been given to us by mistake, taking pay for jobs we did not complete or earn, giving false reasons for mistakes or bad behavior, and many more.

If you will think about these things you will see that this type of dishonesty is caused by *fear*—the fear of humiliation, embarrassment, or loss of money, comforts or goods. In order to overcome these dishonest tendencies, it is important first to gain some moral courage, so that these fears can be overcome. Then, one has to develop a sense of values and be convinced that honesty is worth far more than material goods, comforts, or our personal pride. To be honest in spite of any inconvenience or embarrassment to us is the attitude of a wholesome person who lives a worthy life. There is an old statement, "Do what is right and let the consequences follow." This is the frame of mind necessary for a person who is determined to live an honest life at all costs. And whatever the temporary "consequences" may be, the overall results of an honest life will be rewarding a thousandfold, not only for the strength of character gained, but for the well formed life that comes as a reward.

5. Chastity

Chastity means to be sexually pure, to not indulge in sexual relations with anyone to whom you are not legally wed, or to not engage in immoral sexual practices. The unchaste commit *fornication, adultery* and *homosexuality.* Fornication is the act of having sexual relations when unmarried; adultery is the act of sexual relations by a married person with someone other than his own wife or husband; homosexuality is to have sexual attraction, feelings, or engage in sexual practices with one of the same sex. To be sexually unchaste is called *sexual immorality.*

Sexual immorality is an old problem which dates back to the beginning of time. The prophets throughout the ages have cried out against it, warning the people of dangers involved. This practice continues in present society, sometimes under the name "the new morality." In reality, it is "the old immorality." The only thing new about it is that those who engage in it are pleading for society to accept their sins as "proper conduct," to ease their burning conscience. Past generations have accepted their sins as sins.

This new morality claims that there is no harm in sexual immorality if these intimacies are practiced between two consenting adults who receive satisfaction from it. They blame society for the feeling of guilt imposed upon them and are urging society to accept these evil practices to ease the pain of an outraged conscience and are ignoring the real harm that comes to themselves and to society because of promiscuous sex. Homosexuals also are seeking this acceptance for their sins. The widespread question seems to be "what harm is there in sexual immorality?"

Harm in Sexual Immorality

1. *Sin in Eyes of God:* Thou shalt not commit adultery was given to Moses for his people and written in tablets of stone. This instruction was reinforced in scripture many times. Throughout Bible history sexual immorality was considered a sin of great gravity and in some

periods punishable by death. The punishment is no longer death, but in God's eyes the sin is just as serious.

2. *Distraction and Deviation:* Sexual sin is a distraction to the individual, to a man in his work and to a woman in her devotion to her family. As the interest and energies are focused upon immorality, the responsibilities of life are neglected. Neglect of important work, neglect of family, can lead to failure in many areas of life.

3. *Damaged Relationships:* Attachments formed in promiscuous sex, especially by the woman, can lead to damaged relationships, broken homes and family ties. Oh, how many homes immorality has broken. In communities where "swinging" has been practiced (sexual parties of several married couples), whole neighborhoods have been disrupted resulting in broken homes and families. The damage has been awesome.

4. *Emotional Illness:* We live under spiritual laws which emanate from God. Whether we understand these laws or not does not free us from ill effects when these laws are violated. When we commit an immoral act, we come into conflict with spiritual laws, resulting in a feeling of guilt, pained consciences and emotional distress. I again quote the words of psychiatrist Dr. Max Levine, referred to in the last chapter. "There cannot be emotional health in the absence of high moral standards."

When immorality is committed over a period of time, the conscience can become callous, in which case the emotional pain is greatly reduced. However, the numbing of the conscience destroys the finer, more noble elements of the spirit. And, as the conscience is eased, it ceases to function as a warning, leaving the individual free to indulge in other sins, one sin provoking another.

5. *Lose the Spirit of God:* Those who commit immoral acts will be cut off from the spirit of God. The Holy Scriptures warn, "If any shall commit adultery in their hearts, they shall not have the spirit, but shall deny the faith and shall fear." Being cut off from communication with our Heavenly Father is a major loss. The spirit of God is greatly needed to guide us to a successful life, to help us make wise decisions, lay sound plans, and use good judgment. When we lose the spirit, we are left to grope along life's path alone. This can bring failure in all areas of living.

6. *Eternal Punishment:* We read in 1 Cor. 6:9, "Know ye not that the unrighteous shall not inherit the

kingdom of God? Be not deceived; neither fornicators, nor idolators, nor adulterers, nor effeminate, nor abusers of themselves with mankind." The initial day of judgment at the Second Coming of our Lord Christ, as recorded in Mal. 3:5, "will be a swift witness ... against the adulterers and they shall be burned as stubble." Why God has placed such severe punishments on this particular sin may not be entirely clear to many, but in His noble purposes, which are to bring about the happiness, development and eternal life of man He follows undeviating principle. In emphasizing the next point I would again like to quote from my husband's book, *Man of Steel and Velvet:*

7. *Downfall of Nations:* "The greatest threat of any country lies in immorality, and especially in sexual immorality. Like the columns of the temple of Gaza which Samson pulled down, causing the entire temple to collapse, so will immorality lead to the weakening and eventual destruction of an entire civilization. Sexual immorality was the principle cause of the disintegration of the Roman Empire, Greece, Persia, Babylonia, and the cities of Sodom and Gomorrah, and many others. It is the greatest threat in America today as well as many other countries and supersedes all other problems. It does, in fact, create most of them. If for no other reason than love of country and love of life should we avoid immorality and run from it as the greatest enemy of mankind. It will tear from us all that is near and dear."

In addition to the sins of adultery, fornication and homosexuality, there are other sexual immoralities. Related are the sins of pornographic literature, sensual movies and stageplays, and sensual thoughts. These, too, bring discord to the spirit of the individual. Some justify by saying, "We must know what is going on in the world." But in becoming familiar with these evils, they are subject to the same negative effects. When they interfere with the mechanism of the spirit by transgressing spiritual laws, they bring discord to themselves. If beautiful music, art, literature, and the beauties of nature can affect mankind favorably and enhance the spirit, then bad music, literature and art can affect the spirit in a damaging way.

6. Patience

There are four ways we need patience:

1. *Patience with People:* There is no better place to

learn patience with people than in the home, dealing with our own family. Little children do such things as put gum in their hair, spill pins on the shag carpet, bring in mud on their shoes, or quarrel with each other. When they are teen-agers, they have a new set of problems, such as leave their room in a mess, talk on the phone too long, or don't eat right. The husband may be late for dinner or neglect his yard work. Facing these situations with calm is a mark of a virtuous woman. There are two things a woman can do to help develop patience. First, *"make allowances for these situations"* and count them as "daily living"; and second, *"minimize problems."* Let me give an example which illustrates both. "A little girl spilled fingernail polish on her white bedspread and ran to her mother in tears. Instead of the mother becoming upset, she said, calmly, 'Well, honey, we have lived through worse things than this, haven't we.' "

2. *Patience with Responsibility*: The home is a place to develop this virtue also—cooking three meals a day, washing that never ends, housecleaning that keeps repeating itself. When a woman has patiently performed these tasks for years, she is certainly a better woman because of it. Women show lack of patience by complaining about their work or failing to do it. Lack of patience is the reason that so many women reject their homemaking role and seek relief outside the home in careers. But in so doing, they deny themselves the opportunity of personal growth of character.

3. *Patience with Desires:* It requires patience to work for the fulfillment of certain goals or desires. It may be a new home, furniture, or a vacation. Many women "want it now" and fill their desires at the expense of their family. They may make demands of their husbands or go to work to get these things for themselves.

Or, a woman may want time, time of her own to develop talents or for other personal desires. If she is raising a family, she may feel this time will never come. Because of lack of patience, she may try to do everything *now*, denying herself the enjoyment of her present experience. How unwise. The time will come when her little ones will be gone and she will have time on her hands. As Shakespeare has said, "How poor are they who have not patience to wait."

And when we do have time, it takes great patience to develop talents or create works of art. I remember watching a lady making a hooked rug. I asked her how long she expected it would take to complete it. "Oh, about a year," she said. My comment was that I would never begin something I could not finish in a day or so. About a year later I conceived the idea of writing this book. I learned patience in the endless hours and even years it took for its completion. We can learn patience by watching nature in her methods of reaching her objectives. If you will take a trip to a limestone cave, you will see the beautiful patterns built by drops of water falling from the ceiling. It takes centuries to produce this beauty.

4. *The Brighter Day:* There is another kind of patience we need—the patience to look for a brighter day. Periods of our life may be filed with sorrow, discouragement or disappointments. We should have the patience to "let this time pass by," and to know that life has its cloudy moments, but if we live right principles, a brighter day will inevitably follow.

7. Moral Courage

Moral courage is the courage to do that which is *morally right,* or to follow correct principles at the risk of consequences. These consequences are such things as criticism, humiliation, loss of friends, loss of prestige or position, loss of money, or even bodily harm. It is one thing to set standards for ourselves and quite another to have the moral courage to be true to these standards in the face of unpleasant consequences.

One of the most outrageous examples of a lack of moral courage took place in America about 1967, when a young woman was murdered while a number of people stood by watching, and failed to come to her rescue. They did not want to become involved because of danger to themselves. Contrast this with the Good Samaritan who, when he found the wounded man on the road to Jericho, nursed his wounds and saved his life, despite robbers nearby who could endanger his life also.

It is our duty to defend another when we see them abused, or see someone defame their character or spread malicious gossip about them. It is always easier to not want to get involved—to stay at arm's length from someone else's problem, rather than to defend what is just and right. We should also "take a stand" when we observe some moral wrong such as cheating, stealing or lying. No one likes to get involved, but if wrong can be brought to light and justice rendered, then we should not hesitate to take action.

Another situation is when a woman has a husband who is immoral and having an affair with another woman. The wife may lack the moral courage to "take a stand" and call him to task for his immorality. She may fear that she will lose him, or that her marriage will end in divorce and she will be left with a family to support. Of course, in Fascinating Womanhood we teach the wife to first look to herself to see if she has made mistakes which drove him away; but after these are corrected, if the husband continues to be immoral, she should take a stand with him. This sometimes takes considerable courage because of the reasons mentioned.

Sometimes there are serious moral or political issues which come before us. These could be such things as abortion, sex education, the population explosion, racial problems or sexual immorality. We would have convictions which would lead us to defend or oppose some of these issues. Our own viewpoint, however, may be unpopular in the community. If we are attending a P.T.A. meeting or an open forum where we have a chance to express ourselves, how many of us have the moral courage to speak out or how many may hesitate due to fear of criticism or being tagged as a radical?

There is a tendency for young people to lack moral courage. For example, a young person may determine not to drink or smoke, but when friends pressure him to do so, he may lack the moral courage to say "no" because he fears loss of friends or being "in with the group." A young person may also determine to not be sexually immoral, but may relinquish his standards to save a relationship. Older people are not above lowering standards due to fear of criticism or losing friends.

If we have committed a wrong or made a mistake, it may take great moral courage to be honest, to tell the truth, when our confession would be humiliating to us or cause us a loss of money, position or advantage. I am reminded of all the people who have been aligned in courts of justice. How many of them have had the courage to tell the truth? And how many of us who have committed offenses or moral wrongs have had the courage to speak the truth?

It takes moral courage to have a family, not only

because of the work involved, but because of criticism of large families in present times. It takes courage to say "no" to people who try to occupy your time. For example, you may determine that you want to spend more time with your children or with your homemaking responsibilities, and you place these things in top priority. But friends may pressure you to spend time with them, to do things you do not want to do and which you may consider a waste of time. You may lack the courage to say "no." Or someone may waste long spans of your time talking on the phone, and you may lack the courage to cut the conversation off. In summary, we can say that it takes moral courage to defend the abused, take a stand against moral wrong and bring justice to bear, express our convictions when they are not popular, hold to our ideals or principles, admit our wrongs or mistakes, do the things we feel we should do and not let others push us around.

8. Benevolent Service

There is nothing which will so enrich a woman's life and make her a better person and a better mother as giving benevolent service beyond her own family circle. This virtue was extolled in the Bible in the description of the perfect woman ... "she stretcheth out her hand to the poor, yea, she reacheth forth her hands to the needy." (Proberbs 31:20) A woman's first obligation is in the home, building a happy marriage and family life, but giving beyond this is also part of her duty. We all share a certain social responsibility for the urgent problems of society. Especially should the fortunate and the morally strong assist the less fortunate and the weak. There are three keys to true benevolence I would like to stress:

1. *Perceive the Needs of Others:* It will do little good to do a thousand things for someone, if we fail them in their most important needs. Each one of us needs to develop a *sensitive awareness* of the real needs of other people. We should be able to detect the needs of a small child, or notice the downcast eyes of a teen-ager who is in trouble, or the housewife who is overworked, going without or in some way facing trying problems. This sensitivity usually arises out of a real compassion, wherein we are moved to deep emotion when we see the struggles and suffering of our fellow men. If we value human life, we will be moved to action when we observe the oppressed or

discouraged. Learning to be aware of real problems that people face and in which ways we can be of greatest service is essential to benevolence.

2. *Give When the Need Occurs:* Many real needs in life are urgent and must be filled at the moment. If we wait until a more convenient time, we may miss the golden opportunity to be of real service. We must be willing to rearrange our schedules, stop in the middle of our work, or switch plans to meet an urgent need of someone else.

3. *Sacrifice:* Benevolence requires a willingness to be inconvenienced, to give up one's own comforts, or to go to extra trouble for the benefit of another person. How often do we hear the statement, "Oh, I hope this was no trouble for you," or "I hope this did not inconvenience you too much." In truth, we *should* be willing to go to extra trouble for another, for without this sacrifice there is really no benevolent service.

In rendering benevolent service, I am not suggesting that a woman neglect her overall responsibility in the home. There may, however, be temporary neglect if there is to be giving and sharing. And other members of the household will be expected to make sacrifices, to go without and be inconvenienced as they support their mother in stretching forth her hand to the needy. But in so sacrificing, their lives will be enriched, also. Only by setting an example of benevolence can we teach our children what "the gospel of love" is all about.

If you will remember in the story of *Little Women,* on Christmas morning the family prepared a delicious breakfast for themselves with their favorite food, "popovers." Just as they were about ready to serve, the mother asked her daughters to help her gather up the food, put it in a basket and take it to a poor and sick family. The disappointed girls reluctantly complied with the mother's request, but in following her unselfish example and in making their own portion of the sacrifice, they were benefited.

One day my own little daughter complained about my giving some of my time and energy for a worthy cause. She said, "Why can't you be more like Mrs. Carter? She pays attention to her children all the time." This hurt me for a moment, and I had to stop and weigh out what I was doing with careful thought. Then I thought of Mrs. Carter. She was truly a devoted mother. She gave her children the best birthday parties in the neighborhood and the most lavish Christmases. They took lessons of all kinds, and so she was always driving them places or picking them up. Whenever there was a community project where children were involved, hers participated. Never have I seen a woman lavish more time and devotion on a family. And I, too, wished I could be more like Mrs. Carter. But, I could not set aside the importance of the service I was rendering for the benefit of mankind.

So I sat down and talked to my little girl and tried to explain to her the meaning of service. I told her about three mothers: Mother "A," I said, loved her children; but she got a little bored tending them all the time. She felt she deserved to get away from them part of the time, so she would go shopping for long hours, golfing, go out of town on vacations or do other things she wanted to. Sometimes the children got a little lonely and even felt neglected, but they felt she really loved them.

Mother "B," I said, loved her children very much. She spent most of her time with them. They had the best birthday parties in town and the best Christmases. She took them places, laughed with them, played with them, took them on long walks or bicycling. (I was really describing Mrs. Carter.)

Mother "C," I explained, really loved her children, but she loved other children, too, and other people and wanted to help them with their problems. She took good care of her children, spent a lot of time with them and did all of the really important things for them. But, she shared some of her time with others—helping those in real need. Then, I asked my daughter which mother she thought was living the most Christian life. She could immediately understand the meaning of service and has supported me in benevolent causes ever since, sometimes at considerable sacrifice.

The real enemy to benevolence is "self-centeredness," or an over-concern for our own little nest—our children, our house, our husband or our problems. There are some who derive all of their satisfaction in life from their own family circle. I knew a couple who loved to garden. They spent most of their time working in their yard and created a beautiful array of plants, flowers and garden details. One day they decided to sell their house and moved into an apartment. They felt lost without the garden and really could not find enough to occupy their time. So, they bought another house, planted another garden and were content. They gave no thought to the needs of others in their self-centered lives.

Strange that some people must fill in their time when there is so much that needs doing. We are surrounded by people who are in desperate circumstances, needing a helping hand, material assistance, a word of wisdom or encouragement. I received a letter from a young mother in which she reflected back on earlier hard years. "Both of our children in their infant years were sickly and ran temperatures. Our little daughter had an eye defect and almost died from a high fever and severe convulsions. After this I was scared to leave the children. My husband and I needed desperately to get away for a short time, but neither my mother nor my husband's mother wanted the responsibility for their welfare. We just could not afford a nurse nor would I leave them with a young baby sitter." It seems that we all have a responsibility to search for those in need and even to pray that they will be made known to us, and that somehow we will develop the wisdom and character to help them in a way that is needed. And in this way we will follow the admonition of the Apostle Paul when he said, "Bear ye one another's burdens and so fulfill the law of Christ." (Gal. 6:2)

9. Self-Dignity

A woman with self-dignity has a proper respect for herself, never considers herself as inferior to another, nor will she allow anyone to treat her as an inferior or reduce her to an inferior position. This self-dignity is not something we can superficially achieve by deciding we are going to respect ourselves. It arises from a genuine feeling of self-worth based upon a worthy character and a worthy life. It would be impossible for a weak, lazy, irresponsible person to have a genuine self-respect. But the main point I wish to stress is this: There are people who *do* live worthy lives so that they should have a proper respect and self-dignity, and yet they lack this quality such as in the following ways:

1. *Appearance:* The woman who neglects her figure, or her hair or her clothes or make-up, will naturally be put to a disadvantage with her associates and cannot help but feel somewhat inferior. If she is to maintain a real self-dignity, or feeling of queenliness, she will have to work to give this impression, both to herself and to others. Often

just trimming ourselves down and dressing ourselves up immediately helps our feeling of self-respect.

2. *Depreciate Oneself:* Each woman is a child of God and as such owes a certain respect for inherent characteristics. It is wrong for her to discredit herself by pointing out flaws such as lack of intelligence, lack of talent or physical defects. I have heard women depreciate themselves by saying, "Oh, I'm so stupid," or "My nose is too big," or "My hair is too stringy," or "My legs are too fat." These negative statements although they may have intended to portray humility, only reaffirm a woman's weak points, both in her mind and in the minds of her listeners, and indicate a personal disrespect.

3. *Being Too Servile:* A woman can show lack of self-dignity by making a slave of herself for her family. For example, she may be called upon to do this or that and is never known to hesitate or complain. And, although she is already overworked, her husband brings home some of his office work for her to do. Friends and relatives also impose, expecting her to tend their children, help them with sewing or do special favors, pushing work off onto her which rightly belongs to themselves. In her efforts to please others, she neglects important needs of her own. But, the surprising thing is that instead of being thanked for all of this, it is more or less expected, and she is treated with grudging toleration. Why? Let me take sides with the family and friends:

When we see a woman, queen of earth's creatures, transformed into a mechanical drudge, we can't help feeling a certain contempt for her for falling so far below our standards. In her slavery to others, she seems to be only paying a natural tribute of an inferior to her superiors and, accordingly, is undeserving of either thanks or respect. On the other hand, if a woman has a personal regard for her own worth and needs, then her efforts to take care of her family become a noble sacrifice, and she is admired for it. But, let's not misunderstand. No task should be regarded as too menial or too disagreeable for a woman to do in serving her family. Remember that the Savior knelt before his apostles and washed their feet, but he did so with great dignity and self-respect.

4. *Too Willing to Please:* A woman may strive earnestly to please her husband while neglecting her own personal needs. She may cater to his whims and desires, save her nickles and dimes for special luxuries for him,

always remember his birthday (while he usually forgets hers), and approve of his luxurious spending and indulgences, while she goes without things she needs. A man never appreciates such sacrifices. She thinks too much of him and too little of herself. She has spoiled him, when a better relationship exists when the husband spoils the wife.

Once in a while almost all of us meet a person who strives valiantly to please us. They meet us with ingratiating smiles, listen eagerly every time we open our mouths, anticipate our every wish, laugh mirthfully at every joke, and magnify our every accomplishment. They humble themselves to the point that we are afraid they are going to "lick our hands"; and in spite of a hundred things they do for us deserving of gratitude, we can't help but dislike them for their lack of self-dignity—because they appear as our inferiors rather than our equals. Their fault lies in thinking too much of us and too little of themselves. We are glad to accept the approval of equals, but are little flattered by those who consider themselves our inferiors. If the person happens to be a woman, we can't help expecting her to respect herself as a human being, queen of all earth's creatures and the equal of every other human being.

5. *Easily Mistreated:* Another lack of self-dignity is to be easily pushed around, walked on or abused. It is not in human nature to respect those we can trample on, and men especially do not appreciate this deficiency in women. They admire women who have a little spunk and enough self-dignity to defend themselves. A later chapter will deal with this problem and outline the right way to handle these situations in a way that will preserve self-dignity and strengthen a relationship with a man.

10. *The Gentle, Tender Quality*

The gentle, tender quality is a combination of several virtues—understanding, sympathy, benevolence, compassion, forgiveness, patience, long-suffering, kindness and love, or any of those virtues which soften the spirit of a woman. This quality is vital to our ideal of Angela Human and is the foundation of true femininity. We study femininity as a "human" trait, but in reality it has its roots in character.

I would like to stress that gentleness promotes feminine charm, whereas lack of it destroys it. A woman who has a hard or critical character may have perfect physical features, yet there will be a hard expression about the mouth, a coldness in the eyes, an irritation to the otherwise fair forehead or a bitter tone in the voice that spoils her beauty. The shadowy hint of a harsh character will mar the beauty of an otherwise perfect face. On the other hand, the woman with a gentle character will have a serenity in the face, a softness in the eyes and expressions and a calmness to the voice and manner that is appealing. "Beauty is the mark God set on virtue."

I have known some gentle women in my lifetime. They have been soft spoken, kind and patient under the most trying circumstances, and created such a spirit of peace and harmony in the household that I almost weep when I think of them. These are the angels men speak of in their memoirs, whether they are wives, mothers or sisters. They have earned the deepest respect from their families even when their gentle dispositions seem to be the only thing remarkable about them. But who is ever moved to tears when they remember a woman who has been harsh, critical or impatient? She may have done a thousand things for us worthy of appreciation but we cannot erase from our memory her disagreeable disposition.

11. Responsibility

A quality of true character is to have *responsibility*—to do our part in the world's work, in that portion which rightly belongs to us. Those women who can roll up their sleeves and take hold of the jobs that need to be done, no matter how unpleasant or tiring, and who will do so without whimper or complaint, show signs of real character. Let us consider for a moment the woman at home, scrubbing floors, doing dishes, tending the children, washing diapers or cooking the meals. She may enjoy this domestic work, as many women do. But what if she does not? The woman with a keen sense of responsibility does not ask herself if she enjoys her work or wants to do it. She realizes that here is a job that must be done, that the job belongs to her, and she must see that it is done. Whether she enjoys it or not is beside the point. Her children or servants may assist her, but she is responsible and has a certain pride in filling this obligation.

The woman who fails to assume her domestic duties

shows a weakness in character—laziness and irresponsibility. If she has failed to do her work because it was boring, unpleasant or tiring, this is not a valid justification. The job belongs to her, and she alone is responsible. Failure on her part is a serious dereliction of duty. Our responsibilities also extend beyond the home to any job that a woman assumes in the community, the church or as a volunteer. These duties are secondary, however, and should never be filled at the expense of the greater home responsibilities.

Is Good Character Beyond Your Reach?

Do not think that a fine character is beyond your reach. Your character is not fixed or unchangeable. It was made to grow. We never know what is in our character—it is always more or less an unexplored mine. We are familiar with only a few surface details which trick us into imagining we know ourselves; but let a great crisis come, let us be thrown upon our own resources, let a dear one meet with disaster, or let a great responsibility be thrust upon us and there can arise from the unexplored depths, qualities of character which neither ourselves nor others ever suspected.

"But," you may insist, "I am just an ordinary human being with serious faults. I cannot aspire to 'the living form of a benediction.' I can never hope, with my ordinary character, to be an angel and to arouse such reverence and adoration as Deruchette or Amelia." But, are you so far from being an angel as you think? You may not have done anything in the past deserving of particular reverence, but how do you know what you can do in the future? Look at the millions of ordinary girls who have become our world's extraordinary mothers; or wives who have proved to be the inspiration of their husband's success and greatness. These angels were once ordinary girls whom no one particularly recognized as noble in character. They only *became* great mothers and wives. Each one of us has within us the seeds of fine character if we but believe in ourselves and work to bring it into being. In the words of Ella Wheeler Wilcox:

Trust in thine own untried capacity
as thou wouldst trust in God Himself.

Thy soul is but an emanation from the whole.
Thou dost not dream what forces lie in thee,
Vast and unfathomed as the boundless sea.

How to Acquire a Worthy Character

There are many other virtues of character. These are only some of the most essential. You can acquire a worthy character in the same way that you would acquire any other accomplishment, by diligent effort. However, with worthy character, it would be difficult to make any measure of progress without the assistance of earnest and daily *prayer*. The goal is too high and the forces of opposition too strong to gain any real success without the guidance of God from day to day. You may be able to become a good pianist, a good tennis player or public speaker by persistence and exercise alone, but the perfection of a wonderful character is not entirely within our reach without faith in God, and His divine assistance.

How to Quickly Fall from Your Pedestal

1. Lower your standards.
2. Be critical of your husband.
3. Raise your voice at your children.
4. Be faultfinding of others.
5. Neglect your housekeeping.
6. Neglect your appearance.
7. Fail to stick on your diet.
8. Be selfish and self-centered.
9. Acquire a proud look in the presence of the less fortunate.

Essentials of Character

1. Self-mastery
2. Unselfishness
3. Humility
4. Honesty
5. Chastity
6. Patience
7. Moral Courage
8. Benevolent Service
9. Self-dignity

10. The Gentle, Tender Quality
11. Responsibility

Assignment

Make a self-analysis of your character. List your strong points. List your weak points.

14

The Domestic Goddess

A "Domestic Goddess" is a woman who is a good homemaker. She keeps a clean, orderly home, has well behaved children, cooks delicious meals and is successful in her overall career in the home. But, the term "Goddess" implies something more than these domestic achievements. It relates to the woman herself, indicating a glory which she has added to the home which causes her to appear as a goddess. In other words, a woman may achieve success as a homemaker and yet fail to be a goddess. The Domestic Goddess must, of course, be a successful homemaker, but beyond this accomplishment she gives a spirit to the home which adds a special quality to her calling as a homemaker.

The quality of the Domestic Goddess is found in our studies of Agnes, Amelia and Deruchette. Agnes was as "staid and discreet a housekeeper as the old house could have." Amelia was a "kind, smiling, tender little domestic goddess whom men are inclined to worship." And Deruchette's occupation was "only to live her daily life." Hugo compared her to a little bird that "flits from branch to branch, or rather from room to room."

Qualities of the Domestic Goddess

The Domestic Goddess serves faithfully as the understanding wife, the devoted mother, and the successful homemaker. She is skilled in the feminine arts of cooking, sewing, cleaning, organizing, managing a household, caring for children, handling money wisely, and a few other things. Not only does she do these jobs, but she *does them well*, going beyond the call of duty and doing more than is required.

She is *a good manager of time and values*. She is not necessarily the most *perfect* housekeeper in town, or the best cook, or even the most devoted mother. But, she does succeed in her *overall* responsibility in the home, dividing her time and devotion between her husband, children and homemaking, putting the emphasis where it counts the most—at the moment. Of course, she *may* be the best housekeeper in town, or the best cook. It all depends upon her situation. But a woman with a family is not a Domestic Goddess if she spends most of her time cleaning house while she neglects the needs of her family. On the other hand, if she plays with her children most of the day while her housework is neglected, she is not ideal. She must balance her time where needed.

The Domestic Goddess adds some *feminine touches* to her homemaking—gingham curtains, a wooden bowl of fruit, soft pillows, a cozy rug at the door, flowers, a row of plates above a cross beam, cheerful wallpaper, and other things that give a "homey" feeling to a house. She adds feminine touches to her meals, also—cheerful tablecloths and dishes, and delicious aromas to her cooking. I have talked with many men who long remember the aroma of their mother's cooking—homemade bread baking, onions frying, cinnamon rolls, beef stew, and many others.

The Domestic Goddess has another important quality: She gives a *warmth* to her household. It is she who makes a *house* a *home*, filling it with understanding, love and happiness. She is the central figure in the home, its heart, its "tree of life." She radiates this warmth to her household. Deruchette, you will remember, radiated warmth. "Her presence lights the home; her approach is like a cheerful warmth; she passes by and we are content; she stays awhile and we are happy." She also "sheds joy around," and "casts light upon dark days." Without Deruchette, the house would have been an empty shell. This warm presence is what every man needs when he returns from his work and what every child needs when he returns from school. The home is their refuge, their source of comfort and understanding.

A Domestic Goddess looks with *pride* on her position in the home. To her it is a place of honor and importance. She is filling a function that no one else can fill. Creating a happy marriage and family life and raising well-adjusted, honorable children are the greatest contributions she can make to the well being of society. And even though she does nothing more than to just "live her daily life," she will be doing something worthwhile.

The Domestic Goddess is also *happy* in her homemaking role. She is not bored. She is not looking for some challenging achievement in the world of men for fulfillment. Her glory is the success of her husband, the happiness of her children, and her overall success in the home. She may serve humanity in some additional ways outside the home, but she is not dependent upon this as a means of fulfillment. In summary, we can say that the Domestic Goddess has the following qualifications:

Qualifications of the Domestic Goddess

1. Does her jobs well, beyond the call of duty.
2. Is a good manager of time and values.
3. Adds feminine touches to her homemaking.
4. Adds warmth to her household.
5. Has pride in her role in the home.
6. Is happy in her role, is fulfilled.

How to Find Happiness in Homemaking

An essential quality of the domestic goddess is her ability to find joy and satisfaction in her work. This satisfaction comes as a result of her attitude towards her work and her ability to control her life's activities, as I have expressed in the following thoughts:

1. *Attitude Towards Drudgery:* Just as we learn to accept people as part good and part bad, we must accept our work in the home as part enjoyable and part unpleasant. There are some jobs that are just plain drudgery, and certainly not joy-producing. We can't expect a job as varied as homemaking to be all pleasant. But if we look around us, we find that almost every occupation has its boring, monotonous tasks, and it is best to face them for what they are, necessary responsibility. It can be insulting to an intelligent woman to tell her she must find joy in washing diapers and scrubbing floors. Her happiness comes in the over-all accomplishment.

Many of our duties, however, are a source of real enjoyment. Caring for children, cooking delicious meals, and cleaning the house can all be a happy experience. Some women delight in scrubbing the floors, washing, ironing, and cleaning closets. Actually little of our work is unpleasant, but when it seems so to you, it is best to face it with an honest attitude, realizing that the world's work consists of a certain amount of drudgery.

2. *Don't Become Crowded for Time:* If you want to enjoy homemaking, don't become involved in too many

outside activities. One of the most time-consuming is assisting the husband in any part of his masculine role, especially if the wife works at full time employment. Or she may assist her husband at his place of business or even assume some of his home duties, such as yard work, painting, handling money problems or accounts.

Also, don't become involved in too many activities such as clubs, service organizations, self-improvement programs, education classes, lessons, etc. Although these programs are a very fine thing if you have the time for them, if they consume more time than you can afford, then they may rob you of the time you need to enjoy homemaking.

Activities within the home may also crowd you for time to do the more essential work. Too much time spent talking on the phone, browsing through magazines, watching T.V. or even extensive sewing or canning can cause you to be short on time and in a last-minute rush for the important things. When such is the case, it is difficult to enjoy your work. *When any outside activities crowd you for time to do your work, so that you hurry through your jobs just to get them over with, it is difficult to enjoy them.*

If you will observe little girls as they play house, you will notice that they do not hurry to get their work finished. They will fold and refold the little doll blankets and when they have tucked them neatly around the doll in the crib, will take them all off and start all over again. They are so unconscious of time that they enjoy what they are doing. I believe that our natural instinct is to enjoy the domestic work, as little girls do, but that "being crowded for time" has robbed us of this enjoyment. If you find yourself saying, "I do not have time to play house as little girls do," then ask yourself what you are doing that is more important than your joy in homemaking.

I do not wish to imply that we live self-centered lives, focusing only upon our own comforts and satisfactions. Giving of ourselves in the service of others is a sacred obligation and brings us satisfaction in return. But, there is much time wasted on foolishness, and therefore it is wise to measure each activity for its value, always placing home duties and their enjoyment as of major importance.

3. *The Second Mile: If you will find joy in your tasks, do them well.* This doctrine was taught hundreds of years ago by Jesus when He said, "If anyone compel thee to go one mile, go with him twain." Going the second mile,

or beyond the call of duty, lifts the burden out of work and makes it seem easy and enjoyable. To do well those tasks which are the common lot of all is truest greatness and in return brings satisfaction and happiness.

Many women fail to find happiness in homemaking because they go only the first mile. They give only the bare stint of requirement—just enough to get by. They feed and clothe the family and keep the house reasonably clean, but not an ounce more. Their meals are all "quick and easy," and then they are off to some outside diversion to try to find their satisfaction from life. No woman who ever gave just enough to get by ever enjoyed homemaking. There is no joy in the first mile. You have to give more than is required to enjoy any responsibility. This is what the Saviour taught when He said, "He who loseth his life for my sake, shall surely find it." Only when we lose ourselves in an important responsibility, not thinking of our own reward, but giving wholeheartedly, beyond the call of duty, do we find real enjoyment from it.

Fundamentals of Good Homemaking

Often the difference between a good homemaker and a poor one is a matter of following basic principles which lead to success. The following are some of the most fundamental principles which, if followed, will lead to a clean, uncluttered, well organized household:

1. *Concentrate:* The management of a household requires concentration. One cannot daydream or ponder problems and at the same time expect duties will be performed with efficiency. There is some work like ironing, cleaning windows, and doing dishes in which daydreaming is possible, but most of our work requires thought as well as hands, especially organizing and meal preparation. So, put other things out of your mind and concentrate on the jobs at hand. What is often interpreted as lack of homemaking ability is usually mental laziness.

2. *Simplify:* You cannot become a good housekeeper if you have *too many things,* such as too much furniture, too many dishes, unnecessary clothes, old papers and magazines, too many toys, objects or ornaments, or old treasures which are handed down from generation to generation. "Priceless objects," you may say. They may be valuable if they are useful or add beauty to the home; but they are not priceless if they make life difficult. For

greatest efficiency, households should have only enough goods to serve the family. Anything more only clutters and burdens the homemaker.

If you have a cluttered household and would like to turn it into an organized one, the first step is to simplify by getting rid of things you do not need. A good suggestion is the following: Set aside a day for "whittling life down to the bone." Get three boxes and label one "throw away," one "give away," and one "can't decide." Go through all of your cupboards and drawers quickly, keeping only things you know are essential and discarding the rest in the three boxes. Also consider all objects sitting on open shelves, tables, or hanging on walls. When you have covered your entire household, put the "can't decide" box (or boxes) in the garage or attic and leave it there for about two months. In this time you will be able to see whether you have needed the items or not. Then, sort through the box when convenient.

In simplifying a household, remember a basic principle: Everything in a household should be either *useful* or *beautiful*. And you should have only *enough* useful and beautiful goods to serve your needs. In other words, an egg beater is useful and glasses are useful, but you do not need two egg beaters or forty glasses to serve your household. *Better to have too few than too many*. And, as for beautiful ornaments or pictures, not only should they be beautiful in themselves, but should enhance the beauty of your home. In other words, the home should not be a place to just "store" beautiful objects. And as for family heirlooms, art treasures and things of sentimental value, if they burden your life rather than enrich it, how can you justify their possession?

3. *Organize:* Basic good homemaking depends upon being organized. This means having a *place* for everything and a *time* for everything. If you have "simplified" your household as I have just described, then you should have a *place* for everything. But the important thing is to always put things back in that particular place. A household should be so well organized that you should be able to get up in the night, without turning on the light, and find something you need. This means that the dishes, bowls, glasses and pans should each have a place of their own and be put back in the same place.

As for organizing time, this should be less rigid and more human, but the following is recommended: 1) for *routine jobs,* work out *schedules*—weekly and occasional schedules. To work out these schedules, list all routine jobs of the household and then arrange them on the two schedules. 2) For *non-routine* jobs, follow a *calendar* or *dated diary.* In this, record phone calls, appointments, daily menus, and things to do which are non-routine. Also work in things on the occasional schedule. (The weekly schedule should be memorized.) I have produced a dated diary for women, especially designed to fill the above purpose. It has space for all of the above-mentioned and examples of weekly and occasional schedules. For information about this diary, called the *Domestic Goddess Planning Notebook,* write to Pacific Press, Santa Barbara, P.O. Box 219, Pierce City, MO 65723.

4. *Priorities:* Also important is to work out "wise priorities," or put *first things first.* This means to concentrate on the more essential jobs while placing as secondary those things of lesser importance. To arrange priorities, list your six most important homemaking responsibilities and then arrange them in order of importance. Consult your husband and children for their opinions. For example:

A. Appearance
B. Regular Meals on Time
C. House neat
D. Washing and ironing
E. Imperative Shopping
F. Auxiliary things:

Auxiliary jobs would be such things as care of children, doctors' appointments, transporting children to music lessons, scouts, etc. If there is an infant in the family, it would be in top priority, and small children would come high on the list. The next step would be to create a secondary list which would include such things as general cleaning, sewing and mending, training of children, time for self and others.

One of the most important things to remember in keeping priorities is to *avoid time wasters,* such as talking on the phone for long periods, sewing to excess, spending hours of time browsing through shops, and many more. These habits can cause a failure in following through on priorities. Some may justify these habits on the grounds that they enjoy them. Such may be the case, but if one determines to reach the high goals of the Domestic Goddess, such personal sacrifices will have to be made.

5. *Work:* Although you may concentrate, simplify, organize, and have your priorities well in mind, you will not reach success unless you are willing to work. Good homemaking requires effort, as does any worthy achievement. The only way to run a household is to roll up your sleeves, take the broom, and go to work.

6. *Make Him Comfortable:* With all of your perfection in homemaking, if you want to be a Domestic Goddess, let your husband be comfortable. Remember, *his home is his castle.* When he comes home, let him have the freedom to toss his coat on a chair, sit where he wants to sit and lie down on his own bed without concern for the spread. This does not mean that he be allowed to be slovenly to the point of imposing on you—but just to be comfortable in his own home. I knew a lady who made a grave mistake in this respect. No one was comfortable in her home! When guests were present, she followed them around picking up after them, straightening the pillows or rugs. Guests tolerated this treatment well enough, but her husband was a victim of this all the time. Finally he tired of this foolishness and divorced the lady. He married a woman who was the opposite. She was a good housekeeper, but allowed him to relax and be comfortable. In comparing the two women, he said, "The change in wives was like taking off a pair of tight shoes and putting on a pair of soft, comfortable slippers." So, allow your husband to relax, to stack papers on his desk, hang his diplomas on his walls, place his shoes under the bed if he wishes, and other personal freedoms. If you treat him like the king in his castle, *he will treat you like his queen.* Children are not in the same position as their father. They are subject to your instructions and training.

Motherhood

A quality of the Domestic Goddess is her love for children and her joy in bearing them and nurturing them. This is a natural instinct of the feminine woman. You do not have to teach her to be this way—it is *inborn.* She is like Rachel and Hannah of Biblical days who cried unto the Lord for children. Theirs was an inner yearning to fill the measure of their creation in bearing offspring.

The feminine woman also has a natural instinct to care for her little ones. She has an instinctive concern for their physical welfare, to see that they are properly fed and bathed, and would never allow them to go hungry, cold or unprotected if within her power to prevent it. She takes pride in their appearance, is gentle and loving, teaches them how to be happy, and offers them praise and understanding, giving them bread for their souls as well as their bodies.

Now how does a man view all of this? Men naturally respect women who delight in bearing children. The man himself may complain about this responsibility and even oppose the birth of more children, but he does not admire women who complain. Men admire women who respect their function and will not dishonor it by a negative attitude. How pained a man can feel if his wife complains, "Oh, I'm pregnant again." No matter how justified she may be, her remarks are *unwomanly*.

Meal Preparation

I wonder if women realize how very important meals are to husbands and children. Imagine how they feel as they come home hungry after a busy day, to be able to count on good wholesome meals as a regular part of family life. It is not necessary to have elaborate food, but it is highly important to have the meals *regular, on time,* and *taste good*. Beyond this, the wife has a responsibility for the health of her family in planning nourishing meals, but the family will expect them to taste good, regardless.

Of all household tasks other than the care of little children, the most urgent is feeding the family. Other things can wait, but meals are a daily demand. The best way to face this job is with the spirit of the second mile, going beyond the call of duty. You will not enjoy cooking if you do a halfhearted job—you have to achieve something good. This can be done by reading cookbooks, health books, and combining the ideas. Remember, it takes *time* to cook good meals. You cannot skimp by in a last-minute rush and expect good results. Also important is an attractive table setting, with a tablecloth if possible. This gives the "homey" feminine touch of the Domestic Goddess.

Unfortunately, there are many women who fail in meal preparation. They get by with "quick meals," with an emphasis on speed. They rely upon cold cuts, weenies, packaged mixes, macaroni, and other quick and easy foods. There are some families that do not have regular meals together—just piecing in between. A woman is far removed from being a Domestic Goddess, if she skimps by with such inferior meals. It takes a wholehearted effort to prepare meals that really please the family, and although we must balance this duty with all of the other demands made of us, when we achieve well balanced, delicious meals, we have added a very important quality to family life.

Housekeeping, a Matter of Character

You may never have thought of it before, but keeping the house clean, preparing meals, and running the household is a matter of character. *The woman who fails in these areas shows a weakness of character,* in the following ways:

1. *Self-centeredness:* Poor homemaking is usually traced to self-centeredness, wherein the wife thinks too much of her own comforts and pleasures, spends her time talking on the phone, watching T.V., primping, or just being lazy, rather than on things that would make her family more comfortable and happy.

2. *Lack of Organization:* Lack of order is a serious fault. God, who is our pattern of perfection, sets before us the work of His creations—a work which is a masterpiece of organization and system, from the human body to the planets in the heavens. He has said, "I am a God of order, not confusion." Failure to follow this eternal example indicates lack of character.

3. *Lack of Knowledge:* Poor homemaking may result from a lack of knowledge. This is understandable in the newly married. But, if a woman fails to *seek* knowledge where needed, this can be a serious weakness of character, just as it would be for a man to fail to seek knowledge needed to provide an adequate living. Knowledge can be had. We are taught in the Bible, "If any of you lack wisdom, let him ask of God, Who giveth to all men liberally." (James 1:6) There is no excuse for lack of knowledge in the domestic world. If a woman does not know, *she can learn.*

4. *Lack of Responsibility:* One of the major reasons for poor homemaking is a *lack of responsibility,* or a failure to assume a duty that belongs to us as was explained in the last chapter.

Don't Let Life Become Narrow

There is a tendency for women who focus all of their time and attention on their own household to become narrow in viewpoint and therefore stunted in personality. They tend to be material-minded, thinking too much about food and household goods. Their conversation may be very limited, not being able to talk beyond the antics of their own children or the latest floor polish. Even their own husbands may find them uninteresting, and they may be dull or even boring to strangers who are trying to get acquainted with them.

The Domestic Goddess should constantly guard against letting her life become too narrow, by extending her interests beyond her own home and family. She can do this by keeping up with current events, reading widely, being interested in other people, and having activities beyond her own sphere. One of the finest ways to keep from being narrow is by giving benevolent service to the needy, or to a needy cause.

Beyond Her Role as the Domestic Goddess

1. *Benevolent Service:* A woman can be an active part of the life beyond her home by giving of benevolent service to those in need. I explained in the last chapter how giving service can enrich a woman's life and help her develop character. I wish to stress here how it will also broaden her horizons and keep her from being narrow in viewpoint. Although making a success of family life should be her first concern, it can be a narrow existence if continued indefinitely with no thought of others. We all owe a certain public good to the world. If the homemaker can increase her efficiency so she can help the needy, she will become a better person and even a better wife and mother.

2. *The Gifted, Talented Woman:* There are women who have great talent to give the world, as artists, writers, designers, actresses, and even in the sciences and technical fields. Should they pursue their talents when they have a family at home? The main thing to consider is her responsibility in the home. Her foremost duty is to her family, making a success of marriage and family life. This is her greatest contribution to the well being of society and surpasses any gift of talent she may offer the world. Here,

in the home, she must succeed. If, beyond this, she has the capacity to give more in the way of talents, then she is justified. But there is a great tendency for her career to be competitive with her role in the home, to be demanding of her time and interest. If her work divides her interest from her family so that they are second place to her work, as is often the case, then she is making an unwise choice to pursue a career. *No success in life can compensate for failure in the home.*

3. *The Older Woman:* When a woman's children are grown, she will have much more time to give outside her home in benevolent service or giving her talents to the world. If she stays home, she may experience empty hours. It may not seem right to her to spend her time knitting or idling away her time when she could be doing something more useful. Even if she is not especially talented, she may feel a need to be engaged in important work and may seek a full time job for this purpose. Will this diminish her as a Domestic Goddess? If the older woman does not neglect her family, she can work without harm, if she limits her work to the feminine fields such as secretarial, nursing, school teaching, clerical, and many others. She should avoid the more masculine fields or executive jobs, as we will learn in the next chapter, since they will reduce her femininity. The main thing to consider is the motive. If she works to fill empty hours and give service, she has just reason for working.

There is another thing to consider in the older woman working. If she has children, even though they are married, she is still their mother. A woman is a mother all of her life. Her children and her grandchildren may need her, her counsel and sometimes even her help. If she is tied up in full time employment, she cannot give them this help. There is a great shortage of grandmother assistance, since so many grandmothers are working. In the strains of family life, there is no one for the young mothers to turn to for relief from their burdens, even temporarily. How great it would be, what service, if their mother could temporarily give them a helping hand. And the influence of a grandmother in the lives of her married children and grandchildren can be vital, helping them over some of the great problems of life. I have often heard people say that they felt the influence of their grandparents was more profound than that of their parents. And the older woman still has a husband to care for and a household to manage.

Working may greatly divide, not only her time, but her interest and devotion from her family.

Women's Liberation

There are some women who find little satisfaction in their domestic role as the wife, mother and homemaker. They are rejecting this role in the home and seeking fulfillment in the world of men by following careers. I would like to review some of their complaints against domestic life:

Some women feel that the work in the home is inferior to the work that men do. They say that there is no glory in it, little thanks, and that it is monotonous and drudgery. They feel like second-class citizens—*not like goddesses*. They think that the only important, exciting work is done by men, and therefore they seek their happiness and fulfillment in careers. Let me quote from their own words: "While my husband has the freedom and opportunity to be out in the working world, experiencing new people, new ideas, and perhaps the creative joy of seeing the world change for the better by the fruits of his own efforts, I am at home in the isolated household with no one to talk to but little children and friends in the same situation as myself."

There is a general feeling that housework diminishes a woman or frustrates her development. Again let me quote from their words: "I am assuming a role (wife, mother and homemaker) that frustrates the development of my own capabilities and prohibits me from being a companion who can truly understand my husband's experience and feeling through direct experience of my own." And another. "In too many cases women are a shadow to their husbands and a servant to their children."

Women of high intelligence and education complain that homemaking requires no mental gifts. Because of their own talents, they feel their calling must be outside the home, to make some great contribution to society such as did Madam Curie, or to find a cure for cancer, or develop something in the scientific or technological fields. They may wish to serve their country in politics and thus help make the world a better place. Now I would like to challenge all of these complaints.

As for the woman's intellect being wasted in the home on menial tasks, I will agree that it takes little intelligence

213

to merely feed and clothe a family and do the bare minimum requirements. But it requires real mental ability to make a "smashing" success in the home, as a Domestic Goddess would achieve. To be the alert, all comprehending wife, ever in tune to her husband's needs, always knowing the right thing to say at the right time—this requires I.Q. And to be the wise, understanding mother who guides her children through the pitfalls of life, moulds them to be useful citizens and teaches them how to be happy, making a secure home for them amidst a world of turmoil and uncertainty—I say this requires mental capacity beyond comprehension. And in this way she experiences "the creative joy of seeing the world change for the better."

But the mind is not all that is required to succeed in the home. What about the heart? Isn't giving your heart equally as important as giving your mind? Those dear little women who are experts in giving love, kindness and patience to their families are giving as much, yes, more, than their I.Q. Isn't the product of the heart equal to the product of the mind? Doesn't it do as much or more for the betterment of society? The ladies who donate their I.Q. to society may render a service, no doubt, but if in so doing they rob the home of its mind and heart, what then can compensate for this loss? And those ladies who feel that they have a gigantic brain must realize that unless they match it with a gigantic heart, they are only half a woman, and it would be far more important for them to stay home and educate the heart than to leave the home and go into the world to share their intellect there. Their contributions of the heart will do more for the well being of society than their contributions of the mind.

The world is not short of brain power. We already have men walking on the moon. The world is short of love and kindness and spiritual values—and this a woman contributes in the home, for she is its heart and soul. Several years ago I talked to a "brain girl." She was highly educated, but now was settled down with five small children, devoting her life, she felt, to menial tasks. One day as she was pushing a mop around, she said to herself, "I should be out in the world doing things. My education is being utterly wasted. I want to contribute something worthwhile, to make the world a better place." I'm afraid she did not listen to my good advice, for her marriage ended in divorce. She did not use her mental powers to

214

build a beautiful marriage and family life. Now sh...
preparing to give "something to the world," but what c...
she give to make up for her failure in the home? If she had
given both mind and heart to make her home a success,
she would have made a real contribution. Remember,
someone must do woman's work. Someone must tend the
children. Isn't the mother and wife the logical one? And to
quote from a great lady, Leah D. Widstoe:

"The training of the human soul for advancement and
joy here and in the hereafter calls for the greatest possible
powers of mind and heart. Psychologists and students
generally admit that the first years of life are crucial in
determining what shall be the future of the child physically, mentally, and spiritually; that grave responsibility belongs by right of sex to the women who bear and nurture
the whole human race. Surely no right thinking woman
could crave more responsibility than that.... Theirs is the
right to bear and rear to maturity as well as to influence
for good or ill the precious souls of men."

To be a successful mother is greater than to be a
successful opera singer, or writer, or artist. One is universal and eternal greatness and the other merely phenomenal. Of course, a great mother could become a great opera
singer or artist. But if such secondary greatness is not
added to that which is fundamental, it is merely an empty
honor. One day my young son said to me, "Mother, boys
are more important than girls, aren't they, for they can
become presidents and generals and famous people?" I
replied, "But it is mothers who *make* presidents and
generals and famous people. The hand that rocks the
cradle is the hand that rules the world."

Women should never feel that their work is less
important than men's work. The role of the wife, mother
and homemaker is not inferior to the man's role as the
breadwinner and builder of society. Both are essential
building blocks. In fact, every woman can make a worthy
contribution to society through her children, but not every
man can, through his work. Some jobs that men engage in
are relatively unimportant and some even destructive, such
as the liquor business. And remember that both man's
work and woman's work have their menial tasks. It is not
all interesting. And if women feel that they must serve
their country—the best way they can serve is in the home,
making a success of family life. Calvin Coolidge, former

215

J.S. President, said, "Look well to the hearthstone: therein lies all hope for America."

The career in the home may be a different kind of glory than men enjoy. Few great mothers are famous or even widely appreciated. Theirs is a quiet, unacclaimed honor. Remember, *a woman's glory is the success of her husband, the happiness of her children and her overall success in the home.* But the domestic role is the path to rich fulfillment for a woman and to Celestial love. What greater compensation could she ask for? And now, here are some true experiences to prove the rewards of the woman's role:

Nothing but a "Yes, Dear" Dummy

"I now know what I am doing on this earth and what happiness can come to a woman. Before, I never felt a woman was anything but a 'yes, dear' dummy. I couldn't be happy this way, and it resulted in my being in competition with men and especially with my husband. I made the decisions for us and tried to help my husband, and made every effort to convince him that I had a brain on my shoulders. All of this sent me further from what I really wanted—his love.

"How much easier it is now. How much more fun it is to have my whole day to do for him the things I should. I hated to lose the romantic days of our engagement and early marriage, but it's coming back, just as you said it would. I now enjoy being a woman. It's really fun."

I Felt Like a Drudge

"I believe most women have a crisis in their life, or reach a point when they come face to face with the realization that they do not feel fulfilled. I would guess this is why so many women leave home for the glamour of the working world. I had no such desires, but did feel rather like a drudge. I was seeking for the true purpose of woman. Was it just to bear children and do the never ending housework? I felt somewhat indispensable and yet I couldn't convince myself that this inferior role was my lot in life. Fascinating Womanhood has taught me the heavenly possibilities which are in store for women. I have been so thrilled with the results."

A New Spring in His Step

"In the past, I have felt that motherhood was about the only real joy of womanhood for me. I used to envy men and their role in life and society. I felt trapped at home and resentful that women were placed in obedience to men. This new concept and respect for my sex is one of the most wonderful things that has happened to me. Already my marriage is happier than I could have believed possible. My husband has a new spring in his step and a new note of authority in his voice which is thrilling to behold, and I am finally really satisfied and happy with being a woman."

I Thought It Was a Women's Lib Course

"During the first Fascinating Womanhood class, a lot of things the teacher said grated on me. But I was having trouble with my marriage and thought that maybe my thinking would change. I came into this class thinking it was a women's lib oriented course. I was frustrated with working full time at a job I enjoyed and yet having to do all of the household duties myself. I was hoping to find ways to get my husband to help with domestic duties. Well...needless to say, I've undergone a catharsis. Our marriage has improved now that I've read Fascinating Womanhood and been gathered up into the enthusiasm of our teachers and class members who really believe in two sexes.

"The most important change was when I began accepting my husband's small 'faults' as part of him and realized that he probably never would change. It has relieved me from the feeling that I must tutor him until he realizes the 'right way' to do things. I also was helped by the direction of my teachers to offer sympathetic understanding. All my married life, my husband has talked endlessly about buying an airplane. I've always argued about the safety factor, cost of maintenance, frivolousness, etc. Finally I said (and meant), 'Wes, you've wanted an airplane all your life. I really think you owe it to yourself to buy an airplane.' Well, he was *so* happy. The next day he told me that he really didn't think he should buy one at this point in time (energy crisis, our financial situation)— some of the same reasons I'd been harping on for years.

nd it all happened because I supported him rather than fought him. I'm also happier with housework. Thank you so much!"

Qualities of the Domestic Goddess

1. Does her job well, beyond the call of duty.
2. Is a good manager of time and values.
3. Adds feminine touches to her homemaking.
4. Adds warmth to her household.
5. Has pride in her role in the home.
6. Is happy in her role, is fulfilled.

How to Find Happiness in Homemaking

1. Have a proper attitude towards drudgery.
2. Don't become crowded for time.
3. Go the "second mile," doing more than required.

Assignment

1. List in order of importance your six most essential responsibilities. If you are not certain how they should be placed, consult your husband for his interpretation.
2. List your strong points in domestic skills.
3. List your weak points. Give thought to a special project for improving these areas.
4. Read from the Bible: Proverbs 31:10-31

Part II

The Human Qualities

1. *Femininity*

2. *Radiates happiness*

3. *Good health*

4. *Childlikeness*

The Human side of woman fascinates, amuses, captivates and enchants man. It arouses a desire to protect and shelter.

The Human side of the ideal woman refers to her appearance, manner and actions. It is her femininity, girlishness, joyfulness, vivacity, and dependency upon men for their care and protection. Add to all this a glow of vibrant health and a dash of spunk and sauciness and an underlying attitude of trust and tenderness and you begin to build a delightfully human creature—one that will win a man's heart.

The human qualities have tremendous appeal. They fascinate and amuse men and arouse a tender feeling—a desire to protect and shelter. If you think the human qualities are foreign to your nature, remember that they arise from a woman's natural instincts. If you do not have them, it is because they have been suppressed. They are not unholy for they enrich a man's life and, when combined with the Angelic, awaken Celestial Love.

15

Femininity

Femininity is a gentle, tender quality found in a woman's appearance, manner and actions. It is a sort of softness, delicateness, submissiveness, and dependency upon men for their masculine care and protection. More than anything else, it is a *lack of masculine ability*—a lack of male aggressiveness, competency, efficiency, fearlessness, strength, and *"the ability to kill your own snakes."*

Femininity has great appeal to men, for it is such a contrast to their own strong and firm masculinity. This contrast, when brought to a man's attention, causes him to feel manly, and this realization of his masculinity is one of the most enjoyable sensations he can experience. Femininity is acquired by *accentuating the differences between yourself and men*, not the similarities. There are three phases of femininity which we will now study: 1) The Feminine Appearance, 2) The Feminine Manner, and 3) Feminine Dependency. We will devote the remainder of this chapter to a study of the first, The Feminine Appearance:

The Feminine Appearance

The feminine appearance is acquired by *accentuating the difference between yourself and men, not the similarities*. If you would like to be attractive in a feminine way, wear only those materials and styles which are the least suggestive of those used by men and which therefore make the greatest contrast to men's apparel. Men never wear anything fluffy, lacy, gauzy or elaborate. Use such materials, therefore, whenever you can. Men seldom pay much attention to the latest style in men's clothes, but they expect women to be in tune with the styles, providing they are modest and becoming. In developing a feminine appearance, observe the following rules:

1. *Materials:* Avoid such materials as tweeds, herringbones, hard finish woolens, denims, glen plaids, faint

dark plaids, pin stripes, shepherd checks, and geometrics, since these are materials that men wear. These materials can be used, however, if distinguished by feminine style, color or trim. Otherwise they can give no help in making men realize how un-manlike—how womanly—you are! They cannot strive to bring out any contrast between your nature and his.

Do wear soft woolens, soft or crisp cottons, soft synthetics, floral prints, polka-dots, animated designs, etc. The extremes of femininity are such things as chiffon, silk, lace, velvet, satin, fur, angora and organdie. Try to include some of these in your wardrobe. These can be worn when trying to appear the most feminine.

Colors which are feminine are pastels, soft colors, rich or clear colors. Colors to avoid are the drab and dull colors used by men, such as browns, greys, deep blue and charcoal. These colors may be used effectively, however, if they are cut in a feminine style, or trimmed with feminine touches.

In selecting floral or designed prints, avoid anything which is overly loud and gaudy and therefore lacking in good taste. Men do tend to like vivid colors on women, but not those that are dominating. Therefore, use care in selecting a print, to make sure that it is good design.

2. *Style:* Avoid tailored styles or any suggestion of masculinity such as buttoned cuffs, lapels, and top stitching. These styles can be used, however, if combined with a feminine color or material. Extreme feminine styles are such things as full skirts, ruffles, scallops, puffed sleeves, gathers, drapes, flowing trains, and many others. These styles are not always in fashion, nor are they practical for all occasions. There are, however, feminine styles always available. The dress itself is feminine, since men do not wear them. It is difficult to advise a feminine style which would be suitable for all women, since we vary in figure. A safe rule is to accentuate the difference between you and the men and to avoid any style which has a suggestion of masculinity unless softened in some way by a feminine effect.

Should women wear pants? They are not the most feminine of dress, but are necessary for things such as sports, outings, and mountain climbing. If they are worn for other occasions, they should be of a feminine material. You can soften the effect of pants by wearing a feminine shirt, scarf, or ribbon in your hair. The most feminine pants for special home occasions are of such things as lace, satin and brocade. They can be beautiful and are very feminine.

3. *Trim:* Trim can give a feminine effect to an otherwise plain dress—lace, ribbon, colorful tie, fringe, embroidery, beads, and braid.

4. *Accessories:* Avoid purses which resemble men's brief cases and shoes of masculine style. Wear soft scarves, flowers, jewelry and ribbons.

In achieving a feminine appearance, the important thing to remember is the "over-all impression" which you make. It is not necessary to wear ruffles and lace, but do work for a striking contrast to masculinity. The effect can be fascinating as in the following true experiences as written to me:

A Hat with Pink Feathers

"When I was a little girl, my mother dressed me in high top shoes, long underwear, long stockings and braids. I suppose this is where I began to feel that I was unfeminine. I soon found out that other girls did not wear these things. (This was in sunny California.) I remembered one girl in particular who wore frilly ribbons and was so cute. Oh, how I envied her! But I took pride in the fact that I could beat most of the boys in punching bag.

"As I matured I tried to wear nice clothes, but from my early experiences I concluded that I wasn't the feminine, dependent type. While in college I met and married my husband. Soon after, I came in contact with Fascinating Womanhood and attended a class. I so desperately wanted to become the Ideal Woman it describes, but realized that to do so I must be feminine. I really wanted to be.

"Well, to me one of the most feminine things a woman can wear is a hat, with gloves, scarf, etc. Not just any hat, but a feminine one. However, my husband said that hats were a waste of money and he didn't see any sense in them. I let it go at that because I felt I would not look good in one anyway because I wear glasses.

"But one day when my husband and I were shopping, we passed a ladies' hat section in a department store and I tried one on, then another. Then one struck me as particularly lovely. It had pink feathers on it. When I tried it on, I can't explain the sudden excited feeling I had—I guess it

223

was like something awakening inside of me. I said 'Honey, Honey, look at me!' He got a funny look on his face and said, 'We'll take it!'

"I had a dress at home that was a perfect match, but went along for several months, debating whether to wear it or not. It just did not seem like the real me. But the ladies in the Fascinating Womanhood class and my husband encouraged me to wear it. The very next Sunday I decided to wear it, even though I was afraid I would be the only one in a fancy hat. My husband was ill and could not go, but he encouraged me to wear it. Well, I gathered up my courage and stepped outside. Immediately I heard two boys across the street give some long whistles. I decided that I must look good. This gave me courage, so off I went.

"You should have seen the heads turn when I walked into church. Afterwards several women came up to me to say how wonderfully feminine I looked. They wanted to wear hats and I had given them courage to do so. When I arrived back home, I was so excited about the 'new me.' And do you know what my husband said! 'I think I'll get you a new hat about every four months.' My new feelings of femininity have not come about overnight. But, I make sure that whatever I buy or make is feminine, and it is so fun. I have learned to be feminine and dependent and I am sure that, no matter what a woman's background, she can learn these principles, too."

The Old Brown Bag

"I have to tell you how discarding a simple brown dress changed my marriage. I have a particular brown dress which I find much pleasure in wearing. It's a house-dress and oh, so comfortable. After I had worn it for quite some time, my husband let me know of his great dislike for it, I continued wearing it anyway, thinking, Oh, well, it's only at home.

"Then I noticed that my husband began to come home with what seemed to be a negative attitude. Then the thought occurred to me, I had been wearing that awful brown dress quite a lot lately, due to spring cleaning. My home sparkled, but I did not look like springtime.

"Well, I got busy and bought a pattern for a very feminine housedress, soft gathers at the scooped neckline and peasant sleeves. I made several of them so I would have no excuse. That night when my husband came home, the look of approval on his face was something to see. I had even bothered to slip a string of pearls around my neck. He smiled and asked if this meant that I would throw the 'old brown bag' away. Yes, even a dress can change a marriage. Isn't it an interesting beginning!"

I Wore Pants and Boots

"When my husband and I worked in our yard or lemon orchard I used to wear pants, boots and a sweat shirt. My husband expected a man's work from me. After studying Fascinating Womanhood I have been dressing with more care and thought, even when I do yard work. I lowered the neckline of my sweat shirt, added rickrack and try to wear crisper looking clothes when helping him. Now he does not expect as much of me. In the evening I change to a long folk dress or something soft with ruffles and sometimes beads to match. He seems to enjoy me more and to my surprise seems to respect me as someone special—a person to be loved and cared for."

What a Feminine Appearance Does

As we can see, a feminine appearance will bring about a favorable reaction in your husband, will please him and cause him to respect you more. Your children will also have more respect for you as will people generally. There is another value in the feminine appearance. When a woman dresses in womanly clothes it encourages her to act more feminine in the way she walks, her gestures, the way she sits and conducts herself. The outer clothing and appearance seem to create a positive inner feeling of femininity which encourages a feminine manner. It also increases self-esteem and makes her feel good about herself.

Good Grooming

Another part of the feminine appearance is to be well groomed. We need not dwell on this, since there is much emphasis on grooming in our modern times. We need only mention that clean, well-groomed hair, a clean body and clothes are essential to the feminine appearance. This is not to say that men should not be well-groomed also, but they expect women to be even more immaculate than they are themselves, and somehow it seems more of a disgrace for a woman to be slovenly and careless than for a man to be. If you see a young man who has just been playing basketball sit down and relax before he combs his hair and straightens his clothes, it seems excusable. When it comes right down to it, men are inclined to be less concerned about their appearance and clothes than women. But they expect women to be the opposite—tidy and immaculate. In bringing out the charming contrast between yourself and men, you must have an all-absorbing pride in your appearance; you must endeavor to appear at your best every minute of the day and under all circumstances.

Modesty

Still another part of the feminine appearance is modesty. In spite of the emphasis in our times on the "sex symbol," men do not respect women who expose too much of their bodies to the public. Not only should the body be reasonably covered, but also the underwear. Men dislike hanging slips, bra straps that show, and exposed underwear when a girl sits on a chair. Higher types of civilization have always been modest—it seems to go with intelligence and refinement.

Assignment

Make or buy an especially feminine dress. Add soft hairdo and some feminine touches, such as a ribbon or pearls. Watch your husband's reaction.

16
The Feminine Manner

The feminine manner is the *motions* of a woman's body, the way she uses her hands, the way she walks, talks, the sound of her voice, her facial expressions and her laugh. The feminine manner is attractive to a man because it is such a contrast to masculine strength and firmness. David Copperfield was fascinated by Dora's enchanting manner; the way she patted the horses, spanked her little dog, or held her flowers against her chin were attractive to him. "She had the most delightful little voice, the gayest little laugh, the pleasantest and most fascinating little ways."

I have pointed out the importance of a feminine *appearance*, but if you do not add to this a *feminine manner*, the total effect can be disappointing or even amusing. For example, if you put a frilly feminine dress on a woman who has a stiff, brusque manner, she just doesn't fit the dress. We have all seen women who wear the most feminine dresses, but who wear them as if they were on the wrong person. They do not carry themselves generally in a way to harmonize with their clothes. They are *"professors in chiffon, bears in lace, or wooden posts in organdie."*

A Glimpse Into Femininity

In the novel *The Cloister and the Hearth* by Charles Reade, is an illustration of the feeling the feminine manner can awaken in a man.

"Then came a little difficulty: Gerald could not tie his ribbon again as Catherine (his mother) had tied it. Margaret, after slyly eyeing his efforts for some time, offered to help him; for at her age girls love to be coy and tender, saucy and gentle by turns ... then a fair head, with its stately crown of auburn curls, glossy and glowing through silver, bowed sweetly towards him; and while it ravished his eye, two white supple hands played delicately upon the stubborn ribbon and moulded it with soft airy touches.

227

Then a heavenly thrill ran through the innocent young man, and vague glimpses of a new world of feeling and sentiment opened to him. —And these new exquisite sensations Margaret unwittingly prolonged; it is not natural to her sex to hurry ought that pertains to the sacred toilet. Nay, when the taper fingers had at last subjugated the ends of the knot, her mind was not quite easy till, by a maneuver peculiar to the female hand, she had made her palm convex and so applied it with a gentle pressure to the center of the knot—a sweet little coaxing hand kiss, as much as to say, 'now be a good knot and stay so!' 'There, that was how it was!' said Margaret, and drew back to take one last survey of her work, then looking up for a simple approval of her skill, received full in her eyes a *longing gaze of such adoration* as made her lower them quickly and color all over."

This experience is an example of the tremendous feeling a woman can awaken in a man by the feminine manner, and in this case by the hands alone. Imagine how attractive she becomes when she adds a gentle voice and sweet expression. The feminine manner is one of the most important traits that makes a woman attractive to a man.

My main purpose is to teach women how to be attractive to their own husband. However, if femininity is to be natural and consistent, even to your own husband, you will have to form the habit of being feminine around all people. Another point is this: A man has a certain pride in his wife's femininity, is happy to introduce her to his friends if she has this quality. In contrast, a man may be reluctant to introduce his wife if she is unfeminine—if she is brusque, firm or in other ways unwomanly. So strive to be feminine around all people you meet and your husband will be proud to introduce you as his wife.

How to Acquire a Feminine Manner

You acquire a feminine manner by *accentuating the differences* between yourself and men, not the similarities. Since men are strong, tough, firm and heavy in manner, women should be delicate, tender, gentle and light. We show this by our walk, voice, hands, and the way we carry ourselves generally.

1. *The Hands:* Avoid stiff, brusque movements.

Don't wave your hands in the air or use them firmly in expressing yourself. Never pound on the table to put over a point and never grasp the sides of a lecturer's stand. Never slap anyone on the back. Learn how to shake hands with men. Never shake a man's hand with strength and vigor, regardless of how happy you may be to see him. Shake hands gently, but with enough firmness to convey friendship.

2. *The Walk:* Avoid a heavy gait or long steps such as men take. Avoid slanting forward or rounding the shoulders or walking with knees bent, as this appears heavy and matronly. Keep head back over spine, chest and chin high. Your manner of walking should be *light*. One way to induce a light walk is to imagine you weigh only 95 lbs. Walking with knees slightly straight also encourages a lighter walk.

3. *The Voice:* Usually a woman who is learning to walk and use her hands correctly will automatically modulate her voice to harmonize with her manner. But, if you discover that your voice is spoiling the impression you are endeavoring to create, take a little time and effort to change it.

The ideal feminine voice is gentle and variable, with a clear ringing tone and an air of self-assurance. It is not a voice which is overly soft and timid, for these qualities suggest a lack of self-assurance, something unattractive in women. The main thing to avoid is loudness, firmness, or any of the qualities that men have. You must not let your voice suggest mannish efficiency, or coarse boldness. No man likes a coarse, loud, or vulgar tone in a woman any more than a woman likes an effeminate tone in a man. And no man likes a mumbling, dull, monotonous or singsong voice, because such a voice indicates to him that the character behind the voice is equally dull and uninteresting.

If you have any difficulty with your voice, a few weeks' practice ought to help you greatly. Speaking aloud to yourself or reading aloud in the privacy of your room, endeavoring all the time to eliminate the objectional features in your voice, should be effective. A half-hour devoted to this once every day ought to be sufficient, if it is kept up for three or four weeks. When reading, read with expression. Put laughter into your voice in the humorous parts, sorrow in the sad parts, enthusiasm, delight, eagerness, wonder, love, pity, and every sentiment or emotion. And when you think of it, practice consciously the same expressions of voice in your conversation.

4. *The Laugh:* It is more difficult for a person to change his laugh. Avoid things, however, which resemble men's laughs, such as loudness or a deep tone. Also avoid facial contortions, opening the mouth wide, throwing the head back, slapping your hands on your thighs, roaring or anything coarse or vulgar. If these extremes are avoided, the laugh will probably be at least acceptable.

5. *The Cooing or Purring Quality:* Typical of a feminine woman is a cooing quality in the voice when talking to babies, little children or animals. This is sometimes known as "baby talk." Deruchette "made all kinds of gentle noises, murmurings of unspeakable delight to certain ears." A lady told me that when her new baby arrived her husband loved to wake up early just to hear her talking to the baby.

6. *Facial Expressions:* Avoid harsh or bitter expressions, hard frowns, or tightness across the lips as these all destroy femininity. Women who are feminine in appearance and manner who suddenly take on a hard expression are always a disappointment. The feminine expression is gentle, kind, soft.

The feminine expression has its real roots in character, in "the gentle tender quality." If you have a gentle character it will be easy to convey a gentle expression. If you do not, if you tend to be harsh and critical, to lose patience with people, it will be difficult to keep these unwholesome traits hidden from view. It will be wise, therefore, to work on character, to acquire a better philosophy of life, a better understanding of people, to learn to accept them, to forgive them and be patient with them. The real key to this change of heart and attitude lies in *humility,* for through this virtue we learn to accept, to forgive and not to judge.

In the meantime, while you are working on character, try to control your facial expressions. This will help to train your character within to be more gentle. The face, then, acts as a sort of teacher to the character, reminding it to be patient and forgiving. It will be difficult, however, to keep this practice up for long, if you continue to hold grudges and have ill will towards people.

7. *Conversation:* You can do a great deal to strengthen your femininity through conversation. If some-

one unfortunate is the topic for discussion, show forth sympathy and love. Do not make the mistake of giving an unsympathetic remark like, "Well, he deserves it" or, "He had it coming to him." Take every opportunity to defend people, to be long suffering and understanding, and in this way show forth your gentle feminine nature.

Avoid talking about people you dislike as you may be tempted to make an unkind remark. It will be difficult enough to remake your attitude towards this person without inviting temptation by bringing him into the conversation. Also avoid subjects which may lead to heated arguments. By avoiding negative statements and concentrating on kindly expressions, you can do a great deal to enhance your femininity and therefore your attractiveness.

Feminine Conversation with Children

To be feminine a woman should be gentle and tender with her children. Do not wait for some extreme emergency to show tenderness for your children. When your little boy passes by, pat him on the head or take your little girl in your arms and say, "You are just the kind of little girl I always wanted." Or rest your hands on your older son's shoulders and say, "What a fine boy you are, I am so proud of you." Be kind, sympathetic and understanding with them in their special problems, and deliberately see that they have a steady diet of tenderness from you. This will help keep your children from going astray, and will develop your feminine side. Bossiness, crossness and harshness do not make for good behavior, and they destroy feminine charm.

The Tiger's Whisker—An Old Korean Tale

The tender, feminine approach of a woman can tame the most difficult man. The following story will illustrate: The story is of Yun Ok, a married girl who came to the house of a wise sage for counsel. Her problem was this: "It is my husband, wise one," she said. "He is very dear to me. For the past three years he has been away fighting in the wars. Now that he has returned, he hardly speaks to me, or to anyone else. If I speak, he doesn't seem to hear. When he talks at all, it is roughly. If I serve him food not to his liking, he pushes it aside and angrily leaves the room. Sometimes when he should be working in the rice

231

field, I see him sitting idly on top of the hill, looking towards the sea! I want a potion," she said, "so he will be loving and gentle as he used to be."

The wise sage instructed the young woman to get for him the whisker of a living tiger, from which he would make the magic potion. All night, when her husband was asleep, she crept from her house with a bowl of rice and meat sauce in her hand. She went to the place on the mountainside where a tiger was known to live. Standing far off from the tiger's cave, she held out the bowl of food, calling the tiger to come and eat, but the Tiger did not come. Each night she returned, doing the same thing, and each time a few steps closer. Although the tiger did not come to eat, he did become accustomed to seeing her there.

One night she approached within a stone's throw of the cave. This time the tiger came a few steps toward her and stopped. The two of them stood looking at one another in the moonlight. It happened again the following night, and this time they were so close that she could talk to him in a soft, soothing voice. The next night, after looking carefully into her eyes, the tiger ate the food that she held out for him. After that, when Yun Ok came in the night she found the tiger waiting for her on the trail. Nearly six months had passed since the night of her first visit. At last, one night after caressing the animal's head, she said, "Oh, generous animal, I must have one of your whiskers. Do not be angry with me." And she snipped off one of the whiskers.

The tiger did not become angry as she had feared that he might. She went down the trail, running with the whisker tightly clutched in her hand. When she brought it to the wise sage, he examined it to see if it was real, then tossed it into the fire, causing the poor girl to become disheartened. Then the sage said, "Yun Ok, is a man more vicious than a tiger? Is he less responsive to kindness and understanding? If you can win the love and confidence of a wild and bloodthirsty animal by gentleness and patience, surely you can do the same with your husband."

Refinement

One of the marks of feminine woman is refinement. This means that she has "good social breeding" and a sensitivity to the feelings of others, that she never offends

232

anyone by being rude, impolite, inconsiderate, crude, or socially negligent. She is tactful, diplomatic and considerate.

To be refined, you must never use coarse or vulgar language, profane, swear, tell vulgar jokes, etc. What these habits do to your character is one thing, but what they do to your feminine image is more serious in the eyes of men. Although these coarse habits are not becoming in men, either, they are somehow more easily overlooked—less offensive than in women. Here again, men expect women to be the more refined creatures of the human race. Indulging in loud, coarse or vulgar talk not only causes a woman to fall from her pedestal but to fall from being the idol of femininity in men's eyes. Men have always expected women to be cultured and refined and have considered it beneath feminine dignity to utter coarse language. They are naturally disappointed, if not repulsed, by a display of crudeness.

Still another mark of refinement is to show a courteous appreciation for everyone you meet, regardless of age, situation, financial or social standing. Every person is a human being who is entitled to respect and reverence. The higher your conception of human beings generally, the higher will be your tendency to refinement. To show a lack of courteous appreciation of anyone is only to show a decline in the quick intelligence and perception expected of a cultured person. Nothing is more quickly calculated to give you a coarse, unrefined character than to ignore or shun another individual.

In order to demonstrate a real consideration for people, it will be essential that you never do anything to hurt their feelings. Never, for example, show indifference for the opinions of another or downgrade things he says or does, especially things he considers important. Be considerate of all the feelings, opinions, accomplishments, ideas, traditions, religious customs, or "ways of life" of others. If, for example, you happen to meet a little old lady who has spent a lifetime devoted to a worship of traditions, don't show disrespect for her feelings by trampling on those traditions. Or if you have dinner with some honest soul who takes pride in her cooking, don't refuse a second helping or give any indication that you are any less than delighted with her meal.

If you are in the home of an exceptionally cultured or refined person, do not show a disregard for her way of life

233

by boisterous conduct or heated arguments. On the other hand, if the hostess is fun-loving and set on everyone relaxing and having a good time, show consideration for her thinking by being lighthearted yourself. The greatest mark of refinement you can show is a genuine delight in the company you keep with a respect and consideration for their way of living.

Also, learn to respect another person's *enthusiasm*. For example, if a gentleman happens to be telling you of an adventurous journey he is about to take and gets into a state of excitement as he unfolds the plans, do not "throw cold water" on his enthusiasm by acting coldly indifferent. Even worse, do not make a negative remark which would destroy his enthusiasm altogether, such as reminding him how expensive or foolhardy it might be. Instead, share his enthusiasm. Or if he is merely eating a piece of pie which he enjoys heartily, do not make a cold remark like, "Oh, I can't stand that kind!"

Still another lack of refinement is "cheekiness," an old-fashioned word which means to be nervy or to impose on people. Cheekiness is an attitude of "expecting" favors, with a lack of consideration for the imposition it might be on the other person. Young people especially are apt to be guilty of this practice by asking for things to eat while in the homes of their friends, or by asking to borrow clothing, perfume, cars, or even money. This is not to say that there are not emergencies when we are justified in asking these favors, or that others are not willing to grant them, but borrowing is ordinarily considered nervy and unrefined.

Also, be tactful and diplomatic in your remarks to people. Blunt honesty is never appropriate. Anything which must be said can be said with a kindly consideration for the other person. Refined women never ignore social invitations without a thoughtful acceptance or apology. They are courteous, with a respect for the feelings of everyone.

Bewitching Languor

Languor is a feminine characteristic and is a relaxed, calm, quiet air, similar to that of a cat relaxing before a fireplace. It is like a touch of velvet and is calming and appealing to men. "Deruchette had at times an air of bewitching languor." Languor is a means of varying other feminine mannerisms. The opposite of languor is the nervous, high-strung woman who is always biting fingernails, jingling her keys, twisting her handkerchief or twisting her hair.

Outdoor Parties

One place that women tend to let down their femininity is at outdoor parties and games. This may be due to the way they are dressed, usually in pants and casual clothes, which puts them in the spirit to be lax in their actions, also. It is here that we are apt to see women slap men on the back, whistle, yell or speak loudly, laugh noisily, gulp their food down, sit with their legs apart or one leg resting on another as men do, roar at jokes, throw their head back when they drink, etc. Here is the time to really watch your femininity.

You Need Not Be Beautiful to Be Feminine

You need not be beautiful to have all of the charms of femininity. There are thousands of rather plain women with irregular features and faulty builds who succeed in being attractive to men because they are models of femininity. On the other hand, there are thousands of other women who are beautiful in their faces and features but who, because of woodenness or masculinity of their manner, never impress men as being especially attractive. When a girl is tender, soft, fun-loving, lovable, and also innocent and pure, who stops to inquire if she has beauty in the classical sense? Regardless of her feature or form, to most men she will seem a paragon of femininity. To them she *is* beautiful!

Even when the woman is so homely that the fact cannot be overlooked, the men are often attracted nevertheless. While they may not consider her beautiful, they may consider her pert, cute, charming, dainty, lovable and saucy and everything else that is highly fascinating. Very often such a woman has the most enchanting personality of all and succeeds in captivating the most sensible men, the more vivid and virile characters for whom beauty without personality has no attraction; and frequently such a woman can make a merely beautiful woman seem insignificant beside her. You must not, therefore, let the absence of beauty discourage you; nor must you let the

235

possession of beauty, if you have it, lull you into a false
security. The presence or the absence of beauty is of minor
consequence in the attainment of true femininity.

Don'ts for the Feminine Manner

1. Don't use your hands in a stiff, brusque, efficient,
   firm or strong manner.
2. Don't walk with a heavy gait, long steps, round
   shoulders or slanting forward.
3. Avoid the following qualities in the voice: loudness,
   firmness, efficiency, boldness, over-softness or timidity, dullness flat tone, mumbling, monotonous,
   singsong.
4. Don't laugh loudly or in a vulgar manner.
5. Don't use facial expressions that are hard, harsh,
   bitter or unyielding, etc.
6. Don't indulge in conversation that is harsh, bitter,
   critical, impatient, crude, vulgar or unrefined.
7. Don't slap anyone on the back.
8. Don't whistle.
9. Don't yell.
10. Don't talk loudly.
11. Don't roar at jokes.
12. Don't gulp food or eat noisily.
13. Don't drink by throwing your head back.
14. Don't sit with legs apart or with one leg horizontal
    across the other.

Assignment

1. Analyze your feminine manner. Take your weakest point
   and work on it for at least a week—a month is better.
2. Express to your sons and daughters your tender feelings
   for them, accompanied by a soft look, soft tone in the
   voice, pat on the shoulder, or some act of affection.
3. Express to your husband your tender feelings for him.

17

Feminine Dependency

A good definition of Feminine Dependency is *a woman's need for masculine care and protection.* Women were designed to be wives, mothers and homemakers and therefore in need of masculine help to make their way through life. The men were assigned to fill this need for women by serving as their guide, protector and provider. Feminine dependency is very attractive to men. Dora was rather helpless and dependent upon men and for this reason made a strong appeal to David's gentlemanly heart. Agnes was too lacking in this ability. She was too self-sufficient, and independent, to win David at this stage in his life.

Do not think that protecting a dependent woman is an imposition on a man. *One of the most pleasant sensations a real man can experience is his consciousness of the power to give his manly care and protection. Rob him of this sensation of superior strength and ability and you rob him of his manliness.* It is a delight to him to protect and shelter a dependent woman. The bigger, manlier and more sensible a man is, the more he seems to be attracted by this quality.

How Men Feel in the Presence of Capable Women

What happens when the average red-blooded man comes in contact with an obviously able, intellectual and competent woman manifestly independent of any help a mere man can give and capable of meeting him or defeating him upon his own ground? He simply doesn't feel like a man any longer. In the presence of such strength and ability in a mere woman, he feels like a futile, ineffectual imitation of a man. It is the most uncomfortable and humiliating sensation a man can experience; so that the woman who arouses it becomes repugnant to him. *A man cannot derive any joy or satisfaction from protecting a woman who can obviously do very well without him. He only delights in protecting or sheltering a woman who needs his manly care, or at least appears to need it.*

How Men Feel in the Presence of Dependent Women

When a man is in the presence of a tender, gentle, trustful, dependent woman, he immediately feels a sublime expansion of his power to protect and shelter this frail and delicate creature. In the presence of such weakness, he feels stronger, more competent, bigger, manlier than ever. This feeling of strength and power is one of the most enjoyable he can experience. The apparent, need of the woman for protection, instead of arousing contempt for her lack of ability, appeals to the very noblest feelings within him.

Amelia

An excellent illustration of feminine dependency is found in the character of Amelia in *Vanity Fair*. "Those who formed the small circle of Amelia's acquaintances were quite angry with the enthusiasm with which the other sex regarded her. For almost all men who came near her loved her; though no doubt they would be at a loss to tell you why. She was not brilliant, nor witty, nor wise over-much, nor extraordinarily handsome. But wherever she went, she touched and charmed everyone of the male sex, as invariably as she awakened the scorn and incredulity of her own sisterhood. I think it was her *weakness* which was her principle charm; a kind of *sweet submission* and *softness* which seemed to appeal to each man she met for his sympathy and protection."

Mrs. Woodrow Wilson

Mrs. Wilson was a tender, dependent woman, for her husband wrote to her, "What a source of steadying and of strength it is to me in such seasons of too intimate self-questioning to have one fixed point of confidence and certainty—that even, unbroken, excellent perfection of my little wife, with her poise, her easy capacity in action, her unfailing courage, her quick efficient thought—and the charm that goes with it all, the sweetness, the feminine grace—none of the usual penalties of efficiency—no hardness, no incisive sharpness, no air of command or of unyielding opinion. Most women who are efficient are such terrors.",

The Capable Woman

In describing the capable woman, let me first state that I am referring to a woman's being capable in the *masculine things*. I am not suggesting that a woman be incapable in her own feminine sphere of work. As a homemaker, she must be efficient to succeed. But to be feminine, a woman must eliminate any tendency to masculine capabilities such as efficiency in running an office, skill in fixing a motor or changing a tire, or masculine courage in braving danger. To have such masculine capabilities is to *turn off feminine charm*. This is a widespread problem in our times which needs our consideration.

There are many women, in all walks of life, who possess great personal magnetism, whom all, including the men, admire as great and powerful characters, but who can never change a man's admiration into love. One such woman, a famous Sunday School teacher of young men and women, illustrates this situation. Her magnetic personality and noble character were so much admired that hundreds of young people sought to join her class and thousands of men and women of all ages attended whenever she gave a public lecture. In spite of this almost universal respect and admiration, the average man would never think of seeking her private company, indulging in an intimate conversation or of making her his "little girl" to cherish and protect throughout a lifetime. Everyone knows of such women, healthy, charming, enjoyable, whom men admire greatly but whom they do not seem to be fascinated by. The reason for this is that they lack an air of frail dependency upon men. They are too capable and independent to stir a man's sentiments. The air of being able to "kill your own snakes" is just what destroys the charm of so many business and professional women. And it is the absence of this air that permits many a "brainless doll" to capture an able and intelligent man whom one would expect to choose a more sensible companion.

The kind of woman a man wants is first an angelic

being whom he can adore as better than himself, but also a helpless creature whom he would want to gather up in his arms and cherish and protect forever. The admirable women that we just mentioned fulfill the first requirement but fail to fulfill the second. Though it is absolutely necessary to fulfill the first, you cannot afford to do as these women do and neglect the second.

What if you happen to be a big, strong and capable woman, or have a powerful personality or in some other way overpower men? How, then, can you possibly appear to be tender, trustful, delicate and dependent? In the first place, size has nothing to do with the quality of feminine dependency. No matter what your size, your height or your capabilities, you can appear fragile to a man if you follow certain rules and if you will take on an attitude of frailty. It is not important that you actually be little and delicate, but that *you seem so* to the man.

When the Large Woman Attracts the Little Man

Occasionally we will see a rather small short man, married to a large woman. It is interesting to observe that she does not seem large to him because she has given him the impression of smallness. Such a man is even apt to call her "his little girl." She has managed, in spite of her size, to give him the impression of delicacy. By letting him know that she can't get along without him, that she is utterly dependent upon him, she has been able to disguise her rather large, overpowering figure.

If you are a large, tall or strong woman, you will have to work to disguise these features so that men will have the impression that you are little and delicate. And if you are efficient and capable in masculine things, you will have to "unlearn" these traits.

The Capable Woman that Men Admire

Occasionally we may notice men who seem to admire women who are capable and efficient in masculine things. They may be exceedingly skilled in managing a department or have ingenious ideas about how to make the business or industrial world "tick." But don't let men's admiration for these women confuse you. Although the man may have a genuine admiration for such a woman, it does not mean he finds her attractive. He undoubtedly

240

admires her as he would another man—with appreciation for her fine ability.

How to Acquire Feminine Dependency

1. *Attitude:* In acquiring femininity, you must first dispense with any air of strength and ability, of competence and fearlessness, and acquire instead an attitude of frail dependency upon men to take care of you. Always let him know that his masculine help is needed and appreciated and that you could not get along in this world very well without him. Women often display a capable attitude in the things they say. For example, a woman may oppose her husband's life insurance by saying, "Oh, if anything happened to you, I could take care of myself well enough." Or in planning a move or a trip they take no thought, in their plans, of needing masculine assistance, care or protection. Their attitude is one of self-sufficiency, of getting along in the world without masculine aid.

2. *Stop Doing the Masculine Work:* Next, you will have to stop doing the man's work—stop lifting heavy boxes, moving furniture, mowing the lawn, painting, fixing motors, cleaning cars, changing tires, carpentry, or anything which is masculine responsibility. Eliminate *heavy* work which is beyond your physical strength, and also eliminate work which is *inappropriate* for women, or unfeminine. Also stop handling the money problems and worries, bossing your husband around, telling him what to do and when to do it. Stop braving the dark, facing the creditors or making long distance car trips alone. If you are working to provide part of the living, if at all possible stop working. (If you are an older woman who is working to fill in time or for benevolent service, this may be different.) Stop doing the masculine work, not only to increase your femininity, but *so you will have time for your own feminine work.*

In eliminating the man's work, it is best to first explain your intentions to your husband. Tell him that you feel "unfeminine" doing these things and that you want very much to become a truly feminine woman and live within the bounds of your own role. Then, ask him if he will completely take over all of the masculine responsibility which you have been doing. Discuss each one of these jobs so that he will clearly understand. If your request is feminine, he will probably cooperate. He may,

241

however, resist taking over these jobs, or fail to follow through with a job he has promised to do. The man's failure to do his *home work* is a bone of marital contention, one we will now deal with briefly:

Some women are skeptical about getting the man to do the masculine work around the house. They may say, "Oh, I've tried to get him to do the heavy work, but it doesn't work. Why, I stopped mowing the lawn and it grew a foot high. And, if I didn't paint my kitchen it would never get painted. He won't do these things for me, so I have to resort to doing them myself." This is the common response. The trouble here lies in the fact that the woman does not completely stop, but only temporarily. She never *lets go* and turns her back on the man's responsibilities.

"But," the same woman may say, "if I do not do them and he does not, what will happen? Someone must do these things!" But, must they? Must the lawn be mowed and the kitchen painted and the battles' won at the expense of feminine charm? "But," she may say, "I cannot stand for the roof to leak and the door to fall from its hinges and the lawn to go unmowed." If you cannot make these temporary sacrifices, you cannot become the ideal of Angela Human, nor can you awaken the man's chivalry.

When you turn your back on the man's work, don't expect any miracles. If he fails to do his "home work," don't complain, make him feel ashamed or pressure him to get things done. Remember, the jobs are his to do or neglect. If his failures are difficult for you to accept, develop an attitude of humility by asking yourself, "Have I performed my work well today? Was I dressed and well groomed before breakfast? Did I serve my husband well prepared meals on time today? Is my house clean and orderly? Have I been patient with the children? Am I loving and understanding of my husband?" After you have asked yourself these questions, then ask, "Do I have a right to feel resentful because he neglects *his* duties?" Also, try to understand that what may seem to you like an important job at home, may seem insignificant to him when he compares it to problems he is facing in his work. If you hammer the point on small home repairs, you only display a narrow, self-centered and unsympathetic attitude.

3. *If Stuck with a Masculine Job, Do it in a Feminine Manner:* As you are trying to unload the masculine work, there may be times you will feel stuck with a masculine

job—something that must be done and there is no one to do it but yourself. If this is the case, do the job in a *feminine manner*. It is not up to you to perform masculine tasks with the skill that men do. If you must fix the furnace or the leaking roof or handle the finances, do not try so hard to do it with masculine efficiency. Just be your feminine self, and your husband will soon realize that you need masculine assistance. If you can do a job as well as a man can, *he will never come to your rescue.*

4. *Be Submissive:* Another quality of femininity is submissiveness. This means to be yielding, obedient, to yield to power or authority or to leave matters to the opinions, discretion or judgment of another, or others. The opposite of submissiveness is to be defiant, rebellious, unruly, obstinate or stubborn. To be feminine, a woman must be yielding to her husband's rule.

Women should especially guard against having unyielding opinions. Men find it very disagreeable to be in the company of such women. They want them to express their viewpoints and to defend them to a degree, but are offended when a woman takes such a firm stand on an issue that the man cannot convince her of anything, regardless of his sound logic. It is better to be submissive to a man than to try to win an argument with him. It is more feminine. I do not wish to imply that you be yielding in your moral convictions or ideals, but when you find that you clash in principle.

5. *Don't Subdue Fearfulness:* Feminine women tend to have a natural fear of dangers. They are afraid of snakes, and are even known to be afraid of small dangers such as bugs, spiders, mice, the dark, and strange noises, much to the amusement of men. The reason that men seem to enjoy this trait in women is that in the presence of her weakness he naturally feels stronger. If she shrinks from a spider or hops on a chair at the sight of a mouse, how manly he feels that he can laugh at such tremblings and calm her fears. It does a man more good to save a woman from a mouse than a tiger, since he feels so much more superiority over the mouse.

Feminine women are also known to be afraid of the dangers of nature. An illustration of this is the following incident a woman confided to me: Her husband owned a sailboat and was a competent seaman. He loved to take her into dangerous waters and keel the boat over on its side. She was terrified at such times and asked me, "Why

243

does he do this when he knows I am afraid?" I explained that the reason he does is because she *is* so afraid and he is so *unafraid*. Her fearfulness was appealing to him and this is why he kept repeating the dangerous sailing. I suggested that she express her fearfulness in calmer waters and perhaps he would be satisfied and not take her out further. It is a mistake for a woman to subdue the tendency of fearfulness in the presence of men, for to do so is to subdue feminine charm.

Feminine women are also uneasy in the presence of heavy traffic. If you take a tiny child to a busy highway and hold it tightly in your arms while the heavy trucks and fast moving traffic rush by, you sense the tremorous fearfulness of the child. Similarly, a feminine woman approaches an intersection with hesitancy. She does not charge forth with all confidence, but hesitates at the curb for a moment, clings to the man's arm a little tighter, waiting for him to lead the way. Here again, the man appreciates her apparent uneasiness and his ability to give protection.

6. *Don't Try to Excel Him:* To be feminine, don't compete with men in anything which requires masculine ability. For example, don't try to outdo them in sports, lifting weights, in running, in repairing equipment, etc. Also, don't compete with men for advancement on a job, for higher pay, or greater honors. Don't compete with them for scholastic honors in men's subjects. It may be all right to win over a man in English or Social Studies, but you are in trouble if you compete with a man in math, chemistry, public speaking, etc. Don't appear to know more than a man does in world events, the space program, or science or industry. Do not excel men in anything which has to do with the masculine field of endeavor.

7. *Need His Care and Protection:* Let him open doors for you, help you on with your coat, pull up your chair, or offer you his coat in the cold or in a rainstorm. If he does not offer his help, perhaps it is because you did it for yourself too quickly, did not give him time to offer. But if he still does not offer, then work on the other parts of femininity until he does. You can ask him to do some things, like lift in your groceries, open tight jar lids. Take care, however, that you confine your requests to things that women need men for and not for trivial things that women can just as well do for themselves.

8. *Live Your Feminine Role:* Perhaps in no way can

244

a woman develop her femininity more than by living her feminine role as the wife, mother and homemaker. Here, in this area of her life, a woman has a field in which to grow as a woman. Certainly motherhood increases her femininity. And, although she may not realize it, taking feminine work upon her shoulders year after year makes her more of a woman. And if she is a good wife, she will develop understanding, acceptance, forgiveness and sympathy—all gentle traits which make her more feminine.

What Feminine Dependency Awakens in a Man

Feminine dependency awakens in a man *love and tenderness*. As a man begins to do things for a woman, to shelter her and take care of her, this feeling grows. This is true of any individual that protects and shelters any form of life that is in need of protection. Take our pets, for example. Don't we learn to love them by taking care of them? And the more helplessly dependent they are upon us, the more tenderly we feel for them. Take a little canary for example. Don't you love him because he is so trustingly dependent upon you for food and water, because his happiness is so obvious when he is rewarded with a bit of food? He will twist his little head with such an air of interest and alertness and yet is so soft, fluttering and helplessly dependent upon you that you cannot think of trusting his care to anyone else. This feeling, magnified a thousand times, is what every mother feels who protects her child and what every man feels who protects his wife and children.

A woman also takes care of and protects her husband, in a different way. She prepares him nourishing meals, washes his shirts, and watches over him to see that he does not neglect his health. She gives him comfort, understanding and sympathy, and the man grows dependent upon her for these things. She also protects him in her own way. She tries to keep others from taking unfair advantage of his generous nature; tries to keep his foolhardy courage from endangering his safety; and tries to make certain that his manly indifference to detail does not lead him into trouble. Thus, she too feels that he is dependent upon her, and she delights in his need of her and her ability to fill the need of such a big, strong, yet helpless man. She, too, feels tenderness towards the one she is caring for.

Although men are fascinated by frailty in women, there is a balancing quality that they also want to see. They would like the assurance that, with all the woman's helplessness, with all of her dependency upon him to take care of her, to protect her and to wait upon her, that she has somewhere hidden within her the ability to meet an emergency. He would like to know that in such circumstances she would have womanly courage, strength and endurance and the ability to solve difficult problems, that she would not, in this case, be helpless. This is known as the "sweet promise." The man needs to be able to detect it somewhere in her character.

There are many women who show forth this promise when put to the test. Take for example a young widow who is left with several small children to support. What does she do? She sets out single-handed to battle against all odds. She slaves and struggles, she dares and she suffers in her effort to provide for her children. When defeat stares her in the face, she doesn't even whimper, but taking her lot as a matter of course, she grimly grits her teeth and braves the struggle again. No matter what pain she suffers from overwork, she has always a smile of comfort for the childish fears of her little ones; no matter how weary she is, she is always ready to forget her own weariness at the slightest hint of danger to one of her children. Look to the widows of this earth and you will find that many of them compare to the angels of heaven. This sweet promise is a quality which comes from the development of a noble character, for in it are courage, love, determination, endurance, faith, etc.

Should Women Be Trained for Careers?

Many parents feel that they should prepare their daughters to make a living in the event of widowhood, divorce or other compelling emergencies. Consider the seriousness of this step from the following viewpoints:

1. If one of the charms of womanhood is feminine dependency, a girl should not center her education around a career, in which she becomes *independent*. By so doing she will lose one of the elements that attracts men to women—her need of manly care, or financial support. She will, in addition, be in danger of acquiring the efficient

masculine traits that so many professional women have, thus reducing her feminine charm. There are, of course, some professional women who manage to stay feminine, either through a nature so strongly feminine that it cannot be subdued or by conscious effort. But it seems a mistake for parents to encourage a girl in the direction of a career, when disadvantages could arise which she would always have to work to overcome.

2. Training for careers encourages women to work, both before and after marriage. The effort the girl has put forth in training seems wasted if it is "put on the shelf." She will just naturally be tempted to use her knowledge at some time or another, whether there is a need or not.

3. Requirements for employment change from year to year. The woman who is qualified at one time may be out of date a few years later and must return for further training to qualify for her work.

4. The independence which results from the ability to make money can be a dangerous thing for a woman, serving as an escape. Many difficulties may arise in early marriage. The woman who is independent will have less incentive to make the adjustment. Divorce may seem an easy way out, since she can be self-supporting.

5. It does not seem logical that a woman should train for a career in the event of a rare emergency, if by so doing she bypasses a rich cultural education that would give her a broad picture of life and thus better prepare her for her role ahead as the wife, mother and homemaker. A man may as well train for motherhood and homemaking if this logic is sound.

The best way for a woman to plan for her future is to plan a *broad education*. The background of a liberal education will assist her greatly in being a wonderful mother to her children, in helping to educate them and inspire them with an appreciation for life and in helping them to make the proper adjustments and preparations for their lives ahead. It will help her equally as a wife, since women who are educated in a broad sense are more interesting, more open-minded to new ideas and challenging thoughts. She will also be a better citizen, have a greater appreciation for life and a greater capacity for happiness. This is providing she has a *good* education and puts something into getting the most out of it. As for homemaking classes and family living subjects, these can be of value, too. Somewhere along the line she will have to learn to cook, sew and manage a household. Many girls learn these skills from their mothers, but if not, she will need to have training or at least have a determination to learn on her own. But all of her education should focus around helping her fill her feminine destiny—to create a happy home.

As for meeting a rare emergency, the woman with the broad cultural background has developed creativeness, intelligence and wisdom. When faced with an emergency, she usually has enough ingenuity to solve her problems. If she must work, she can usually find her way into the working world and qualify for a job better than can the woman who was trained for a career ten years earlier and now finds that she is "out of date."

Summary

As we come to the end of the chapters of femininity, you should have gained a new insight into the subject. Femininity, as you can see, is much more than ruffles and lace. Although a feminine appearance is important, it is of little use without the feminine manner; and neither of them will be of any merit without feminine dependency. Of all the qualities a woman may possess, this one attribute outweighs them all, as far as men are concerned. Without femininity she may have a magnetic personality and she may have a powerful character, but in men's eyes she will not be a woman. A man isn't interested in a great and powerful character. He *wants a woman,* as evident in the following true experiences:

It Helped Me to Become Feminine

"Before I found out about Fascinating Womanhood, I was extremely unhappy. I had doubts about whether or not I even wanted to get married, because there are so many marriages that fail. I didn't know if I could make a marriage that would not only survive, but *be happy* in the process. I had been raised to be very aggressive, independent, and competent, and added to that was the fact that I am very tall and non-feminine looking. Fascinating Womanhood helped me to realize my mistaken frame of mind and become a truly fascinating woman. My husband has become more of a man through my application of the principles, and he says I have made him so happy he just doesn't know what to do, sometimes. I feel anything that can change a person like I was into a soft, feminine woman needs to be taught to every woman, especially women's libbers! They don't know what they're missing!!"

I Tried to Do Too Much

"My success story is quite different from most. I had been married two times before I found Fascinating Womanhood. Now that I have found Fascinating Womanhood I have married again, and it seems to have been planned to happen this way. My mistake was different from most women's. I tried to do too much. My mother was married and divorced many times; consequently, I wanted to be the 'perfect wife.' Instead, I went to a disappointing extreme.

"The first marriage (to my childhood sweetheart) was when I was 18 and he was 20. He had always been spoiled by his parents and family, and I was convinced I should do every task for him that I could possibly perform. This included washing cars, earning money on two full-time jobs so he could attend night classes at college, handling finances, making all the decisions, serving his breakfast in bed, laying out his clothes each day, etc. He appeared to enjoy this, and I thought we had a good marriage, though he was immature.

"Trouble came after two years of marriage, when I became pregnant. Although we had always planned to have children, this baby was not planned at this time. He simply could not accept the responsibility. (After all, he hadn't carried any of our responsibilities yet—I had 'mothered' him!) He told me I must either get an abortion or immediately sign papers to give the baby away as soon as it was born. He claimed the baby would interfere with his completing college and that we would have children later. He told me if I did not do one of these things immediately, he would leave me. This threw me into a traumatic state of shock, crying, disappointment, and I just can't describe the painful hurt feelings. My world collapsed!

"I decided to leave him. After I moved out, however, I received another shock. I lost the baby. The doctor said it was due to the nervous strain. After that, everything was fine as far as my husband was concerned, and he wanted to reconcile. I just couldn't feel the same, so I continued to live alone. After one year and three months, I filed for divorce, still not realizing I made the mistakes by not letting him 'grow.'

"Later I married a man 15 years older than myself. He was very mature about all things, fun, easy to get along with, kind and considerate, handled the money, and was definitely the 'boss' in our home. He had three children from a previous marriage (8, 10, and 12 years old) who visited us each weekend. The children would always bring three friends their own age to visit them for the weekend in our home.

"We all got along very well, and I became very close to his children, and they seemed to love me also. In fact, they still come and visit me, even though I have remarried. Because of my husband's heavy financial responsibility, I still worked and tried to make things as easy for him as possible. My husband and I had an understanding before marriage that I would work only one year to pay off some of the bills, and then I could get pregnant and we would have 'our' baby. Well, we paid more and more money to the ex-wife and child support, and my husband had a guilt complex that seemed to get worse each year. He bought them more and more gifts, trying to compensate for not being with them through the week. We were behind in all our bills, and didn't even own a home, or even pay the rent on time. I kept trying to come to his rescue and never be any problem myself or bother him with my needs. I just kept quiet and let the tensions and frustrations build up inside, all along thinking I was doing the right thing. The children would call continually with problems and the ex-wife would call, too. At one time my husband even made the statement: 'You can take care of yourself, but they can't.' I should have heard what he was trying to tell me . . . *you don't need me . . . they do!*

"Finally, after three and one-half years I asked him if we could either buy a house for OUR marriage, and have OUR baby, and if not, I wanted OUT! I wanted to start my life rather than finish up his first marriage. Soon after that I had the marriage annulled on the grounds that he had deceived me when we were married, promising children and then refusing. He said he didn't feel he was doing enough for the three he already had, and did not want to bring another baby into the world and have to support it for twenty years thus taking away from his three children he already had.

"After the marriage was annulled I felt pretty empty.

250

I had put everything I had into both marriages, but still failed as a wife; I just didn't understand. I thought I was doing all any woman could. Then I found Fascinating Womanhood. I read it, and after doing so, I took a long time deciding whether to ever risk another marriage. Then I met my 'Mr. Wonderful.' He was only five years older than I, he had no children from his previous marriage, but wanted a family. He definitely was the 'boss' between us, and seemed to be all the things I wanted and admired. We were married eight months later. I had completed my first Fascinating Womanhood course, and was ready to let go and live it. I am a completely different woman in this marriage. I still do very many special things for my husband, and he comes first. I love him handling the responsibilities of his role, and I stay in my role as a woman.

"I have had my fondest wish granted by my husband. He has allowed me to quit working. I had worked for ten years with the Aerospace industry, and held quite a high position. I enjoyed the people and everyone said I would not enjoy staying home, especially with no children. I am busy all day, every day, and I'm happy to say that all those people were wrong. I love being home! I know that Fascinating Womanhood has taught me how to enjoy my home and my role as wife and homemaker. I just light up when 'Mr. Wonderful' comes home for lunch and dinner. We are planning a family, and it is so comforting to have a husband who wants children and is looking forward to our first child.

"I have now completed three Fascinating Womanhood courses and plan to teach in the very near future. Fascinating Womanhood has taught me the true meaning of the happiness in being a woman, and being married to a wonderful man. My husband thinks Fascinating Womanhood is the greatest! He tells his friends if they get a wife only half as good as his, they will really 'luck out.' "

I Stopped Killing My Own Snakes

"Before I started practicing Fascinating Womanhood, our home was anything but happy. Now I can truthfully say that the harmony we have is more than I had thought possible and it is increasing every day.

"Considering the fact that my husband and I have been Christians for 21 years, it really came as a shock to me to find that I was the one that needed to do the changing. Only when confronted with my self-righteous attitude while reading Fascinating Womanhood could I accept it and change.

"Oh, the heartache I needn't have gone through with our oldest son. He is just 20 years old, and he has had mama telling him what to do and when to do it for too long. Now I can see what caused his rebellion in the first place. (Me!) He returned home this summer to work on the farm for his father, and with the help of Fascinating Womanhood, things went smoother than they have for years. Our 15-year-old daughter is responding, too, and our married daughter is a faithful follower.

"I'm saving the best for last, my husband. He takes me to dinner at least twice a week. He has cancelled his big hunting trip to Alaska, which he has been planning for six months. Says he would rather spend the money taking me to Mexico. When I have gone out of town to shop, he services the car for me, without being asked. The other day he even carried my golf clubs to the car because he thought they were too heavy for me. All this for the girl who has been 'killing her own snakes' for years! He knows how I love flowers and has brought me two bouquets he picked himself. This from the man I've always considered as being cold and unsentimental."

Assignment

1. Analyze your life's responsibilities to see if you are doing any masculine work.
2. If you are: 1) Ask him to take it over. 2) Stop doing it and risk the consequences. 3) If you feel stuck with it, do it in a feminine manner.

18
Radiant Happiness

I have already told you of inner happiness which is a spiritual quality and must be earned. What, then, is radiant happiness? Radiant happiness is a *voluntary* quality and can be "put on," like a smile. It is such things as cheerfulness, laughter, singing, joyfulness, smiles, bright eyes, pleasant outlooks, hope, optimism, the ability to radiate happiness to others, and a sense of humor.

There are many women who are happy at heart, but it may never have occurred to them that it is important to show it. Do not make the mistake of putting your happiness *under a bushel* where no one can see it. Instead, *put it on a candlestick* where everyone in the room may benefit.

Radiant happiness is one of the real charms that men find fascinating in women, counting far more than physical beauty of face and form. Beautiful women should not make the mistake of "resting on their laurels," hoping that their pretty faces alone will make them attractive. Without a smile and sparkling eyes, they will have little appeal. Men admire pretty girls as they do beautiful pictures and scenes from nature, but they search for radiant smiling women to be their life's companion. Women who lack beauty of face and form due to irregular features, often turn out to be real charmers because they have worked diligently to make up for these defects by acquiring the qualities that really count with men. Amelia, you will remember, was chubby and stout, with a short nose and round cheeks; yet she succeeded in winning the love of all men who came near her. This was partially due to her smiling lips, eyes and heart.

There is great emphasis in our modern times upon the appearance, especially of clothes, hair styles, etc. This emphasis upon the "outer shell" is all very good, but if radiance is not also added, it will be like serving a beautiful banquet, arranging the table with the finest china, silver and crystal, and then serving an inferior quality of food. For example, a girl can be dressed in the latest styles from the most expensive salons, with her hair arranged in the most feminine and alluring fashion, but if she also appears with a disagreeable or sour expression on her face, she will be a "flop" as far as men are concerned. If, on the other hand, she appears in rather plain clothing and hair style, but a smile of radiance included, let a man notice her and he will be fascinated, and her ordinary appearance will mean very little in comparison with the beauty of her face. This is not to underestimate the value of feminine and girlish clothes, etc., but only to stress that unless radiance is added, the effect will fail to be fascinating.

Deruchette, Amelia and Dora

The most fascinating trait of Deruchette was her ability to radiate happiness to others, to "shed joy around" and "cast light upon dark days." She had in her smile alone a "power" which was great enough to lift the spirits of others. She radiated joy to her entire household, for her presence alone brought a "light" to the household, and her approach was like a cheerful warmth. As the author says, "she passes by and we are content; she stays a while and we are happy."

Amelia was "kind, fresh and smiling, with a smiling heart." Dora had a "gay little laugh and a delightful little voice." Mrs. Woodrow Wilson also had this quality, for her husband said, "She was so radiant, so happy!" Men simply do not want or enjoy women who are glum, depressed, or even overly serious. They seek out women who are vibrant, alive and happy!

Dolly Madison

The longest reigning and gayest of all first ladies of the White House was Dolly Madison. During the eight years her husband presided, she won the hearts of her countrymen and was known as the most popular person in the U.S. and the most loved. In Parisian turban topped with a plume, her neck and arms strung with pearls, she was the perfect hostess—bubbly and natural, tactful and gracious. Her zest for life never ran out. Without becoming ill, one day at age 82 she simply passed from a nap to death. "She sparkled," reported a friend, "up to the very verge of the grave."

Ninon de Lenclos

Ninon de Lenclos of the 17th Century courts of France was another woman of special charm and radiance. Some of the greatest men of the century loved her, and she is said to have won the hearts of three generations of men in a single family, for she lived and retained her beauty and charm into her eighties. The most interesting women of France were her devoted friends. The most wonderful thing about her, everyone said, was her eager delight in everything around her. In her own words she said, "You never hear me say 'this is good or this is bad,' but a thousands times a day I say, 'I enjoy, I enjoy.' "

A Sense of Humor

A sense of humor will not only add to your radiance, but it is a means of handling the rough times in life in a way that will reduce tension and problems. So important is this quality that an entire book could be written about its application in daily living. I only stress here that it is important, will make a woman more radiant, and is a means of turning mishaps into amusing situations. For example, laugh if you spill a plate of spaghetti on the floor, run out of gas on the freeway, tear a hole in your new fall coat, lose a ten-dollar bill, or lock yourself out of your house in your nightgown. Will fretting or being miserable about the situation do any more good to solve the problem? No. In fact, if you can keep your spirits up, you will be much *more* likely to solve your problems.

How to Acquire Radiant Happiness

1. *Work for Inner Happiness:* It will be difficult to radiate happiness to others if you are not happy at heart, or within your spirit. This, then, is the first step.
2. *Make a Conscious Effort to be Radiant:* It is surprising what a voluntary effort to be smiling and cheerful will do. A good suggestion is the following: After you have applied your make-up, stand before the mirror for a few seconds and practice radiance. Remember, your artful make-up will do little good if you wear a glum expression. If you leave the room with a happy face, your friends and family will be apt to reflect back this same expression, and

your day will begin with good spirit and charm. The radiance, however, must be of the lips, the eyes and the entire countenance, and not just a stiff wooden-like smile. After this good beginning, add a cheerful attitude. Try not to be skeptical or dubious about life in general. Certainly some things we must look upon with doubt, but our attitude should be one of optimism, hope, and emphasis on the brighter side of life. It will be difficult to have a smile such as Deruchette, which has the "power to lift the spirit of others," unless we also maintain a bright outlook.

3. *Radiant Happiness to All:* The best way to form the habit of being happy is to radiate happiness to all, and not merely to your circle of family and friends. Deruchette "shed joy around" which suggests that it was for everyone. Radiate not only to the happy, but to the sad, the depressed and disconsolate. The world delights in sunny people; there are more than enough serious ones. A bright smile does more good for the downhearted than food for the hungry. Give sunshine also to the frowning and disagreeable. They need it most of all. Give whether they are deserving or not. Your smile will be even more appreciated because it is such a rare pleasure with those who frown.

4. *Smile Through Adversity:* It seems to be a natural part of life that we have periods of discouragement. It is then that smiling seems much more difficult, and even unnatural. However, as with all Christian and moral teachings, we are expected to do the supernatural thing. It is a mark of true character, and especially womanly character, to smile in the face of adversity. The following lines by Ella Wheeler Wilcox express this trait beautifully:

It is easy enough to be pleasant
When life flows by like a song.
But the one worthwhile is the one who can smile
When everything goes dead wrong.
For the test of the heart is trouble
And it always comes with the years.
And the smile that is worth the praises of earth
Is the smile that shines through tears.

When Not to Smile

There are some occasions when it is best not to be radiant. For example, when you are in the presence of someone who is depressed, your happy attitude *may* suggest a lack of sympathy. In this case, it will be best to be serious and show an understanding for what the other person is suffering. Try to be perceptive of these situations in which gravity and sympathy seem more appropriate. You can tell by the reaction of the person. If they seem offended by your happiness, you can be sure they feel it is not in harmony with their low spirits, and they wish you would stop.

The Real Charm

Inner happiness combined with radiant happiness is an essential part of the real charm that men find fascinating in women. Inner happiness, as we have learned, brings a calm spirit and tranquility which is a peaceful beauty. It is like clear calm water in a pond. Radiant happiness is like the lily pads that add breathtaking beauty. Beneath the flowers you can see the stillness of the waters. The charm is in the over-all effect.

"There is in this world no function more important than that of being charming—to shed joy around, to cast light upon dark days, to be the golden thread of our destiny, and the very spirit of grace and harmony. Is not this to render a service?"

19

Fresh Radiant Health

The foundation of fresh beauty is genuine good health, not only for the health itself, but for the fresh and joyous spirit health sustains in the woman's appearance, actions and attitude. How alluring are sparkling and dancing eyes, lustrous hair, clear voice, buoyancy of manner, and the animation which good health brings to the face and vivacity it communicates to the thoughts. We cannot, therefore, attach too much importance to this qualification.

We all know the importance of good health, but our trouble lies in thinking of good health in terms of not being ill. The perfection of healthy womanhood is more than merely being well. A fresh radiant appearance is a result of *health in rich abundance*. Health, like happiness, is based upon laws and comes as a result of understanding and applying them. The following are the fundamentals of good health:

1. Correct internal disorders.
2. Get enough sleep.
3. Exercise.
4. Drink plenty of water.
5. Get fresh air.
6. Eat properly.
7. Relax—at work or play.
8. Have a healthy mental attitude.
9. Control weight.

1. *Correct Internal Disorders:* It is impossible to attain health if there are internal disorders. Often women will go for years with such things as infected teeth, infected internal organs, disorders of the blood or glands and other malfunctions of the body which cause them to have poor health. Many of these ailments can be eliminated by proper attention.

2. *Get Enough Sleep:* We all know the value of

sufficient sleep, but women often neglect this essential, due to heavy responsibilities. If you are robbed of your sleep by too many things to do, ask yourself if your activities are more important than your health. Many things we do are a waste of time when it comes right down to facts, especially when they are measured against genuine good health.

3. *Exercise:* Exercise is as important as the food we eat in both preserving life and youth and in producing health. You may feel that you have enough exercise in the ordinary activities like walking, bending and reaching. These motions of the body do not bring into play all of the muscles. As a result, many women suffer from poor posture, sagging muscles, fat deposits, and loss of health. If exercise seems like merely an added labor to your already busy schedule, remember that exercise can actually rest a weary person. Calling a different set of muscles into activity refreshes and stimulates the body.

4. *Drink Plenty of Water:* The body is made up of 66 percent water—more than two-thirds by weight and several gallons in all. If you do not drink enough water, your body will be forced to use its water over and over again. Your whole system will suffer unless refreshed frequently with a new supply of water.

5. *Get Fresh Air:* A good air supply consists of three things. The first is having *fresh air with ample oxygen* content, the second is to *breathe deeply enough* to take the air into your lungs, and the third is to make certain that the air *is not lacking in moisture.* Oxygen is our most important food. What good food is to the stomach, oxygen is to the blood. Make sure that you have fresh air in your rooms and also that you breathe deeply enough to take it into your lungs. Poor posture and lack of exercise are responsible for shallow breathing, which leads to a shortage of oxygen in the blood. The purpose of exercise is not only the development of the muscles, but also a healthy intake of air, deep into the lungs.

Most of us realize the importance of fresh air, but many do not realize the importance of moisture content, both day and night. Many modern heating systems dry the air so that even in a fairly moist climate the air in the house may be dry. This overly dry air can cause colds, sore throats, and even lung irritation. The solutions are to either turn the furnace off at night and open the windows, have a moisturizer installed in the furnace, use a vaporizer, or hang a wet towel in the bedrooms at night. The same care can be taken in the daytime if the furnace is used then.

6. *Eat Properly:* What is a safe guide for proper eating? Our appetite is not a safe guide, for even bad foods taste good. There are many foods and products on the market. Which are good and which ones harmful? Many of the studies concerning foods are confusing, and some of them are contradictory.

Nature reveals to us the secrets of good eating. We cannot improve on an apple as it comes from a tree, or a banana, or a potato as it comes from the earth. *Eat foods as near to nature as possible* is the safest rule. There is fresh food available in every season. The summer brings its fruit, vegetables and melons; the fall brings apples, squash and potatoes which last until spring. Early spring brings the navel oranges, late spring the berries and more fresh vegetables. All of these are best when eaten fresh in the season in which they grow. Nature also produces the grains which remain fresh for several seasons. Wholesome foods fall into five categories:

> fresh fruits
> fresh vegetables
> nuts
> grains
> meats

There are many highly processed and refined foods on the market today, many of them containing preservatives. They come in boxes, cans and packages. Some of the vital elements have been removed, and in an effort to make up for this lack, man has added his own created vitamins and minerals. Our Creator's foods have been tampered with. Can man improve upon nature?

7. *Relax:* The secret of being able to relax at work or play is essential to both health and charm, and is an ability which is fairly easy to acquire. The mind controls the body, and this control can cause either tension or relaxation. If you will merely *tell your body to relax*, you will immediately feel a relief of tension. This same technique can be applied in getting to sleep when you are suffering tension.

8. *Have a Healthy Mental Attitude:* The effect of unwholesome attitudes such as worry, fear, anxiety, pessimism, hate, resentments, impatience, envy, anger, or any other irritating mental image can have a detrimental effect upon the human body. Its destructive influence is carried

through the nervous system to the entire body. For example, people have been known to die of anger. Even after the temporary emotion has left, the physical damage may remain. A healthy mental attitude comes as a result of good character. If you suffer from these unwholesome attitudes, it is a sign of weakness in character and a need to develop your angelic side.

In contrast, wholesome attitudes, buoyant and kindly thoughts, have exactly the opposite effect. Faith, optimism, love, kindness, cheerfulness, sympathy, and enthusiasm all harmonize with body function and tend to invigorate the system.

9. *Control Weight:* Often, overweight people tend to become discouraged with their problem, feeling that it is a lifetime struggle and perhaps not worth the continual effort. They may feel that to be slim means to "starve" for the rest of their lives. But take heart with this thought: When a woman finally reaches her normal size, or better still, just a few pounds below her normal weight, it is not the struggle it once was. The appetite at this point tends to become normal, or at least controllable with reasonable effort. You can reach the point that it is not a major problem any longer—for many women have done so to prove it. With reasonable care you can keep that figure for the rest of your life.

After you reach your normal weight, make it a habit to *weigh every day!* If you gain one pound during the day, you can go on a diet the next day with only one pound to lose. This makes weight control easy. You will, however, have to be consistent about weighing each day, without exception, for this plan to work.

There are many good standard diets which will gradually take off the pounds. One is the diabetic diet, which is one of the most wholesome. This can be had from your doctor. Another is the plan followed by "Weight Watchers." I would like to strongly recommend "Overeaters Anonymous." It is based on principles of Alcoholics Anonymous and deals with root problems which cause compulsive eating. It has miraculously helped many people, sometimes when all other programs have failed. For information write to Overeaters Anonymous, P.O. Box 3372, Beverly Hills, California 90202.

One of the best rules to follow if you are inclined to gain weight is to make a determination to eliminate all sweets from the diet for the rest of your life. This would include all pie, cake, ice cream, candy, gum, soft drinks, cookies, pastries, puddings, etc., including such things as syrup on hotcakes or jam on bread, etc. If you will try this drastic elimination of sweets, you will find that in a month or two your desire for these things will lessen, if not entirely leave, and that you will also feel better due to improved health. There is no doubt that this step will do much to preserve your health, lengthen your life, and also help you retain beautiful teeth for the rest of your life, as well as help you keep your figure. Certainly these incentives are strong enough to make this step possible. With this diet, you can eat almost everything else. You can eat all of the vegetables, potatoes and bread that you feel hungry for, within reason. You will have to avoid fats to some extent, but you will find that when you eliminate sweets, you also eliminate many of the foods that contain large amounts of fats.

Another diet suggestion is to not eat after 3:00 p.m. Those foods which you take in your body in the evening hours are more easily assimilated due to your being more relaxed. Before three, you can eat a fairly reasonable diet that is well balanced. You will have to be firm in your determination to not eat after 3:00 p.m., however. If you break the rules for even a few mouthfuls of food, the diet will not "work." If you follow this plan "to the letter," you will lose close to a pound a day. If you do not find it convenient to eat your meals before 3:00, try eating only two meals a day. You can eliminate any one of the three, breakfast, lunch or dinner, but try not to eat late in the evening. Whatever plan you choose, remember that men dislike excess fat and that it will be more difficult for you to appear dainty, feminine, and girlish if you have a chunky figure. Take seriously, then, any excess weight you may have and work with determination to lose it.

If Health Is Beyond Your Reach

There are some who, because of permanent damage, cannot attain this ideal of abundant health. If, however, they maintain a healthy mental attitude, they may appear much more healthy than they actually are. Elizabeth Barrett Browning was an invalid, yet one of the truly charming women in history. Her husband, Robert Browning, adored her. Her physical weakness was not an added attraction, but she had an abundance of other womanly qualities which overcame the physical lack. Radiant health is only one qualification of Angela Human. If you have a healthy mental attitude, you may still be a fascinating woman.

Cleanliness and Grooming

Good health is not the only essential in attaining a fresh, healthy appearance. Cleanliness and grooming are also important. The teeth, the hair, the nails, the feet, and cleanliness of the entire body are vital contributions to the effect of health.

A fresh appearance in clothing is also attractive to men. Such things as fresh starched collars, flowers (real or artificial), clean shining ribbons, polished shoes, and clean, well pressed clothes contribute to a fresh look. Certain materials and colors appear fresh, while others are drab. Clean stripes, polka-dots, ginghams, daisy designs and animated prints suggest freshness.

Make-up is also important in the effect of health. Men are not opposed to artificial beauty if it makes the woman appear more alive and healthy. In fact, your attention to these details only indicates to him your efforts to please him. Eye make-up and lipstick especially help to make the face appear fresh and healthy.

Assignment

Evaluate your health in comparison with the ideal taught in this lesson. If you have a weak point, or points, organize a health-improvement program.

20

Childlikeness

Except ye be converted and become as little children ye shall not enter into the kingdom of heaven.

What is meant by the Biblical statement "except ye become as little children"? Doesn't this imply that children have qualities which we would do well to copy? The greatest childlike trait is that of being teachable, but I believe that beyond this, there are other childlike traits which are admirable. The point I wish to stress is this: *We would do well to copy the manner in which children express emotions,* especially the emotions of anger, hurt, disappointment, sympathy, tenderness and joy. I believe that by so doing, women can solve some of their most difficult marital problems.

In all of the previous chapters, I have suggested that women do a lot of giving. Childlikeness is a balance to all of this. It is the means whereby we keep from being a doormat, or keep from being trampled on. And yet childlikeness is fun. It is the spice and spark of the subject and keeps the perfection of the Angelic side from becoming cloysome. Men love this trait in women. It amuses and fascinates them because, like femininity, it is such a contrast to their own superior strength and masculine ability. In this chapter and the next, I will explain twelve important ways of being childlike.

The first is that of *childlike anger.* The most urgent need a woman has to be childlike is in dealing with anger, especially if she is angry with her own husband. She can relieve some of her most distressing problems by handling them with childlikeness. But, before explaining this method, I would like to review the feeling of real anger and how it is usually dealt with.

Anger is a very real feeling which we must deal with in one way or another. It is an inner turmoil which feels like steam gathering in a teapot. If intense, it can be sickening, frustrating, and even painful. What do we do with this uncomfortable feeling? Here are the usual ways we handle our angry feelings:

1. *Self-control:* We can be in control of our actions, refusing to give way to ugly words and expressions. The violent temper may still be there but is held firmly in check by tight lips, counting to ten, and other methods of self-control. This method causes pressure to build within as steam pressure in a teapot. You may be in control, but there is an inner turmoil. Such a trapping of emotions can cause severe frustration and can even be damaging to the health and emotions. It has, in fact, caused heart attacks.

2. *Suppress It:* We can suppress the emotion of anger by subduing our hostile *feelings.* There may be a struggle within, an effort to ignore feelings or thrust them down inside where they will not have to be dealt with and will no longer cause us trouble. Many women have learned to thus deal with emotions, from childhood. They have been taught that if they are to be nice little girls, they must not be angry. Although this may be better for society than ugly violence, there are two harmful consequences we would do well to observe:

First, when we subdue miserable feelings, we tend to form *resentments* which may last for hours, days, or even years. This can be responsible for a sullen attitude in women and causes much damage to relationships. Second, suppressed anger can be *damaging to the emotions.* We learned in our study of "man's pride" that those who suppress emotions tend to acquire a self-induced numbness which dulls the sting of pain. But in dulling the pain it also numbs the pleasurable sensations. Thus, when we suppress anger we reduce our ability to enjoy pleasant things such as beautiful music and the beauties of nature. We turn off the fire from the teapot, but in doing so we cause it to become cold. When we consider these consequences, we have to recognize that there has to be a better way of dealing with anger.

3. *Release It:* When we are angry we can lose our tempers and express violent emotions. But when we do, we

must realize that this explosive action is ugly and destroys feminine charm. It is like the steam gathering in the teapot to the point of forcing the lid to fly off. This reaction is probably responsible for the expressions "blowing her top," or "flying off the handle." This means of expressing anger can cause deep wounds and sever relationships in a way as to be almost irreparable. There must be a better way to express anger.

4. *Talk Things Over:* We can sit down and talk things over with our husband, reasoning, accusing, criticizing, implying, appealing, and especially telling him how he needs to treat us better. These attempts almost always fail because the man takes a defensive attitude. And if the man is more clever than the woman, he will succeed in putting the blame on her for everything. This method usually amounts to a quiet civilized argument. None of the above methods of expressing anger are successful, since they cause damage to the woman, to her husband or their relationship. The only successful method of dealing with anger, to my knowledge, is the following:

1. Childlike Anger

Her very frowns are fairer far
Than smiles of other maidens are.

AUTHOR UNKNOWN

What is childlike anger? It is the charming, expressive anger, spunk or sauciness of a little girl. There is no better school for learning childlike anger than watching the antics of little children, especially little girls who have been given an abundance of love. They are so trusting, so sincere, and so innocent, and yet so piquant and outspoken that they are often teased into anger. They are too innocent to feel hate, jealousy, resentment and the uglier emotions. When such a child is teased, she does not respond with some hideous sarcasm. Instead, she stamps her foot and shakes her curls and pouts. She gets adorably angry at herself because her efforts to respond are impotent. Finally, she switches off and threatens never to speak to you again, then glances back at you over her shoulder to see if you thought she really meant it, only to stomp her foot in impatience when she sees that you are not the least bit fooled.

A scene such as this will invariably make us smile

with amusement. We feel an irresistible longing to pick up such a child and hug it. We would do anything rather than permit such an adorable little thing to suffer danger or want; to protect and care for such a delightfully human little creature would be nothing less than a delight. This is much the same feeling that a woman inspires in a man when she expresses anger in a childlike way. Her ridiculous exaggeration of manner makes him suddenly want to laugh; makes him feel, in contrast, stronger, more sensible and more of a man. This is why women who are little spitfires—independent and saucy—are often sought after by men. This anger, however, must be the sauciness of a child, and not the intractable stubbornness of a woman well able to "kill her own snakes."

How to Express Childlike Anger

1. *Character:* To express anger with the innocence of a child, there must be an absence of bitterness, resentment, hate, sarcasm, or the ugly emotions. If harsh feelings are present, or you are a woman who has an explosive temper, it is likely that you will not be able to express childlike anger until you work on character and overcome these serious weaknesses.

2. *Manner:* Next time you are angry with your husband, why not try some childlike mannerisms: Stomp your foot, lift your chin high and square your shoulders. Then, if the situation merits it, turn and walk briskly to the door, pause and look back over your shoulder. Or you can put both hands on your hips and open your eyes wide. Or, beat your fists on your husband's chest. Men love this! Or, there is the timid, frustrated manner of pouting, looking woeful or looking with downcast eyes while mumbling under your breath, or putting both hands to your face, saying "Oh, dear!" These are only a few of the childlike mannerisms you can adopt.

Some of these actions may seem unnatural to you, at first. If they do, you will have to be an actress to succeed in childlike anger, even if only a ham actress. But, remember, you will be launching an acting career which will save you pain, tension, frustration, a damaged relationship and perhaps even save a marriage. Is any acting career of greater importance? So, turn on the drama. It is guaranteed to ease tension and bring humor into your life instead of pain.

3. *Use Adjectives:* Acquire a list of expressions or words which compliment masculinity, such as "you big, tough brute," or "you stubborn, obstinate man," or "you hairy beast." Other appropriate adjectives are—unyielding, determined, difficult, hard-hearted, inflexible, unruly, stiff-necked, indomitable and invincible. Be certain that your words compliment masculinity and will not belittle his ego, such as the words little, imp, pip-squeak, insignificant, weak, simple-minded, etc.

4. *Exaggerate: Exaggerate his treatment of you* by saying, for example, "How can a great big man like you pick on a poor little helpless girl like me!" or "So this is the way you treat a poor little helpless girl," or "Oh, what a dreadful thing to do!" or "You are the meanest man in town." Or, *be charmingly defensive* by saying, "I'm just a poor, erring, wayward little human being," or "Everyone has at least one little fault. Nobody's perfect!" Or, *make childlike threats by saying,* "I'll never speak to you again," or "I won't do anything for you anymore," or "I'll tell your mother on you." Be sure that your expressions represent a trustful, feminine woman of high character and not a vulgar or suspicious one. Do not, for example, use words that are crude or insulting, such as nasty, wicked, dumb, ridiculous, hateful, rude, etc.

It is interesting to note that the reason children tend to exaggerate is due to their impotence—their feeling of littleness or helplessness in the presence of superior adults or even in the presence of other children. Unconsciously, in moments of frustration, they feel they must make up for their smallness by exaggerations. Therefore, when a woman uses this same method, she gives the man the impression that she also is impotent and helpless and therefore childlike.

Dora's Anger

A good illustration of childlike anger is found in the story of *David Copperfield.* In this particular situation which I shall review, Dora responded to David's criticism with the charms of both exaggerations and adjectives. Here is the situation: David had criticized Dora because she did not manage the hired help well and, because of this, one of them had stolen Dora's gold watch and fallen into further difficulty. David put the blame on Dora. The hired help was a young boy—a page, as he was called.

"I began to be afraid," said David, "that the fault is not entirely on one side, but that these people turn out ill because we don't turn out very well ourselves." "Oh, what an accusation!" exclaimed Dora, opening her eyes wide, *"to say that you ever saw me take gold watches. Oh! Oh! you cruel fellow, to compare your affectionate wife to a transported page! Why didn't you tell me your opinion of me before we were married? Why didn't you say, you hard-hearted thing, that you were convinced that I was worse than a transported page. Oh, what a dreadful opinion to have of me! Oh, my goodness!"* Notice that Dora uses adjectives—*cruel* and *hard-hearted* and that she exaggerates his treatment of her.

Becky Sharp

Another illustration of sauciness is found in the story of *Vanity Fair*, the story in which we find the character of Amelia. Becky Sharp also succeeded in charming men throughout the story. On the occasion I shall mention, Amelia's brother, Joseph, had tricked Miss Becky into eating hot peppers. "I shall take good care how I let you choose for me another time," said Rebecca, as they went down to dinner. "I didn't know men were fond of putting poor little harmless girls to pain." "By Gad, Miss Rebecca, I wouldn't hurt you for the world," was Joseph's apology.

When You Have a Right to Be Angry

You have a right to express anger *when you have been mistreated*—when you have been insulted, criticized harshly, imposed on too far, treated unfairly, ignored, teased, etc. But you do *not* have a right to express anger *when the man has failed in his world of responsibility*, when he has made a stupid mistake in his work, lost his job, neglected to cut the lawn, balance the budget or wash the car, etc. He has a right to be himself, to be weak, lazy, to neglect his duty or even to fail. That is his department. He does not, however, have a right to *mistreat you*. This is where we draw the line.

You should also *not* express anger *when you feel the emotions of hate, bitterness, resentments and ugly emotions*, as I have already explained. At least, you should not express this anger to your husband. If one experiences

269

these violent emotions, it is better to pour out angry feelings to a trusted friend or parent, or engage in hard physical work. Then, work to develop character, especially the qualities of humility and forgiveness, before you express anger to your husband. Only when ugly emotions have been overcome can anger be effectively expressed without damaging relationships.

Express childlike anger at the *moment of offense,* not sometime later when you have time to think things through and decide just what you are going to say and do. This means you will have to think quickly and plan some reactions ahead of time. If you *do not* respond "at the moment," then you can consider it your own failure, and you may as well forgive and forget. Review the situation and be prepared wih a response next time. Remember, don't blame your husband. If you do not express anger "at the moment," it is *you* who has failed.

Also do not use childlike anger as a means of *reforming a man,* thinking he will stop insulting and neglecting you, etc. He may, but on the other hand, he may continue to mistreat you. If he does, keep on responding with childlike anger. The only purpose of childlike anger is to give vent to feelings, to communicate a message, and to be fascinating.

Express anger at times of *medium* offenses. In other words, it is best to overlook *trifles,* lest we appear "picky." *Major* offenses may be so disturbing that they are difficult to approach with childlikeness (not impossible). But, do apply childlike anger in times of *medium offenses.* Now, I would like to comment about the *major offenses:*

Major Offenses

There are some serious ways in which men sometimes mistreat women—infidelity, physical abuse, gross neglect, non-support, and lack of respect for human rights and liberty, etc. When a man thus mistreats his wife, she needs to live the entire philosophy of Fascinating Womanhood for a period of time, to soften his heart and try to bring about a reformation in his behavior. Men's ugly actions are sometimes the woman's fault, sometimes due to her lack of acceptance, admiration, sympathetic understanding, and her failure to place him No. 1. When she so neglects his greatest needs, she can bring out his ugly side.

But, in addition to living all of Fascinating Woman-hood, major offenses can sometimes be handled with childlikeness. For example, a woman wrote to me the following experience: "One night my husband was out with another woman. As I waited in agony for him to come home in the early morning hours, I determined to react with childlikeness. When he came home, I ran to the door to meet him, threw my arms around him weeping, and said, 'Oh, how could you do this to poor little me?' My husband was aroused to compassion and took me tenderly in his arms. This was the beginning of a new life for us."

A Word to Those Who Resist Childlike Anger

If you find it *unnatural* to express anger in a childlike way, remember, as a child this response was natural to you. It was only in growing up that you lost it. You need only recapture that which belongs to you by nature. Many women who have felt silly expressing their anger as I have instructed, have accepted the challenge, worked on this quality, and been surprised to find an inborn talent return.

Some women claim that they *do not need* to express childlike anger, that life is going along fine for them now. This may be true in some cases, but as long as we have men who are thoughtless and critical and as long as we have sensitive women who become upset, angry or resentful towards their husbands, we need childlike anger.

There will be some who will try to solve their anger problems *in a different way*—by changing their husbands. There is a human tendency in all of us to try to reduce our feeling of anger by changing the person who offends us, or at least *trying* to change them. "If he would only change," we may reason subconsciously "if he would only stop doing the things which make me angry, my problems of anger would disappear." This seems to be the easier way. However, this is not the right way. The change should come within ourselves. It is always safer in human relationships to change ourselves rather than to depend upon someone else to change. We should *let men act themselves*. We women should *learn how to react*. I am not implying that men do not need to improve; only stating that they may not, and we therefore need a successful way of dealing with problems such as anger.

There are a few women who think the *idea of*

childlike anger ridiculous. How can they, as grown-up women, take the part of a little girl who stomps her foot, shakes her curls and pouts. Can they look adorable in such a scene? I challenge women to try it—even once. Remember, it may seem ridiculous to you, but not to a man. Of course, if you do not play your part well, if you laugh and make a joke of it, you will make a fool of yourself and the man will, of course, think it is ridiculous. Or, if you fail to appear as a child, you will not get the message across and the man will be unimpressed. But, if you will apply these principles as I have taught them, and with sincerity, acting the part of the little girl, the man will be charmed.

You do not, however, always have to stomp your foot and shake your curls. There are other methods of childlike anger. You can still use adjectives, exaggerations and amusing statements that will charm him. But, if you feel you cannot express yourself in any of the ways I have suggested, *do* find some acceptable means of expressing anger, so that you will not form resentments towards your husband and thus harm your marriage relationship. In fact, *you owe it to your husband,* as well as yourself, to express anger. You do him no favor to smother your angry feelings and then form resentments and grudges towards him. Eliminating these problems is my main purpose in teaching childlike anger. It builds better marriages.

How to Overcome Anger

As long as we are angry, as long as there is the miserable feeling within us, we should seek effective means of dealing with this problem or releasing the inner turmoil. But, there are things we can do to overcome the tendency to anger, such as the following:

1. *Spiritual Growth:* We can overcome the tendency to anger by growing in spirit. As we learn to be forgiving, understanding and patient, as we acquire humility, allowing for the mistakes and human frailties of others, we overcome the tendency to anger. We no longer experience the turmoil and distressing feelings which accompany anger. Through spiritual growth, we overcome this human trait. However, in the process of becoming angels, we are still human beings, prone to anger. We must, along life's way, have some means of dealing with this human fault.

2. *Self-respect:* Those women who have a wholesome self-respect, or a good self-image, are less likely to be

offended and therefore less prone to anger than women who do not have this virtue. With self-respect comes a certain "invulnerability of spirit" which keeps the person from being hurt by other people, even their husband. It is a sort of "sticks and stones may break my bones, but words will never hurt me" attitude. A woman who is invulnerable to criticism or abuse will feel "I know you neglect me, criticize me, or treat me unfairly, but I know that you like me too much to do this intentionally." In this way she is marvelously freed from the damaging effects of offenses and keeps her relationship intact.

For an illustration, I was in the company of a lady and her husband when he criticized her in a way that I thought was rather severe. He told her, for example, that she never cooked, sewed, or cleaned the house and that he had to hire a housekeeper to do all of this for her. Then he told her that she never even taught the children anything and he thought she should stay home more and do these things. I was surprised to see the lady smile and even laugh a little. She told him that he was right and very soon she would turn over a new leaf and improve. Do you know why she was invulnerable to his criticism? It was because she had a wholesome respect for herself. She knew these weaknesses, but she also knew her virtues. She was actually a wonderful wife and loved her children. They all knew this and so did she.

But here is another thought: Even if we grow in spirit and have a wholesome self-respect so that we are invulnerable, it is not morally right for us to allow someone else to push us around or trample on us *too far*. We should respond to mistreatment in such a way as to preserve our human dignity. This we do in a proper and feminine way by expressing our emotions with *childlikeness*.

When Men Mistreat Others

When men are unkind to us, we can respond with "childlike anger," but what about when they are unkind to *someone else*? Many of these situations can be handled beautifully with childlikeness. For example, let me refer you to the story of *The Little Minister*, by James Barrie:

Nanny, a little old lady was to be evicted from her house and taken to the poorhouse due to lack of money. The Little Minister and the doctor, who were responsible for this eviction, were calculating and somewhat cold, moved only by a sense of justice, as men often are. As they were taking Nanny to the doorway, Babbie walked in. Nanny fell at her feet sobbing, "Do not let them take me away, do not let them take me." With fire in her eyes, Babbie faced the two men. "How dare you," she said, stomping her foot. The two men quaked like malefactors. "You who live in luxury would send her to the poorhouse. I thought better of you." Then, turning to Nanny, "You poor dear. I won't let them take you away."

Not only did she save Nanny from the poorhouse, but it was then that the Little Minister first loved her, for he saw the strength of her noble character and was charmed by her spunk. A little later on in the day, the Little Minister said to Nanny, "She has been very good to you, Nanny. She has an excellent heart!" Similarly, we can bring about compassion and mercy by defending the mistreated with childlikeness. But here again, we must take care to not feel bitterness, or insult or demean the man who has been unkind.

When the Husband Is Angry

In marriage there are two sources of anger. One is when the wife is angry with her husband. The other is when the husband is angry with his wife. Always keep these two situations separate and don't confuse them. When the wife is angry with her husband, the suggested response is childlike anger or sauciness. But *when the husband is angry with his wife*, remember, this is another situation. Sauciness can be successful in some instances but is not always appropriate. Here are some suggestions to consider:

1. *Do Some Thinking:* First, flash in your mind, "He has a right to be angry. He is only human. I become angry, why shouldn't he? If his anger seems more severe and harsh than mine, it is because he is a man." Remember, to expect him not to be angry is to expect him not to be human.

2. *Let Him Express Himself:* Let him pour out his angry feelings, and even encourage him to do so. Remember, in so doing he will rid himself of resentments. If he does not express himself in an acceptable way, try to overlook it. Later on you can teach him some of the

techniques of childlike anger, or how to express anger in a more acceptable way. Men, however, should express childlike anger in a masculine manner.

3. *If You Are Guilty:* Tend to agree with him by saying, "Oh, that was so stupid of me," or "How have you put up with me all of this time?" These expressions are childlike because they are absent of bitterness or hostility and are exaggerated and amusing. Then apologize and ask forgiveness.

4. *If You Are Not Guilty:* If a man is angry with you and you are not guilty, still let him express himself. Remember, even if you are innocent, he *thinks* you are guilty and will have some pent-up feelings which he needs to express. During this time, do not try to defend yourself. Just let him do the talking. After he has finished, you can offer an explanation and clear yourself. But don't embarrass him or make him feel cheap for his false accusations, and don't use cutting words to "get even." Let him know you consider it a misunderstanding and forgive as you would any other error.

5. *Return a Gentle Word for an Angry One:* A feminine response to a man's anger is to speak kindly. If he is harsh, speak gently to him and thus soften his anger. There is a Christian hymn which reads, "You can speak a gentle word to the heart with anger stirred." This is feminine and angelic. One must not, however, take on a "beaten down" attitude in which dignity of spirit is missing.

6. *Teasing Playfulness:* If a man is only mildly angry, cross or irritable, a woman can respond with teasing playfulness, which I will explain in the next chapter. It is a childlike method.

7. *Sauciness:* If your husband's anger really hurts you and seems unjust, then you can respond with childlikeness—a pout, mumble a few words with downcast eyes, or even shed a few tears or any of the methods suggested in this chapter.

Any of the seven methods of dealing with a man's anger will relieve tension and promote good relations. Often anger is intensified by a feeling of frustration due to a need to express anger and a conflicting fear that it will cause problems. If we can allow men to express their anger without fear, we can help them to reduce their angry feelings.

275

2. Childlike Hurt

The second way of being childlike is that of being *hurt*. The feeling of being hurt is a crushing or cutting sensation as being cut with a knife, only the wound is in the spirit rather than the flesh. When hurt, one does not feel the emotion of anger, or feel tempted to lose one's temper. Instead, there are two tendencies—one to *cry* and the other *withdraw*. The trouble is that when tempted to cry, women usually over-react, displaying deeply wounded feelings and emotional turmoil. This can be frustrating to a man. He is often at his wits' end to know how to comfort her. I have known men who, in their desperation, walk away and leave a woman alone due to a feeling of inadequacy as to how to handle the situation. Or when a woman reacts in an opposite way—withdrawing into her shell, she forms resentments and breaks communications. In either case there is harm to the marriage relationship.

The best way to express ourselves when hurt is to again copy the mannerisms of little children. When children are hurt, the lips quiver and a tear or two trickles down the cheeks. Or they look with downcast eyes, pout, mumble a few broken words, tremble, rub their foot along the carpet and look rather helpless in their predicament. Or, if the occasion merits it, the cry can be more expressive, with exaggerations and heaving of the breast, but with an absence of bitterness. Childlike crying is amusing and charming and arouses tenderness in men. It is a marvelous way to handle human frailties and build good marital relationships.

When a woman reacts in a childlike way, however, she must be certain that her actions resemble the showy outbreak of a child and not the emotional turmoil of a deeply disturbed woman. If she is unable to rid herself of deep emotional pain, this is a signal for her to work on her character, to build a good self-image, inner happiness, and to accept her husband and learn forgiveness and humility.

It is interesting to note that hurt feelings usually arise when the man has mistreated his wife, especially when he has insulted, criticized or neglected her, the same causes as when angry feelings occur. These are the times to express oneself and not when the man has failed in some area of his life. And if a woman cannot learn to express herself in a childlike way, as I have described, I encourage her to find some acceptable means of dealing with hurt feelings so that she does not form resentments towards her husband or injure relationships.

3. Disappointment

The reaction for disappointment is very much the same as for hurt feelings, with a pout, a tear or two, downcast eyes, etc. The trouble is that with most women there is an entirely opposite reaction. When disappointed, she demands her rights, reminds the man of his moral obligation to fulfill his promises, and expects a detailed explanation of the circumstances.

How refreshingly different and charming when a woman will, instead, react as a child, when she will realize her position with the man and trustingly accept the situation, request no explanation, make no demands, clamp no unwholesome obligation upon him to follow through, but merely expresses her human but charming disappointment. How childlike, and yet how womanly.

Conclusions

In this chapter we have covered three ways to be childlike—in anger, hurt or disappointment, all *unpleasant* emotions. In reviewing these subjects, let me again state that we are human beings, prone to anger and all unpleasant emotions. These can be distressing feelings which we must handle in one way or another. Although we should constantly try to improve our character so that we overcome these weaknesses, in the process of becoming angels we are still human beings.

Childlikeness is difficult for some women to apply, but I must stress that it is one of the most important parts of all Fascinating Womanhood, for it helps us handle human frailties (our own and our husband's). Sometimes little irritations which are really insignificant can grow to be mountainous in size. Childlikeness will reduce these problems and turn what could have been pain, into pleasure. It will make a woman happier; the man can relax and be himself; his wife will react to his behavior in a charming way; they will have an improved relationship; the woman acquires a fascinating charm and vitality of spirit which arouses the man's tenderness. There is conclusive proof that childlikeness "works" as I have claimed. Evidence is in the following success stories submitted to me. If you have further doubt, I challenge you to try this method in your own life and see for yourself that it can "change the night to day."

Saucy

"When I tried a saucy response to my husband's thoughtlessness, he said, 'That was so cute, let's do it again.'"

A Pout

"I had my doubts about applying Childlikeness, for I didn't think I could do it. Then one time when I was offended I just stuck out my lower lip (just slightly) and my husband said, 'You look so cute when you do that,' and we both forgot what we were upset about."

The Kitchen Floor

A wife scrubbed and waxed her kitchen floor and when finished her husband walked across it with muddy shoes. She said in a little girl voice, "Oh, dear, see what you have done, see what you have done! Oh, what will I do?" How much better this was than for her to say nothing and hold a grudge, or to mumble some complaining words under her breath, or even worse, to "fly off the handle," and say in a disgusted voice, "Look what you have done!"

Picked On

"My husband had been home all day and was in a bad mood, criticizing me on every turn or making some kind of complaint. I was really ready to cut loose with my anger. A brief moment of thought about his meanness made me decide a little childlike anger might be a better answer. The next time a nasty comment came from him, I said, 'You big bully, you've been picking on me all day. Just because you're bigger and stronger than I am you think you can push me around.' With that I turned on my heel and stomped my foot. With no change in voice from his gruffness of all day, he said, 'Get over here and kiss me, then.' Our day was suddenly better."

Neglected Me

"My husband is very involved in practicing Judo, sometimes to the point (I feel) of neglecting me. When I have felt neglected, I have become cool and refused to take an interest in his activities. This has made him feel guilty, but has not caused him to spend more time with me and the children. After our lesson on childlikeness, I decided to try this method of venting anger when the next problem arose, to see if it would bring better results.

"Last week he went to Judo three times, and on the nights he didn't go he was too tired to be really good company. On Saturday morning he got up and announced he was going to the club again and would be gone most of the day. I had planned all sorts of things for us to do as a family and at this announcement became furious. But, instead of holding back my feelings, I pouted, stamped my foot and called him a big meanie. He finally said, 'O.K., I'll stay.' But I said, 'No, you just go to your darned Judo, I don't want you with me. Just go ahead!' At this, he began to laugh and turned to the kids and said, 'Isn't Mommy funny?' And when they agreed, he said, 'But she's cute.' He then got the kids ready and took us shopping, bought us lunch, and on the way home stopped at a flower shop and bought flowers for me and also our daughters. He made the remark when we were preparing for bed that night, 'Gosh, I enjoyed our day!' "

The Silent Treatment

"In early marriage I had an explosive temper. I would blow my top and he would bolt for the door, slam it shut and go off in the car for hours. When he came back I could count on him not speaking to me for a week or so. I soon learned to keep my mouth shut when I was angry, but I would smolder inside. He gave me the same silent treatment but at least he didn't leave the house. This method of non-communication continued until Fascinating Womanhood. With childlikeness I learned to release my feelings while building up his ego. I say 'You big mean brute, you hurt my feelings.' He laughs good naturedly and is no longer silent towards me."

A Chuckle

"The most valuable lesson in the whole of Fascinating Womanhood for me was the section on childlikeness. It is wonderful to be able to channel my anger properly so that I receive from my husband a delighted chuckle instead of a temper tantrum! During the two months I have been living Fascinating Womanhood I have been showered with presents, compliments and attention. Obviously my husband is convinced that I am for him and no longer against him."

From a Little Girl

"I am ten years old and going into the sixth grade. My mom has the book Fascinating Womanhood. One day about two months ago she told me to take Fascinating Womanhood to my teacher and let her read it. But it was too late. Her husband had died about six years ago. But it still didn't hurt for her to read it. She didn't have time to read it in class because she was too busy getting mad at some boys who had been playing hookey the day before. I told her she could take it home with her to read and she did. The next morning she came to school with a real pretty dress on. She says, 'That's a fantastic book. If more people would read it and do what it says there wouldn't be any more divorces! Can I borrow it again?' 'It's o.k. with me,' I replied. Now, whenever she gets mad she uses sauciness and has a soft voice. Thanks to Fascinating Womanhood for everything."

Until Daybreak

"One evening while visiting my sister, two of my friends dropped by to see me. It was very late. My husband had retired and when I could see that the conversation would be a long one, I excused myself to see if my husband objected to my staying up late. When I walked into the bedroom, he was irritated and said, 'Well, what's going on downstairs?' I lifted my head high, straightened my shoulders and said, 'Well, I came up here out of kind consideration to see if you would object to my staying up late. But, since you are going to be so hard-hearted and disagreeable, I *will* go downstairs and I won't come back until daybreak.' I turned quickly and swished off and just as I came to the door I glanced back over my shoulder and could see that my husband had raised up on one elbow, half smiling. Then, I quickly turned my head and went downstairs. And I did stay until daybreak. When I returned to the bedroom I felt kindly towards my husband—with no feeling of resentment. Had I not expressed myself, I would have felt mistreated. The following day we returned to our home 250 miles away and while driving he held my hand all the way home and was especially kind and tender."

The Tease

"When entertaining friends my husband brought out old pictures of me to show the guests. I did not have a particular liking for the pictures and resented his showing them. I tried to rescue them, but since he was bigger and stronger, I couldn't. Then he picked me up, carried me into the bedroom, and locked the door. I pounded on the door and threatened, 'I'll never speak to you again. I'll go downtown and spend all your money.' I could hear my husband laughing. The children were standing nearby and were laughing to see their parents quarrel in this amusing manner. They told their friends about the cute way their parents quarrel."

How to Express Childlike Anger

1. Develop character so you eliminate the ugly emotions of hate, bitterness, sarcasm, resentments, etc.
2. Use childlike mannerisms.
3. Acquire a list of adjectives which compliment masculinity.
4. Exaggerate: A. His treatment of you. B. Your defensive attitude. C. Threats of punishment.

Assignment

1. Make a list of adjectives which compliment a man's masculinity.
2. Create some exaggerated expressions for moments of childlike anger.

21

Childlikeness, Some Additional Ways

I stated in the previous chapter that I would teach twelve ways to be childlike, all of which will solve marriage problems and be charming to men. Thus far we have covered only three: anger, hurt, and disappointment. In this chapter, I will briefly explain the remaining nine:

4. How to Ask for Things

As we live from day to day we women usually need or want certain things in life. There are things we need *to have*, things we want *to do*, places we want *to go* or some things we need *to have done for us*. I am not referring to selfish whims, but to *just desires*. Many of these things we are dependent upon our husbands for. We must ask him for them. Knowing how to ask in a way that he will be encouraged to say "yes" is so simple you will hardly believe it. But, simple as it may be, most women do not know how and therefore ask in the wrong way and are more often than not turned down. Consider the following mistakes women make in asking and why they often fail.

Mistakes Women Make

1. *Hinting:* A common mistake a woman can make is to offer a gentle hint, hoping her husband (who is supposed to adore and cherish her) will heed her wishes just to please her. If he overlooks it, as he often does, she will likely interpret his indifference as a lack of love. This can cause her to feel neglected and resentful. She may say to herself, "If he really loves me, why isn't he interested in helping me get the things I really want, especially if I drop a hint?" The reason this method of asking fails is that most men are too preoccupied with their own problems to give much thought to hints. They may even count them as

womanly whims. A man often, in fact, does not remember hints from one day to the next.

2. *Suggestions:* Common suggestions are, "Let's do this," or "I think it would be nice if we were to do this," or "Wouldn't it be nice if we could build a bookcase in this end of the living room?" or "Don't you think we should enlarge the patio?" Such suggestions are fine if you are not quite sure of what you want and are really seeking his opinion. But, if you know what you want, don't expect this approach will bring forth an agreeable answer unless he just happens to be in the frame of mind for it. It will, in fact, most likely provoke an opposing view.

3. *Convincing:* If a woman really wants something, she may first spend some time thinking of all the reasons she is justified in asking for it. Then she takes the matter to her husband and tries to convince him. The trouble is that this tends to provoke opposition, wherein he thinks of all the reasons she has *not* justified. But, here again, if she is not sure of what she wants, it may be better to discuss the matter with him and see who comes up with the more sound reasoning. But when a woman really wants something which she feels justified in having, this is not a very successful method of getting it.

The reason trying to convince a man so often fails is because the woman will appear as an *equal partner* to him. Appearing as an equal in decisions places the man in the frame of mind to say "no," just to show his *authority*. He may actually be in favor of granting a request but says "no," automatically. He seldom realizes that the reason he took such a stand against it was to preserve his position as the leader.

4. *Demanding:* Because some women become frustrated in their relationships with men, they feel there is no alternative but to demand their rights. When a man feels pressure from his wife, he may give in, but it is never in good spirit, and thus, it becomes a "bone of contention" in marriage. No real rewards come to either the man or wife when she must demand what she wants. This method fails because the wife *usurps authority,* or at least does not show proper respect for his position as the leader. When the man feels his position is threatened, nothing in all the world is going to make him *want* to do things for his wife, even though he may "give in."

Because women have had such a difficult time getting what they need from a man, many of them become frustrated and give up entirely. They would rather do without than to go through the ordeal of trying to get a man to do things for them. But the real problem in her "giving up" is that she cannot help but feel resentments towards the man. She may feel that she *gives so much* to him that it is not fair for him to ignore her simple requests. But, please, *do not give up.* Important to any man-woman relationship is that they be "in tune" to each other's heartfelt desires. Instead of "giving up," learn how to ask in the right way so the man will want to do things for you. Here is the method suggested:

The Right Way to Ask

When you ask a man for things, copy this art, again, from little children. How do they get what they want? They just *ask for things,* in a trusting manner. They do not justify, explain, or argue a point, for they are too dependent and incapable in the presence of adults. A little girl, when she wants something, will approach her father trustingly, realizing that he has the power to say "yes" or "no." She will say, "May I please?" or "Will you please?" or, "It would mean so much to me," displaying a *dependent* attitude and causing her father to feel big and masculine and in the position of the leader. All kind-hearted parents are inclined to say "yes" to such a childlike request.

When you approach a man with a request, and ask for it in a trusting, childlike way, it places him in the proper position of leadership and makes him feel more masculine. When he realizes your respect for his position and your dependency upon him for all that you have, he will be more considerate and is psychologically encouraged to do the utmost to fill your requests. He will enjoy doing things for you, because of the way it makes him feel. If you ask in the right way, he will jump at the chance to do things for you and will love you more because of it. As I have said, *men have often broken their necks to cater to the whims of femininity* just because of the wonderful way it makes them feel. And, although I am not suggesting "whims," I do advise you to ask for things which are needful and important for your well being. It will promote a better relationship, and your husband will feel more tenderly towards you and be charmed by your childlike trust which makes him feel manly. And you will feel more kindly towards him for heeding your heartfelt desires.

What Not to Ask For

There are a few things you should not ask for. Do not ask for things which are *selfish* or which he *cannot afford*. Do not ask for *love* or *tenderness* or *affection*. *These attentions are of value only when given voluntarily. Also, never ask a man for a gift or to take you to dinner.* This is too aggressive. Also, do not ask for things which would be in *conflict with his responsibilities*, or for which he would have to *neglect some important duty*. Do not ask for things which would be *against his convictions, his judgment or his principles*. Do not ask for anything which would place a heavy *burden upon him*, or a *worry*. Also, it is best not to ask for things if you have *not been doing your part as a wife*. If you have been neglectful of your homemaking, his meals, your appearance, or failed to be a good sex partner, it is best to not ask him for anything special until you make these improvements.

If a man says "no" to your requests, do not be alarmed. Ask yourself if you were selfish or imposing or if in any other way you did not have the right to ask. If you are at fault, then you will have to forget it and be better prepared in the future to make only justified requests.

Practice this art of asking for things on your husband and you will see for yourself his immediate response. Not only will he willingly oblige, but you will notice a warmth in his response and a strength in your relationship. A man loves a woman more when he does things for her. Be sure to always thank him and he will delight in catering to your requests. But, you will have to make certain that you do not use this as a manipulatory "art" in which you take unfair advantage of him to get things that are selfish, for this would destroy the objective of Fascinating Womanhood.

The Self-Sacrificing Wife

Unfortunately, many women make the mistake of unnecessarily going without things they need, thinking it is angelic of themselves to do so. For years they may have wanted something, but subdue every impulse to ask for it, usually so there will be more money for the benefit of their husband or children.

Now what does her husband think of all of this? During an emergency a man will greatly appreciate his wife's willingness to set aside personal needs to solve problems. But, when there is no urgent reason for her to go without, he does not want a self-sacrificing wife. She is his queen, deserving of the best he can offer. He does not want her to place his comforts, nor those of the children ahead of her important needs.

Another point is this: Women who are self-sacrificing rob their husbands of experience which would make their love grow. There is a natural response in all of us to love those whom we serve. Likewise, we tend to cease loving those we neglect. For example, if we neglect the care of an animal we tend to lose love for it. Women who neglect their children, find love more difficult. So, you owe it to your husband and to your marriage relationship to see that you obtain in life those things which mean so much. But, you must ask. A man is not a mind reader.

An Old Promise

After having been taught this philosophy, a woman wrote the following: "My husband has been the kind of man who has always said 'no' to everything I have ever requested. I remembered an old promise which he had made to me voluntarily and which he had carelessly never kept. I had never felt right about it, and it was something which I still wanted with almost a burning desire.

"I went to him trustfully and in a childlike manner. I reminded him of the old promise, but I assured him that I recognized his right to say yes or no. Then I said, 'All that I have in life I am dependent upon you for. And this desire I cannot have without your consent. Will you please consider granting it now?'

"My husband acquired a most pleasant look on his face and laid his pen down, for he had been writing. He motioned for me to come over and sit on his knee. Then he affectionately kissed me and said, 'Do you know how you make me feel? I feel like I am a big judge and that you are some poor young thing who has come to plead her case.' Then he said fondly, 'Anything that you want in life you can have.'" When a woman has such an effective method of obtaining her heart's desire, she is rather foolish to use any other.

Still Another Way to Ask—Expecting Things

There is another method of asking for things and, although it is not childlike, it is effective for some purposes. It is an attitude of expecting things. This, however, applies to only certain situations and must be done in the right way. An illustration of this is of Abraham Lincoln's stepmother, Sarah.

Abraham Lincoln's real mother, Nancy Hanks, lived for years with her husband and children in a little log cabin with a dirt floor. She was a meek little lady, and her husband, Tom Lincoln, was negligent and somewhat lazy. He never got around to building a wooden floor for her.

After she died, Tom Lincoln married Sarah. She was a very fine person, but very different from Nancy. When Tom brought her home to the log cabin, she brought with her several wagonloads of fine furniture and home furnishings. She took one look at the dirt floor and said, "Oh, my goodness, Tom, I couldn't think of bringing all of my nice things in here on this dirt floor. I will just leave them in the wagons and you can build me a wooden floor tomorrow." And Tom Lincoln did build her a wooden floor the very next day. Wasn't it sad to think that poor Nancy lived all of those years on a dirt floor just because she did not know how to motivate a man to action. Notice that Sarah was *pleasant*, but she was *definite* and placed a time limit on the task. With the furniture sitting outside, there was emphasis to her reqeust. She was entirely within her rights. We do not always, however, have such a convenient situation to make such a request.

5. Childlike Joy

Still another emotion which can be charming to men is that of childlike joy. In studying the joy of little children, you can first observe that it takes very little to make them happy. When they are rewarded with a pleasant surprise or promised a forthcoming good time, what do they do? They become very excited and their eyes sparkle. My own little girl will clap her hands and jump up and down. Children also tend to exaggerate by saying "this is the *prettiest* or the *best* in the *whole* world." The benefactor receives so much enjoyment from this pleasant outburst that he is apt to repeat the act again and again just to see the sparkle in her eyes and the joyfulness of her manner.

A man appreciates a similar response in a woman when he buys her a gift or does something especially kind for her. Exuberant women who get excited over every little thing a man does for them usually have men who pamper and spoil them, showering them with gifts they do not even need. On the other hand, women who respond with a bland "thank you," or "Oh, how nice," or "Oh, how thoughtful of you," do nothing to encourage a man's generosity. Even worse, some women receive these favors from a man as though he "owed it to them."

Years ago I knew a woman whose husband left her for another woman. Many things came to light about his disapproval of her, one being her inability to appreciate anything which he did for her. On one occasion he had brought her a beautiful dining set which she accepted as though he owed it to her. When a personal friend asked her why she was not more appreciative, she said, "Well, isn't a man supposed to do these things for his wife?" Perhaps a man *is* supposed to do things for his wife, but remember, *his only pay is her joyful appreciation.* What else does he forfeit his hard-earned money for? Certainly not so he will have a beautiful chair to sit on. A man may appreciate an elegant piece of furniture himself, but if money does not come easy with him, he will be inclined to conserve his resources and take less in the way of comfort, if his generosity is not appreciated fully.

There is another way to receive a gift or favor: If a man gives a woman something of unusual value, or does something for her which requires considerable sacrifice on his part, even childlike joy may not be sufficient for such a momentous occasion. A deeply expressed appreciation may be more significant and rewarding, or even "tears of joy."

When He Gives You Something You Do Not Like

A very real problem can arise when a man gives a woman a gift she does not like. Because of this, she may make the mistake of showing disappointment, criticizing it, returning it, exchanging it, or putting it away and not using it. These actions are *unforgivable.* (Exchanging for size is all right.) A moment like this does not need to pose a problem, however, as many women would imagine. Here is what to do:

You need not be insincere and act as though you like the gift when you honestly do not. The thing to do is to appreciate, *not* the *gift,* but the *giver* and the *act of giving.* Your words should be carefully chosen to show appreciation for the man, for his thoughtfulness and his generosity. The gift is of little consequence in comparison to the man, his feelings and the beautiful moment which you may remember for a long time if you handle it wisely. Whatever the gift, be sure to use it, at least for awhile, with deepest appreciation for the giver.

When He Gives You Something He Can't Afford

A woman can make a similar mistake when a man gives her something he should not afford. Some very practical and thrifty women will make unkind remarks about how the man should have known better than to buy something so expensive. I know of a woman who received a beautiful leather purse from her husband for Christmas. She made a slight remark about how "he should not have bought her something so expensive." She was only trying to be unselfish. But instead of being appreciated for her willingness to forego nice things for the sake of economy, her husband was so crushed that he did not buy her another gift for thirty years.

The only way to overcome this tendency is to not be so material-minded, counting everything in terms of money, and learn to count generosity and love as the supreme contributions which we make to human relationships. If you have a husband who is extravagant with you, count it as good fortune. If you feel that your circumstances require that you must curb his tendency to overspend, sometime well in advance of a time he might buy you something, explain that you greatly appreciate inexpensive gifts just as much as if they cost more, because "the act of giving" is the thing which is important, not the gift itself. He will then count it as unselfishness on your part and not consider it a rejection of his gift.

If your husband happens to be negligent about gift-giving, don't let this concern you too much. Perhaps in the past, you have failed to show enthusiasm for his gifts or favors and so he has lost interest in doing things for you.

But whether this is true or not, the fact remains that men are known to be negligent about gift-giving. They lack imagination about selecting appropriate gifts for women and are forgetful of the occasions when gifts are expected. Do not, therefore, attach too much importance to this negligence or interpret it as lack of love. Also, some men have a tendency to dislike the compulsion of gift-giving which has been handed to us by tradition, such as birthdays, anniversaries, Christmas and Valentine's Day. Men prefer to buy something when they feel like it, when it comes from the heart rather than when tradition dictates.

Also, try to understand your own husband's attitude about gift-giving. If it is difficult for him, if he hates to shop for women's things, or if he dislikes the obligation of gifts, accept this deficiency in him and learn to overlook it. Tell him that you do not expect him to give you gifts, that you understand his attitude. He will probably be greatly relieved of the feeling of obligation and will be apt to buy something for you impulsively. But if he does not, learn to accept this, also. Count all that he does do and do not dwell on this insignificant flaw. On the other hand, we should never discourage our husbands from buying things or doing things for us, since pampering and spoiling us a bit makes them love us more. And we can encourage their generosity by receiving these favors with childlike joy.

6. Girlish Trust

Girlish trust is a confidence such as children have in their parents, a confidence that the parents have their best interests at heart and will *always take care of them*. Just as a little girl trusts her father as her leader and trusts in his ability to take care of her, to provide for her, to solve problems and make wise decisions, a woman can show this same trust in a man. She should be careful not to doubt his ability.

She should not, for example, tell him what to do. There is nothing a man dislikes more than a woman who gives him directions or instructions in things that he is supposed to know more about than she does. I remember being in the company of a man and his wife who were trying to show us the city in which they lived. With every turn he made, she was there at his elbow telling him what to do and where to turn. When a man is driving, never make the mistake of telling him where to turn, unless he asks. It is better to let him make a mistake and have to back track, than to give him the feeling that you doubt his common judgment. Especially is this irritating in something as simple as finding his way around in life.

Also, never doubt a man's ability to solve a problem. For example, do not question his ability to fix a stalled car by suggesting that he call a repairman. Or do not doubt his ability to find his way out of a financial problem or other perplexing situation. Also, do not doubt a man's ability to reach a difficult goal such as achieving a high education or advancement in a job. To doubt his ability is to show a lack of trust.

On the other hand, if a man is trying to reach a difficult goal or solve a difficult problem, do not give him the impression that you expect it will be *easy*. For example, if a man intends to go through a difficult education, do not doubt his ability to reach his goal, but on the other hand, do not give an indication that you expect it will be easy and thereby rob him of his potential heroism. What a man wants is for you to *recognize the difficulties of his goal and his problems, but have a girlish trust that he will one way or another be victorious over his problems*. In this way you recognize opportunity for heroism and do not doubt his ability to be a hero. This is girlish trust.

Also, when a man is about to make a decision be careful not to insult his judgment by questioning his motives, suggesting failure or bringing up simple facts that any man should know. And when a man has made a decision that you may question do not demand an explanation or put him in a position where he feels he must justify his actions. To do so suggests a lack of trust.

Girlish trust has a special application for a woman in her relationship with her husband's role. Trust makes her a better follower and her husband a better leader. When the man functions in his role as the guide, protector and provider, the wife with a girlish trust will confidently follow knowing that he will take care of her in all circumstances. *She feels safe with him. She trusts not so much the outcome of events, as the intent of his heart or his motives.*

She knows that, being human, he will make mistakes. But moved by his desire to always take care of her, he will act upon his best judgment. This is all she has a right to expect. And she also knows that since God has given him the responsibility to watch over his family, He will certainly bless him with the wisdom to do so. Therefore, he is better equipped to fill this role than she is. She may be intelligent and may feel justified in voicing her opinions at times, but she does so in a way that will not indicate lack of trust.

You may wonder, how can you trust a man who has made many foolish mistakes? First, it must be remembered that *men learn by making mistakes and that mistakes of the past tend to sharpen judgment for the future*. However, it would be unrealistic to expect that at some future time the man would cease making mistakes. Human error is a continual part of life that both men and women must expect, not only of others but of themselves. Second, the woman should learn to trust, not so much in the outcome of events, as *the man's intent to take care of her*. She must be willing to risk money, security, comfort, and material things in her girlish trust of him, for if the man desires to do right and strives to use the best of his judgment, she cannot expect more of him than this.

It is important to understand just what trust will do. When a woman puts her trust in her husband, it cannot help but make him feel more responsible. He simply must measure up to her expectations of him and never let her down. And what does the woman gain? Girlish trust makes her more childlike and therefore more fascinating and arouses tenderness in the man.

The woman who lacks girlish trust, on the other hand, brings negative reactions. For example, when she doubts her husband's ability to *lead,* she will invariably try to take over and run things her way, thinking she can do a better job. If she is highly intelligent, she may succeed in avoiding a few more mistakes than he did, but she will most certainly diminish him as a man and undermine his confidence. Or when she doubts his ability to *provide her with an adequate living* and takes to the working world, providing her own security and material comfort, she further undermines his confidence in himself. She loses charm and the girlish trust that makes her so much of a woman. She may gain the whole world, but lose out in her own marriage relationship.

7. Teasing Playfulness

Another charming art of childlikeness is "teasing playfulness." You can use this "coquettish" response when a man is overly *serious, stern* or *cross* with you, or when he "sits you down" to *give you a lecture* on how you need to improve, or even *when he ignores you.* In Victor Hugo's admiring description of Deruchette, he mentions that she had "the teasing playfulness of a child."

A perfect illustration of teasing playfulness is found in the character of Babbie in the play "The Little Minister." The dignified little minister looked with horror upon her wild gypsy ways. But when he protested with her about her apparent irresponsibility, she interrupted the serious lecture by teasingly wanting to know which was the taller, making him stand back-to-back to measure their respective heights. And then, when he was ready to burst with indignation at her lack of seriousness, she pouted adorably as if to say, "You're not really going to be angry with poor little me," and flashed at him such a confiding, trustful, "I-am-certain-that-you-like-me-too-well-to-hurt-me" glance and smile that the poor man forgot his indignation completely in a struggle with himself to keep from gathering the adorable creature in his arms and telling her, "No, I wouldn't want to hurt you for all the world."

If you will notice, the first thing that Babbie did was to *change the subject* by wanting to know which was the taller. Then she *distracted his attention* away from his lecture by making him stand back-to-back with her. You can practice a similar teasing playfulness by following these same rules. First, change the subject to something playful and light, then distract his attention by such things as "adjusting his glasses," "straightening his tie," "smoothing his hair," etc. Find ways and means to practice this charming art. Men will find it enchanting, and you will help to drive away the seriousness from their lives.

Another time for teasing playfulness is when you feel ignored or neglected. For example if your husband is spending too much time reading the paper and not paying any attention to you, you can sit on his lap, pull the paper from his hands, pat his cheek or pull his ears, and say, "You are not paying enough attention to me." Or if he is looking out the window while you are trying to explain something to him, you can do the same. The only time this will not be well received by the man is when the wife has been guilty of terrible behavior, when she has been dominating, demanding, critical or in other ways failed as a woman, so that the man may have such a terrible attitude towards her that no action on her part seems charming to him. But if there is a fairly good feeling existing, the woman can be teasingly playful when a man is cross, stern, overly serious, demanding, or neglectful. Teasing playfulness in women, however, does not mean playing pranks. This trait is characteristic of little boys, not of little girls. At times pranks might be fitting for men, but they are never fitting for women.

8. Tenderness of Emotion

Tender hearted women are apt to have tender feelings for little children, animals, flowers, someone who is sick, helpless or needy and are easily excited to pity or sympathy. Amelia, for example, cried over a dead canary, a dead mouse or over the end of a novel. If a man is telling an exciting story which contains an element of danger or distress, a tender hearted woman will sympathize heartily with the characters involved. She becomes horrified or delighted by turns, and can hardly wait for the end to find out if everyone escaped unhurt. This betrayal of girlish tenderness of heart is fascinating to men. They will sometimes concoct the wildest and most heart-rending tales just for the sake of stirring up their tender hearts.

The trouble is that most women feel ashamed of their tender feelings and try to cover them up. While watching a dramatic or tragic movie, or while listening to an impressive poem or incident which arouses sympathy, they hold back the tears and smother their emotions so they will not be detected. Women should not try to hide their tender emotions. Not only would they be healthier, but they would be more attractive.

9. Outspokenness

Another way of being expressive and doing so in a childlike manner is by being outspoken. I do not wish to imply that we have "unbridled tongues," or that we speak too frankly, with little concern for the feelings of others, a fault noticeable in some adults. The childlike manner I refer to is one of being *direct* in conversation and *not evasive*, *"beating around the bush," making excuses*, and *failing to come to the point*.

A little child who has been reared by kind and loving parents of whom he is not afraid tends to be honest and outspoken. He says such things as "I don't want to," or

"Oh, I forgot." He is not afraid to be honest. For example, if you ask a little girl if she would like to go with you to visit a lady down the street and the child really does not want to go, she will say, "I don't want to go." She does not hunt for excuses or ask to put it off until another time, etc. She is honest and direct. This is the response a man appreciates in a woman.

If you are shopping with your husband for such things as furniture or clothes, and he suggests you buy something you dislike, it is not necessary to explain your objections. Be honest and outspoken and say, "Honey, I just don't think I want this one." This comment will not only relieve the situation, but will be appreciated and less likely to insult his tastes than would an elaboration of your ideas. Of course, it is important to please our husbands in home decor and appearance, but in doing so it is not necessary to accept items which clash with our own tastes. Most men want to please their wives, want them to have things they like, and will appreciate outspoken expressions of their desires.

I knew a woman who had this charm of outspokenness. On the occasion I remember, her husband and several other men had just announced plans to sail down the Colorado River on a raft. The girl, thinking the trip extravagant, especially since she had been going without some of the things she needed, said in a girlish manner, "But, what about me! I need some new cotton dresses and some spring shoes." The man looked up in surprised wonder and amusement. How much better this was than if she had complained, accused him of selfishness, or even worse, said nothing and held a grudge. But please note: In some instances a woman should encourage such manly plans with eagerness and excitement; but in this case the trip really was beyond their means, and her outspoken words brought him back to reality and kept him from making a mistake. Since she felt she must express herself, it was wise to do so in a girlish outspoken manner.

10. Changefulness

A woman is more interesting if she is changeful—not the same all of the time. Charles Reade states in *The Cloister and the Hearth* that "girls love to be coy and tender, saucy and gentle by turns." This adds variety to the woman and makes her more mysterious and therefore more interesting to men. If she is unpredictable and he cannot quite count on her mood or her reaction in a situation, she is a more fascinating woman. Deruchette, you may remember, although she was *sweet* and *good*, was teasingly playful, vivacious, and had an *air of bewitching languor* and a *dash of melancholy*.

The *way* to be changeful is in *emotions*. And in this respect we copy the art from little children. I have seen little girls, for example, run to their mothers with tears streaming down their faces and, when comforted with a kiss or pleasant surprise, instantaneously burst into a smile while tears are still wet on their cheeks. Also, children hold no grudges, which is one reason their emotions are free to fluctuate. Also, observe the emotions of children while they are watching a bedtime story. When the story takes a turn for the worse, they display anxiety; but when things work out better, they express delight. Children are not monotonous, but changeful and expressive in emotion.

11. Youthful Manner

The youthful manner arises from a *zest for living* or an inner feeling of youthfulness. There will be a spring in the step, a light-heartedness of spirit, an interested alertness about life and enthusiasm for the future. This is the spirit of youth, but it can be retained into old age. I recently had a conversation with a lady who said, "You know, I am 74 years old but I still feel young and kind of cute." This is what every woman should feel all of her life if she is to be fascinating. It is a spirit which makes her eternally attractive to her husband.

A youthful woman can get excited when she hangs up new curtains, makes her child a new dress, cooks her favorite recipe, cleans the cupboards or smells her clean wash. She "turns on" at the smell of the sea, the first snowfall or a country lane lined with trees. She is excited about life, the wonder of life.

If you want to be youthful in manner the first step is to eliminate any matronly tendencies, especially in the way you walk. Older women tend to slant forward, drop their chin, round their shoulders, walk with legs apart and wobble the upper part of their body. This is the walk of age. So, to appear youthful, do the opposite. Also avoid a dreary look in the face which stems from a sour disposition, foreboding about the future or being bored with life, as these are symptoms of age.

12. Youthful Appearance

To achieve a youthful appearance the first thing to do is to *avoid looking matronly*. Now, what are matronly styles? They differ from generation to generation, but you can count on it that they are the styles which are *out of date*. They are the dresses, the hair styles, the shoes and the make-up that may have been in vogue ten or more years ago, but just are not worn anymore. There is a tendency for women to hang onto these styles that were popular when they were young, and it is this tendency that contributes to a woman looking matronly.

I am not suggesting that we go to the other extreme and go in for fads that quickly change from one season to the next. A well dressed woman always wears styles which are in good taste and which are becoming to her, regardless of the current fashions. And clothes which are in good taste tend to remain in fashion for a long time, but eventually even they are dated.

To avoid a matronly appearance, also refuse to let yourself get "overweight," even ten pounds over. There is nothing which will so destroy the appearance of youth as a chunky figure. It is almost impossible for a woman to appear youthful in either manner or appearance if she is fat. She will not look youthful in her clothes and she will wobble when she walks so that it will be impossible for her to attain a youthful manner.

To accentuate your youthfulness in dress, visit the shops where the young girls shop. You may not end up buying your clothes there, but you will get the picture of what is in fashion. There will be a tendency for these clothes to be "mod" or to come and go as fads, but you will be influenced to youthfulness if you learn what young people wear, because they are always "in style." This is typical of youth.

And if you want to create some youthful styles of your own, especially for housedresses, visit a little girls' shop. There you will see buttons and bows, checks, plaids, pleats, stripes, jumpers, daisies, and even satin, lace and velvet and many other girlish styles. All of their clothes are pretty to see. Another source of girlish styles is in the children's section of pattern books, some of which are repeated in women's sizes. Girlish hair styles are the traditional long styles, braids, pony-tails, curls, and with the addition of ribbons, flowers, bows, bands and barrettes.

If you think it a bit ridiculous for grown women to wear these youthful styles, wear them in your own home and let your husband be the judge. He may not want you to wear them in public, but he will likely love them at home or for informal occasions.

Childishness

Childlikeness should not be confused with "childishness," which is a negative quality. To be *childish* is to copy the *faults* of children; whereas to be childlike is to copy their *virtues*. Some unattractive traits in children are self-centeredness, a lack of responsibility for their own actions, and expecting too much of ordinary human beings. Those who retain these traits in adult life tend to fret when they do not get their way, blame others for their unfortunate circumstances, fail to acknowledge their own mistakes and failures, and make unreasonable demands of their associates. When we were young we expected much from our parents and thought they could do most anything. To project this unrealistic thought into adult life is to expect too much from our associates and is therefore childish. *Childishness* in a grown woman is unattractive.

Conclusions

There are a few women who resist the idea of acting childlike, who consider it an insult to their good sense to expect them to act the part of a little girl. They insist upon believing that really sensible men, the kind of man they admire, would be repulsed instead of attracted to such a childlike creature. The only way to prove to yourself if childlikeness is charming to men is to try it in your own life and test your husband's reaction.

Even when women agree that a childlike woman is the most attractive, many of them mistakenly assume that for themselves the acting of such a part is impossible. Be assured that every woman can become childlike, for we all have this trait somewhere in our nature. It is part of being a woman. Remember that it was not long ago that you were a little girl when these traits were natural to you. You can recapture this manner and charm of youth and make it part of your personality. You will be more charming to your husband and will make him feel bigger and manlier. Remember, *if you are to be loved and treated like a woman, you must make him feel like a man.*

There is a marked tendency when a woman matures to lose this childlike trait, especially when she gets married. She somehow feels that now she must "grow up," without realizing that men never want women to grow up completely. Truly fascinating women never take on the unattractive traits of matronliness, nor do they become skeptical, stubborn, cynical, and overbearing as some older women do who have lost their youthfulness.

Childlike Ways

1. Childlike anger
2. Childlike hurt
3. Disappointment
4. How to ask for things
5. Childlike joy
6. Girlish trust
7. Teasing playfulness
8. Tenderness of emotion
9. Outspokenness
10. Changefulness
11. Youthful manner
12. Youthful appearance

Summary

As we come to the end of the study of Fascinating Womanhood, it may seem that much is expected of you and that you must do a lot of giving. This does not always seem fair. But remember, marriage is not a fifty-fifty proposition. Each partner is expected to give ninety percent. But in so giving wholeheartedly, we receive a rich compensation. *When you cast your bread upon the waters, it comes back buttered.* Similar to the Christian doctrine, "He who looseth his life for my sake, shall surely find it," the woman who lives these teachings devotedly gains a tender, romantic marriage relationship. And this happy marriage is the heart of a happy home. *Fascinating Womanhood makes women happier, husbands happier, and children happier.* This is the promise given to all who live this way of life. And if you have any doubts about it, I challenge you to apply these teachings in your own life and see from your own experience if these things are true.

Some women are greatly concerned about yielding to the man his leadership right and staying out of his masculine role as the guide, protector and provider. If they have shared decision-making, money management, and have been working so that they have money of their own, they may feel that they must give up too much in living these teachings. In answer, remember that when a woman walks away from the masculine role, if she gives up anything, it is headaches, heartaches, frustration, disappointments, hard work, and discouragement. Perhaps she does give up some of her precious freedom, but when a woman surrenders to her husband his leadership position, relinquishing what may appear to her to be rights, she gains every advantage a woman could hope for—a husband who will do anything within his power to make her happy.

A woman is in a precarious position as the wife. When we understand the man's deep needs and his sensitive pride, we can see that a woman is in a position to either build or destroy a man. She destroys him by needling him to change, by stealing his leadership position, wounding his pride and ignoring his important needs. She

300

builds him by looking to his better side, admiring his masculinity, giving him sympathy, understanding, and helping him to excel in his role as the guide, protector, and provider.

The most basic principle taught in this book is this: If you want to awaken a man's love and tenderness, you must 1) *Be a person worthy of that love*, a woman of character who can inspire a worshipful feeling in a man's spirit. 2) *Make him feel like a man.* You do this by admiring his manly qualities, by making him feel needed and adequate in his role as a man, by filling your role as a woman, and by taking upon yourself feminine and childlike characteristics which make him feel manly in contrast. This awareness of the differences between the masculine and the feminine awakens love and tenderness.

In living Fascinating Womanhood, do not become discouraged if you occasionally "backslide" by making mistakes. This is normal. It usually takes about a year to form new habits. But keep going, and you will create a new way of life and find that you are in a "new world," a world that seems like you are looking through "rose-colored glasses." Once you have a glimpse into this new world of Fascinating Womanhood, you will never again be content to enjoy the old one. You may stand astride for awhile, between the two worlds—unable to reach the higher goals but discontent with the unhappy days of the past. But, eventually you will advance to the "banquet of life," never again to "eat the crumbs."

Once a man has experienced you as a Fascinating Woman, *he* will not be satisfied with the "old you" again, either. *Once he has tasted the sweet—he will not be content with the bitter.* So it is better to accept the fact right from the beginning that once you start on the road to Fascinating Womanhood, *there is no turning back.*

You may have wondered why I have not included in this writing instruction concerning sex. My reason is that Fascinating Womanhood deals with the mating of spirit with spirit while the physical relationship is a subject which I feel should be dealt with separately.

I acknowledge that sexual relations are highly important and that problems can be solved and remarkable improvements made through applying correct principles. To help in this area my husband and I have prepared a booklet explaining how to apply Fascinating Womanhood principles to common sexual problems. To obtain a copy please send $2.00 to Family Living International, P.O. Box 189, Pierce City, MO 65723 requesting a copy of "FASCINATING WOMANHOOD APPLIED TO SEXUAL RELATIONS."

Perhaps the greatest encouragement in living Fascinating Womanhood is in reviewing the successful experiences of other women. I have cited some throughout the book, and many thousands more have been written. Here are three more to remember:

Heartbreak—With a Happy Ending

"My husband and I were married when I was 18 years old and he was 19. We went through school together and went together for six months after graduation before becoming engaged. After a one-and-a-half year engagement we were married, and eight days later he was sent overseas by the Air Force. I lived with his parents for the next five months while saving up enough money so that I could join him. His folks were closer to me than my own. He was their only son, and they accepted me lovingly into their home as their only daughter. I thought I knew everything there was to know about my husband when I finally joined him.

"Well, I was wrong, and completely oblivious to the really important things a wife should know about her husband and, most important, herself. I ignorantly stumbled through seven years of marriage. The last four of those years were pure hell for me emotionally, for when our first child was three months old, my husband finally confessed (after a million times I'd accused him of not loving me) that maybe I was right, because he didn't think he did love me anymore. Now it was at last out in the open and we didn't know what to do about it. We are both very conscientious people with extremely high moral standards, and we decided to seek professional help to determine if there was enough left of our marriage to salvage.

"Our minister suggested Family Service Association, and so for two years after that we went weekly to our marriage counselor. We had another baby 17 months after the first, and shortly thereafter I was critically burned in an auto accident, which I know was the answer to my prayers. Dumb? Yes, but I was desperate, emotionally falling apart at the seams. Since counseling obviously was not providing the answers to our problems (my problems, really), I prayed to God every day to help me find a way out, or to take me out of my misery by taking my life, or by making something horrible happen to me, so my husband would be jolted into realization and know one way or the other whether he loved me or not. The constant pressure of not knowing was too much for me to go on bearing.

"Well, it worked, or at least I thought it did for a while. As I lay in the hospital in intensive care, I heard my husband say 'I love you' for the first time in three years. It was wonderful at first and I suffered greatly for that; and that 'I love you' was all that kept me going the whole two months I was in the hospital, for I was sure that when I got home, everything would be wonderful and happy again in spite of my ugly scarred face and hands.

"Again I was wrong. Things were worse than ever, and the next two years I spent praying for the good Lord to show mercy on the wretched human being who was really at the end of her rope. I tried so hard and changed my ways just like the counselor said, but nothing helped. The problem definitely was not solved and I had no emotional control left. I was a complete 'wreck' in every sense of the word.

"Last July, my husband was speaking cruelly and disrespectfully to me in front of our children and I thought that was the very last straw, so I helped him pack his bags and asked him to leave. He did, somewhat to my surprise, and he was ready for it. Merciful peace reigned at last, and I truly felt this was God's answer to my prayers.

"Again, I was wrong. For two months we were the happiest separated couple the world has ever known. The children made great strides in that short time. The baby, now two years old, completely potty trained herself, and the two boys were happier than they'd ever been. Then my sister finally brought me the book Fascinating Womanhood, and I immediately began the most intensive study program I ever partook of in my life. I read slowly, thoroughly, and then I thought and thought and then I'd apply one chapter at a time. An explosive revolution was going on inside me and I was so happy at last to have God's answers to all my problems, but at the same time I hated myself with a passion I never knew existed. 'How could I have been so dumb—so blind—so stupid!!!'

"My husband was everything good I'd ever wanted in

life, and I hated myself for never having understood him as a man. By the time I finished the book I looked in the mirror and saw myself as I really was—how my husband saw me. I despised what I saw. Oh, how ignorant and self-righteous I was. I cried for two days after I read about the Russian author of *War and Peace,* Tolstoi, and how his wife made herself so offensive that he couldn't stand the sight of her. I was sure it was too late to ever repair the damage I had caused my husband. He had a wall of reserve that made the Great Wall of China look microscopic!

"Thank goodness our God is a truly merciful God, for I followed step by step the principles of Fascinating Womanhood and my husband responded miraculously. I will always be in debt to Fascinating Womanhood, Helen Andelin, and God for showing this wretched creature how to make others happy and how to be happy—for just that reason and none other. This is how it happened:

"I called my husband and asked him to stop by one evening on his way to work. I wanted to tell him of my new-found knowledge and tell him all the things the 'ice breaker' said to say as a start. He came, and I stammered for a while until I finally told him that in my loneliness I had been doing a lot of reading and that I was at long last able to see how wrong I had been all the years (seven) of our marriage.

"I told him that I couldn't expect him to forgive me for making his life into a hell on earth, but I wanted to apologize just the same and that I was truly and deeply sorry for the misery I had caused him. I told him I could now see that the failure was my fault and mine alone and he was the best husband a woman ever had. I told him I admired his strength of character and that he never once gave in to my nagging criticism and never allowed me to make him putty in my hands. He had to know this for his future happiness, for I never wanted him to think our marriage failed through any fault of his. He could rest assured that someday he would find someone who could be the kind of wife he deserved and know that he couldn't ever cause any problems because he was the best guy in the world and I hated myself for not seeing it in time.

"All of the while I was telling him these things he just sat there looking alternately into space, not seeing anything and then in blank disbelief at me, and then into space again. When I'd finished, I had tears running down

304

my face and the whole house was so quiet. He didn't move his blank stare and I just sat nearby, waiting, waiting, waiting. That two or three minutes seemed an eternity. His first words were, 'I'm dumbfounded. I don't know what to say.' I told him I didn't want or expect him to say anything but I simply wanted him to know how I felt. He left for work still somewhat dazed with disbelief.

"I did not leave the house for three days, waiting for a call or something, and finally he called to ask if he could come over for his weekly visit with the kids and I said, sure. That night I admired him before the children for his long legs, broad shoulders, manly physique and neat good looks, and he just ate it all up. He'd grin from ear to ear and chuckle and tell the children not to believe everything their Mom told them. After we put the kids to bed, he asked me to a dinner dance a month away and I was once again happy, happy, happy. This meant that there might still be some hope for me to reinstate myself with him, and again I thanked God for being so merciful to such an unworthy human being. Weekly visits came and went and always the children consumed his full attention, but occasionally he would compliment me on the improvements I'd made in my appearance, homemaking, etc. But never a hint about moving back home to us, so in one of my loneliest moments I asked him over to watch T.V. with me, and he came.

"After bedding down the kids, we talked a bit and I told him that I wanted him to know that I truly loved him and saw the error of my ways, that I felt I understood him as a man and that I thought I could make him happy if he could forgive me enough to move home. I told him I certainly didn't expect him to, but that I'd love to have the chance to make him happy and to please think about it. 'I just want you to know that I want you more than anything in this world and that if by some miracle you should want to come home, we love you and would be the happiest family to have you back.' He said it was too soon to decide and that he was sorry I hadn't changed sooner. That's the way it went, and the next two months went by with not one single word or ray of hope from him that he even ever thought of returning.

"It had been seven years since we said 'I do' and five months since our separation when he came up to the house with some papers for me to sign. He had just bought a car and needed my signature as it was to be in our names. I floated around the house for days and days (7 to be exact), clinging to that first ray of hope that he might be considering giving me another 'last chance' to make good our marriage. I was so happy, but never pressed him about it.

"One week later his refrigerator broke down at his apartment and he brought down all of his food to store in ours until his could be fixed. In a joking way, as he was trying to figure out how to work picking up his food each day and plan his meals, I suggested he could move home with us and not worry about all that. He stopped and smiled (to my amazement) and I just waited for his response. When it finally came, I was up on 'cloud 9' because he said, 'Well, I guess I could at that.' I wrapped myself around him and bawled my eyes out with joy and the only words I could utter were, 'You mean it? You mean you would really give me another chance?'

"After several moments when I'd calmed down a bit, he sat me down in a chair and said that before he could move home he had to know how I would be in regard to his new-found and dearly loved 'freedom.' He said that while on his own he realized that his freedom to be himself and to indulge in his hobbies (wood working, electronics, etc.) and not to have to adhere to set schedules was his most precious possession he'd discovered while on his own and that he couldn't give that up for anyone or anything. I told him I understood and I guess he knew I did (at last), and as he walked out the door to get his things, he turned and held out his hand. In his hand was a brand new set of keys for his new car, and he said, 'Here, I guess you'll need these now,' and he left, but only so that he could return again and this time for good. That was three weeks before Christmas and we had the happiest Christmas any family ever had. Since that glorious day, almost six months have passed and not one week goes by that he does not comment in a bewildered way that he just can't believe how much I've changed. (He'd remind me of how I would have reacted before.)

"Fascinating Womanhood has been the salvation of my soul, my marriage, and my family, and I will strive the rest of my days to live up to its teachings. I never did one thing—not one thing—right before, and I have got a lot to learn yet before my old habits and thinking patterns have been wiped out of existence and replaced by the more mature and proper Fascinating Womanhood way. Not one

Fascinating Womanhood applied principle has failed me and I know it's the right way to be even though every day is a challenge; I know it is, because my husband can't believe I have changed so much. I thank God in heaven and you on earth for giving me this 'last chance' to make my family happy. Thank you, thank you, thank you."

How I Won My Husband Back from a Harlot

"Fascinating Womanhood was, literally, an answer to prayer. I remember when the book arrived at my house. I had been praying that the Lord would show me what I could do to improve myself, wherever I was wrong in my crumbled marriage. One day I decided to call an old college roommate, whom I hadn't seen in years. She came over for a visit. When she asked me how my husband felt about the fourth baby I was expecting, I hedged—I knew he was furious about it. I finally broke down and told her he had sued for divorce twice, separation once, and that he had gone to one psychiatrist and a marriage counselor and I had gone to the counselor, a hypnotist, our minister, every friend we had, and my obstetrician, and nobody could say any more than either to pray about it or to get a divorce. And I had tried *so hard.*

"Every complaint he had I had done something about. The house was super clean, the children kept quiet and out of the way when he came around. If he said he didn't like something, I jumped and corrected it. I tried hard not to act pregnant, because I knew how disgusted he was with my situation. I had, in turn, mailed him lovely good-by letters, called him every name I knew, threatened divorce or never to let him have one, not answered the phone, had the children only talk with him, or run to answer the phone myself on the first ring with the sexiest voice I could muster. All the tricks women think of to handle a man, using his weaknesses, I had tried. They brought temporary relief but no change.

"The next night my college friend drove forty miles to bring me The Fascinating Girl. I read a little in a few chapters and was so excited I had butterflies. The next morning I dumped the children in the car and drove twenty miles to the nearest bookstore to buy both Fascinating Girl and Fascinating Womanhood, seriously damaging the family food budget. When I started reading Fascinating Womanhood, I kept it with me all over the house—in the kitchen, bathroom, bedroom—and read it as a man nearly dead of thirst would drink water. My face felt hot and burning when I read about not comparing your man to other men, being happy within yourself, even when he is not, accepting his faults and not trying to change him, looking to his better side, losing your temper in a childlike way, not allowing yourself to be stepped on, accepting him at face value, and what criticizing a man can do to him. You can see that I did not understand men at all.

"About a month after I had read Fascinating Womanhood for the twenty-fifth time came what I had been hoping for—my husband told me I had changed. He didn't know how but he sure liked it. About four months after that, he spilled out to me that in his utter misery in our situation he had picked up a harlot and had been living with her for three-and-a-half years. She was ugly, uneducated, sick, divorced three times at the age of twenty-four, near alcoholic, and wouldn't hold down a job. She had given her only son to her parents to raise. But, she was *fascinating*. My husband was like a god in her eyes. His enemies were hers, his friends were hers. She made him feel important and accepted and understood.

"When my husband confessed his affair to me, I temporarily forgot all about Fascinating Womanhood and completely lost control of my temper. I broke a glass door and a couple of glass-covered pictures and ended up getting beaten and my husband leaving the house, going to a motel and taking about two bottles of aspirin and calling his mistress for comfort. Even after he came home and calmed down, he went on secretly seeing her for a couple of weeks. But, I kept that image before my eyes of taming the terrible tiger with kindness and patience, and eventually the rewards were what I had been praying for the eight years of our marriage. When I began to learn the difficult lessons of how to be *fascinating*, apparently the bottom fell out of my husband's relationship with the harlot—in fact, these were my husband's own words.

"I don't mean to say that these changes were easy to make. My husband had become 'addicted' to this woman, and I had to be understanding and loving and mop his brow when he lay in bed and shook because he hadn't talked to her for three days. When he would lapse into moods or end up referring to her in his conversations, I had to find inner strength and happiness to carry me over it, and sometimes I would truly give way to despair. During this period when my husband was trying to rid himself of his 'addiction,' he brought home a Gideon Bible and started reading it. I was so thrilled. About seven weeks after his 'confession' to me, we were baptized together into our church. In about two months after that my husband became what our church has been praying for, in charge of our "tape ministry" and got it into a functioning and prospering position.

"My husband's Bible reading continued at a phenomenal pace, and he kept growing and growing in Christianity until now, one year later, and he is still growing and studying. He has an understanding of God that I am sure very few men have—it's like living with a prophet, a man like Paul or David in the Bible. He has completely built his own business and in five years has prospered to the point where he told me he has 200,000 dollars in the bank. But he, like Tolstoi, doesn't want to let the world separate him from God, so he won't use the money on material needs. He does not know yet what the Lord would have him do with the money and he talks of adopting some children. Thank you, Mrs. Andelin, and even more, I thank God for sending your message to me and to my family."

I Didn't Love Him Anymore

"George and I have been married for sixteen years. The joy I expected in being married ended with 'I do.' I was sure that if we just tried, we could have a beautiful marriage, even though no one we knew had this kind of marriage. The trouble was George would not try. I read everything I could get my hands on. George would not read it or allow me to read it to him. I would leave magazine articles about marriage around. All to no avail.

"I went to a church-going psychologist six times. He told me 'We never give advice, but if I were you I would leave him. You will not live more than ten years if you remain with him.' But I could not believe that divorce was the answer. Besides, we have three children, and what effect for Christ would I have if I were divorced? Besides I had made a vow, for better or for worse.

"George did not hit me or anything like that, and he was faithful to me. But he totally ignored me and the children. He would not give me five minutes of his time. He was busy with his work and his own interests. He would not help with the children. If he tied a shoe lace when they were small, he acted like a martyr. He would not take me anyplace or buy me anything. Money was not for spending except for outright necessities.

"He would get angry at me over little things which would crush me. This hurt so badly. By threat of divorce I forced him to go to a church-related marriage counselor with me. This really helped change a poor marriage into a good one. But, there was no joy, happiness, or sparkle. After six months I realized I no longer loved him. It was dead, killed by so many years of neglect and hurt. Can you imagine what it is to clean house, cook and take care of the children of a man you do not love? But George always said he loved me. This was difficult to understand. I would remember the lovely friendship we had before we were married. What fun we had together. How we adored each other. And I would wonder what happened. I've wondered why I married him. Thousands of times I've thought, 'Why did I do it? Why did I marry him?'

"Last summer a friend loaned me Fascinating Womanhood. That very day our marriage began to change from good to excellent. I had thought if he would only change. But it was I who needed to change. I had been trying to change him. I belittled him, criticized him, I bossed him in little ways and I was playing mother. I did not admire him (poor guy) and I did not concentrate on his good side. (But I concentrated on his bad side with a magnifying glass.) But I was not all bad. I did keep myself clean and pretty and was a good mother, cook and homemaker.

"When I admire him I feel sort of silly and clumsy and I'm not very good at it, but that does not matter. He is so hungry for it, it doesn't matter how I mess it up or goop it on. He loves it. I have always met his physical needs, sex, clean clothes, clean house, etc. His spiritual needs are met because he is a Christian and reads the Bible every day and prays. But I have not been feeding his soul. I didn't know. Isn't that pitiful? Now I try to feed his soul a minimum of three times a day. I think, 'Did I give his soul breakfast today?'

"George is delighted with the change in me. Recently he said, 'I can hardly believe I finally have the kind of wife I've always wanted to have.' He has taken more interest in the children. He is opening up. He is not so stingy. My love for him is coming back. Thank you, Mrs. Andelin, for Fascinating Womanhood. Thank you, thank you, thank you."

ABOUT THE AUTHOR

It is not surprising that a book which is inspiring new hope in the American woman should be written by a feminine, home-centered wife and mother such as HELEN B. ANDELIN. She is the wife of Dr. Aubrey P. Andelin, and they are the parents of eight children. Her background experience was gained by teaching marriage classes to the women of her community. The success of the classes provided the impetus for her to write a book on the subject so that other women might be benefited. Dr. and Mrs. Andelin have established Family Living International, an educational foundation which sponsors classes in marriage for men and women.